**Patterns in the Folk Speech
of the British Isles**

Patterns in the Folk Speech of the British Isles

Edited by
Martyn F. Wakelin

With a Foreword by
Emeritus Professor Harold Orton
B.Litt., M.A., Hon. Fil. Dr, Hon. D.Litt.,

Honorary Editor-in-Chief of the
Survey of English Dialects

THE ATHLONE PRESS of the University of London
1972

Published by
THE ATHLONE PRESS
UNIVERSITY OF LONDON
at 2 Gower Street London WC1

Distributed by
Tiptree Book Services Ltd, Tiptree, Essex

U.S.A.
Oxford University Press Inc
New York

© University of London 1972

ISBN 0 485 11128 4

Printed in Great Britain by
WILLIAM CLOWES & SONS, LIMITED
London, Beccles and Colchester

Foreword

As co-founder with the late Eugen Dieth of an English dialect survey which, between 1950 and 1961, collected all the information, and much more besides, now being published in the *Survey of English Dialects* (Leeds, 1962–), I welcome most warmly the present series of stimulating articles, most of them by young scholars who have made or are making valuable contributions to this project. Dr Martyn Wakelin, who has been associated with the whole project first as research assistant, then as assistant editor, and finally as co-editor, is to be congratulated most heartily on his initiative in organizing—together with papers by certain established scholars associated with collateral dialect investigations in the United Kingdom—this extensive exploitation of the large corpus of first-hand, pinpointed information about the dialectal speech used by elderly natives over three hundred selected localities distributed over the whole of England. Dr Wakelin's pioneer book of articles by various authors, all of them university or college teachers, is an important contribution to the detailed study of not only traditional regional English but also of English philology in general. I have the greatest satisfaction in recommending this book and hope that it will have many successors.

Leeds   Harold Orton
October 1970

Contents

Contributors

Martyn F. Wakelin, M.A., PH.D.
Lecturer in English, Royal Holloway College, University of London

J. Y. Mather, M.A.
Senior Lecturer in the School of Scottish Studies, University of Edinburgh

Peter Wright, B.A., PH.D.
Senior Lecturer in English, University of Salford

John D. Widdowson, M.A.
Lecturer in English, University of Sheffield

Philip M. Tilling, B.A.
Lecturer in English, New University of Ulster

Robert J. Gregg, PH.D.
Professor of Linguistics, University of British Columbia

David R. Parry, M.A.
Lecturer in English, University College of Swansea

Michael V. Barry, M.A.
Lecturer in English, Queen's University of Belfast

Pauline Duncan, M.A.
Lecturer in English, Sedgley Park College of Education, Manchester

Abbreviations

Abbreviations throughout the book are those commonly in use, but the following should be specially noted.

The abbreviations for the English counties, which occur in the tabulation and listing of material, are as used by the *Survey of English Dialects*, and are as follows:

Bd	Bedfordshire	Man	Isle of Man
Bk	Buckinghamshire	Mon	Monmouthshire
Brk	Berkshire	Mx	Middlesex
C	Cambridgeshire	Nb	Northumberland
Ch	Cheshire	Nf	Norfolk
Co	Cornwall	Nt	Nottinghamshire
Cu	Cumberland	Nth	Northamptonshire
D	Devonshire	O	Oxfordshire
Db	Derbyshire	R	Rutland
Do	Dorset	Sa	Salop (Shropshire)
Du	Durham	Sf	Suffolk
Ess	Essex	So	Somerset
Gl	Gloucestershire	Sr	Surrey
Ha	Hampshire	St	Staffordshire
He	Herefordshire	Sx	Sussex
Hrt	Hertfordshire	W	Wiltshire
Hu	Huntingdonshire	Wa	Warwickshire
K	Kent	We	Westmorland
L	Lincolnshire	Wight	Isle of Wight
La	Lancashire	Wo	Worcestershire
Lei	Leicestershire	Y	Yorkshire

Numerals following the county abbreviations refer to the numbered localities in the *SED* network.

Several works of reference are mentioned so frequently in the following pages that, to avoid excessive documentation, abbreviations for them may be conveniently given here:

EDD Joseph Wright, *The English Dialect Dictionary*. Oxford, 1898–1905.

EDG Joseph Wright, *The English Dialect Grammar*. Oxford, 1905.
OED *The Oxford English Dictionary*.
SED Harold Orton et al., *Survey of English Dialects*. Leeds, 1962–71.
Dieth-Orton *Questionnaire* E. Dieth and H. Orton, *A Questionnaire for a Linguistic Atlas of England*. Leeds, 1952. Subsequently incorporated in H. Orton's *Introduction* to *SED*. Leeds, 1962.

The phonetic symbols used throughout the book, with the exception of some special symbols used by Professor Gregg, are those of the International Phonetic Association.

RP = Received Pronunciation

Note on the Survey of English Dialects

Since several of the essays in this collection are dependent upon material collected by the *Survey of English Dialects*, a general note of explanation on matters connected with the survey may be useful.

SED was planned in 1946 by Professor Harold Orton and the late Professor Eugen Dieth (then Professor of English Language at the University of Zürich), and subsequently carried out from the University of Leeds. As stated in the Introduction to the present volume, its aim—following that of the earlier Continental surveys—was to collect traditional English dialect, that is, the type of dialect normally used by elderly speakers belonging to the same social class in rural communities.

The basic tool of the survey was a questionnaire of some 1300 questions on rural and domestic affairs, designed to establish from the responses gained a reasonably comprehensive description of the vocabulary, phonology, and grammar of the dialect-speakers who were interviewed. The questionnaire, first published by the Leeds Philosophical and Literary Society in 1952, and reprinted in Professor Orton's *Introduction* to *SED* (Leeds, 1962), was put to practical use by nine trained field-workers between 1950 and 1961, who between them covered a network of 313 localities in England (but not in Wales and Scotland). They transcribed the responses to the questions in the script of the International Phonetic Alphabet, and in the same script noted down potentially useful material from the informants' conversation. This 'incidental material' has since proved invaluable as supplementary matter, especially in view of the fact that it emerged not in a formal framework but spontaneously in the course of casual conversation, and may thus reveal forms of words different from those which occur in the responses.

Pending publication of a more expensive Linguistic Atlas of England, the responses to the *SED* questions (together with much of the incidental material) were published in tabular form in four volumes of Basic Material—Northern, West Midland, East Midland and Southern—but definite plans for the production of the Atlas itself have now been laid, and it is hoped that this crowning achievement of *SED* will soon be realized. Much material in the *SED* archives still remains unpublished, however, and thanks must be offered here to the Director of the Institute of Dialect and Folk Life Studies at Leeds University, Mr Stewart F. Sanderson, for allowing various of the contributors to the present book to make use of this material.

Introduction

Martyn F. Wakelin

The study of dialect in Britain can be said only to have begun in earnest with the publication of Part V (1889) of A. J. Ellis's vast work, *On Early English Pronunciation* and of Joseph Wright's *English Dialect Dictionary* (1898–1905), although both of these works came at the end of a long line of dialect monographs and other works on the subject, revealing an interest which went back several hundred years to the sixteenth century. In the nineteenth century, however, the study of dialect in England received a most important boost from contemporary dialectal studies on the Continent (Wright himself had been trained in the Neo-Grammarian school in Germany), which had emerged out of the controversy centring round the Neo-Grammarian principle of the inviolability of sound-laws. The disputes which took place over this matter suggested a new approach to linguistic problems, namely the testing of linguistic theories on the living, rural dialects, where—so it was felt—the reflexes of historical forms could be studied in their natural setting, free from influences such as loans from the written language. The earliest work was done in Germany and France, and the foundations of the subject—the questionnaire, the recording of items in a network of localities and the plotting of these on maps—thus laid. In order to obtain the *traditional* features of the dialect (as distinct from extraneous ones borrowed from elsewhere) which had been present from early times, it has been the practice of most of the dialect surveys so far established to use as informants older members of the population living in relatively undisturbed rural communities. And so it has been in England. Although in more recent years, work has started on urban dialects, sampling cross-sections of the public, educated as well as uneducated, young as well as old, such investigations having an inevitable socio-linguistic emphasis, earlier work, including that of the *Survey of English Dialects* (which began in 1946), was insistent on obtaining what Professor Orton called 'traditional vernacular, genuine and old',[1] and to that end *SED* took special pains over the selection of

[1] 'An English Dialect Survey: Linguistic Atlas of England', *Orbis*, ix (1960),

1

elderly, native informants who would represent this type of speech. This is what is sometimes called 'folk language' or 'folk speech', and it is the type of dialect upon which the essays in the present collection are chiefly based (especially since some of these make use of the material collected by *SED*).

The study of 'folk speech' must, however, always be closely associated with that of 'folk life': the dialectologist may well elicit from his informants such traditional expressions as *pace-egging*[2] or *Old Christmas Day*, terms for parts of the old wooden plough or the cowhouse, but he will need additional information to work out their meaning and implications. It was such considerations that earlier led to the branch of study characterized by the phrase 'Wörter und Sachen'. But—more important, especially for linguistic geography— as Mr Mather points out elsewhere in this book, some dialectologists have suggested that 'external' criteria should be taken into account in determining dialect areas. Thus Uriel Weinreich in a paper quoted more than once in the present book writes: 'Dialectologists have generally switched to extra-structural criteria for dividing the folk-language continuum', and 'ever more impressive results are being obtained in correlating the borders, centers, and overall dynamics of language areas with "culture areas" in a broader sense.'[3] Weinreich goes on, most illuminatingly, to exemplify his point by reference to the 'Eifel Barrier' (the Eifel mountain range) between the Cologne and Trier areas, which, in addition to marking the dividing line between various linguistic features such as *helpe* and *helfe*, *haus* and *hus*, also divides short-bladed from long-bladed scythes, grey bread in oval loaves from black bread in rectangular loaves, the cult of St Quirin as the patron saint of cattle from St Quirin as the patron saint of horses, and so on. In view of the desirable connection between the two fields of study, it was a happy decision of the Univer-

332. In connection with this, some words of Professor Raven McDavid Jnr., Professor of English and Linguistics at the University of Chicago and editor of the *Linguistic Atlas of the Middle and South Atlantic States*, are specially relevant at the present time: 'Consequently, a first-stage general survey of a wide area is bound to stress the older and more stable elements in the population, and the more traditional elements in the language system. To young Turks, impatient to grapple with the language problems of seething urban multitudes, such an emphasis may seem quaint or "ruralistic", but it is a necessary background for their investigations—and of course it has its uses in other kinds of linguistic work, notably in reconstructing the past stages of the language.' ('Two Studies of Dialects of English', *Leeds Studies in English*, N.S. ii: *Studies in Honour of Harold Orton*, ed. S. Ellis (1968), 26.)

2 See the interesting map of egg-rolling districts given by I. and P. Opie in their book, *The Lore and Language of Schoolchildren* (Oxford, 1959), p. 254.

3 'Is a Structural Dialectology Possible?' *Word*, x (1954), 397.

2

sity of Leeds to create, in 1964, an Institute of Dialect and Folk Life Studies, in which could be stored the accumulated materials collected in this country both by Professor Harold Orton and his associates in the field of dialect and by Mr Stewart Sanderson, the Institute's first Director, in the field of folk life, and, although there is no official connection between the Institute and the present collection, many of the contributors are, in fact, associated with it in one way or another. Without being too wildly speculative, may it not well prove that contrasting 'culture areas' in Britain will ultimately emerge from future researches—regions co-extensive with ancient dialect areas such as those delimited by the river Humber (roughly dividing the northern from the Midland dialects by virtue of some important isoglosses, among them the northern *hoose*/southern *house* boundary), by the Watling Street (which roughly divides *ool* from *wool* and *I be* from *I am*, among numerous others), and by some of the old hundred boundaries in Cornwall?

The essays in this book are concerned with aspects of 'folk speech' in Britain, with—in many cases—an emphasis on the material and cultural aspects of dialectology as well as with more purely linguistic ones. Mr Mather's study, on the traditional drift-net herring fishery on the east coast of Scotland, deals with the nomenclature of the net, but also needs to take into account relevant technical and historical factors, as does Dr Wright's essay on coal-mining language. It is, furthermore, particularly valuable to include papers on fishing and mining vocabulary since these are subjects which have so far received little or no attention; for the dialectologist and the scholar of folk life they present complex pictures in that both fishermen and miners have moved around a great deal. According to a report published in 1878, 'it was the *same* men who fished waters as far apart as the Minch, the Scottish east coast, East Anglia and Ballantrae Bank' (which, incidentally, no doubt also helps to explain the presence of East Anglian words in the Cornish fishermen's dialect), and there has been 'frequent and large-scale exchange of miners and mining words between coalfields'. Mr Widdowson's study of proverbial usages adds yet another dimension to dialectal-cultural investigations, advocating the reference of proverbs and sayings to their contexts wherever possible. *Days get a cockstride langer after Old Christmas Day*, for example, is an instance 'of how folk-belief and ancient custom may be preserved in sayings still felt to have a relevance today', while the expression [kɛlks kɔmɪn əfoəɹ] (the) *kirk's coming afore* preserves, fossilized, so to speak, two specially interesting dialectal phenomena, namely the use of the northern word *kirk* in an area where the normal word is now *church*, and the

3

replacement of [ɹ] in that word by [l]. If we go on to ask what seems to be a further pertinent question, whether both of these features partly owe their preservation to fishermen's taboo—by an unwillingness to use the normal word for 'church' or the normal pronunciation of *kirk*—we immediately become yet more aware of the very close relationship between linguistics and popular culture in a broad sense.

All of the foregoing emphasizes that the study of language must always be linked with that of its environment: my own essay on dialect and place-name forms in a particular geographical area attempts to do this, and by thus combining the two types of evidence, to offer interesting conclusions about local linguistic usage in two of its aspects. It is recognized that the relationship between the present state of a dialect and early written forms is a complex one, and that such early forms are not always reliable evidence for the early stages of the spoken language. If caution is needed in dealing with place-name evidence, it is even more necessary in dealing with another form of written material—dialect in a literary form. In his essay on Tennyson's dialect poems, Mr Tilling carefully probes the poet's spellings for their significance, and makes some noteworthy suggestions about them—and thus about early nineteenth-century Lincolnshire dialect—by a comparison with the *Survey of English Dialects* material.

The remaining papers in this collection are more sharply linguistic. Professor Gregg's is concerned with drawing boundaries between different dialectal types of speech in Ulster, Mr Parry's with the formative linguistic influences (English and Welsh) behind the present-day English dialects of south-east Wales. Both of these analyses, however, are obviously related to a geographical and cultural background in which such factors as trade contacts and immigration play profoundly important parts.

Mr Barry's and Miss Duncan's essays are concentrated upon single aspects of linguistic geography—Mr Barry's with the various regional forms of the definite article in England, and Miss Duncan's with the forms of or expressions for the pronoun *she*. But detailed investigations of these single items are no less valuable than full-scale analyses of entire dialects, and such treatments in depth—like Mr Mather's in another sphere—may lead to the definition or substantiation of some most important dialect boundaries.

The unity underlying the essays presented here is thus a geographical one: they are concerned with the geographical distribution of selected features, and with the inferences which can be drawn from the patterning which emerges. The book aims to advance and promote the study of linguistic geography and of folk life in Britain, as subjects between which there is a close relationship as worthy of attention as are the subjects themselves.

1 Linguistic Geography and the Traditional Drift-Net Fishery of the Scottish East Coast

J. Y. Mather

In *Blackwood's Magazine* for March 1842 appeared an article, 'Notes on The Fisheries of the Scotch East Coast', which contained these words: 'The east coast is a fresh field, even to the humble pen of the observer, who collects the material which genius vivifies and groups—making facts pictures, peculiarities characters, and ideas actions.' The author (who was anonymous) had in mind the vivifying genius of Scott and Galt, although he complained that Scott was too busy with the romantic border country to pay much attention to the east coast, and that Galt concerned himself only with the west. What is interesting about the passage, however, is that all the material for an essay in linguistic geography is here: a delimited geographical area, observation and collection of material, and grouping which makes 'pictures' out of 'facts'. It is the first contention of this present essay that the east coast of Scotland is still a remarkably fresh field for study in the patterning of linguistic geography.

From the linguistic material gathered by The Linguistic Survey of Scotland various patterns have emerged. One advantage of a contemporary, synchronic survey (as is The Linguistic Survey of Scotland) is that it is possible to have a synchronic and synoptic *display* of the evidence and, at the same time, to invite a diachronic interpretation of it. This is particularly so with the type of patterning often likened to a geological stratification. Albert Dauzat, for example, in reflecting on a similar phenomenon in France was able to write: 'Mais le fait capital, c'est que la géographie linguistique—et par là elle nous apparaît comme une véritable géologie du langage—reconstitue, si l'on peut dire, par leurs affleurements actuels, les couches successives des mots en grande partie enfouies.'[1]

Furthermore, it is often possible to apply almost completely matching non-linguistic evidence to the stratified linguistic evidence. In Scotland, for instance, as I have shown elsewhere,[2] dialect ver-

[1] Albert Dauzat, *La géographie linguistique* (Paris, 1922), p. 34.
[2] J. Y. Mather, 'Aspects of the Linguistic Geography of Scotland: I', *Scottish Studies*, ix, part 2 (1965), 129–44.

7

sions of the word *chaffinch* can be displayed synoptically as a stratification from south-west to north-east, and the ornithological and
historical evidence—for example, for the progress in the breeding
range and the actual physical presence of the bird in a given area at a
given time—can match this by a historically and ornithologically
certified extension for each stratified dialect word.

The patterning of linguistic geography can therefore often be
simple, vivid, and immediate. It may, indeed, be misleadingly
simple, but when reinforced by the independently known history of
the thing it may serve to emphasize some recent requests from
dialectologists that non-linguistic as well as linguistic evidence should
be accepted and accommodated. There is, of course, the well-known,
although not well-accepted, conclusion of Th. Frings for the coin-
cidence of some political, ecclesiastical, and linguistic frontiers in
Germany.[3] Malkiel has also reflected on the taxonomic techniques
of lexicology and phonology, where 'a scholar organising into a
pattern the names of the lizard needs information not only about
sound and form developments, but also about the lizard itself in
scientific and popular zoology'.[4] Similarly, Weinreich has asked for
an 'external dialectology',[5] and Pulgram for non-linguistic evidence
to be taken into consideration whenever the linguist 'is forsaken...by
the *littera scripta*',[6] and in any case to safeguard him in his interpretation of cases of linguistic congruence without contact.

I propose to consider here some linguistic (specifically lexical)
evidence for the traditional drift-net herring fishery on the east coast
of Scotland from Caithness to Berwickshire. In order to define the
material still further, I wish to present the distributional evidence for
the nomenclature of the net only, but to add to this whatever technical and historical evidence seems appropriate for reasonable interpretation. For both words and things I have had the help of
informants whose experience dates to at least the first or second
decade of this century, although some, in fact, were fishing before this
and in sailing vessels. Since the numbers of such informants must obviously be diminishing quite rapidly, it seemed sensible to collect
words as quickly as possible in their most direct and obvious designation of things and as a simple act of collection. Thereafter, with

[3] Th. Frings, *Grundlegung einer Geschichte der deutschen Sprache* (Halle, 1948).

[4] Yakov Malkiel, 'The Pattern of Progress in Romance Linguistics', *Romance Philology*, v (1951), 278–95.

[5] Uriel Weinreich, 'Is a Structural Dialectology Possible?' *Word*, x (1954), 388–400.

[6] Ernst Pulgram, 'Prehistory and the Italian Dialects', *Language*, xxv (1949), 241–52.

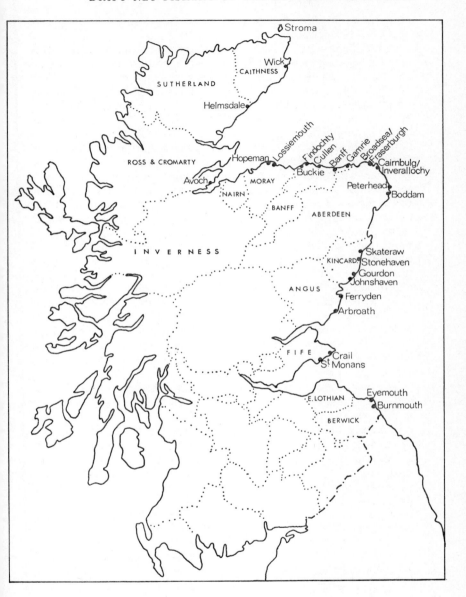

Stroma

Wick
CAITHNESS

SUTHERLAND

Helmsdale

ROSS & CROMARTY

Hopeman Lossiemouth
Findochty
Cullen Banff
Gamrie
Broadsea/
Fraserburgh
Cairnbulg/
Inverallochy

Avoch
Buckie

MORAY

NAIRN

BANFF

ABERDEEN

Peterhead

Boddam

INVERNESS

Skateraw
KINCARD Stonehaven
Gourdon
Johnshaven

ANGUS

Ferryden

Arbroath

FIFE

Crail
St Monans

E. LOTHIAN

Eyemouth
Burnmouth

BERWICK

more time for reflection, the ways in which they might be connected could be considered.

In the linguistic geography of Scotland there are, of course, very many cases—*chaffinch* is one of them—where the relationship of words and things is relatively simple and where the patterning (a stratification, perhaps, or a spear-head) can be interpreted in terms of a very simple image. For the theme I have chosen the non-linguistic evidence, at least, seems to suggest that the patterning will be more complicated, if only because the progress of the herring fishery, especially in the nineteenth century, has clearly been away from the *locality* and from the conservatism which this seems to imply. The historical evidence is that fishermen of the most varied local origins have, at a certain point of time, begun to operate from a centre like Yarmouth, or Lerwick, or Castlebay for at least some part of the year and, as the industry has progressed and become more and more specialized, in many instances throughout the entire year. For example, by 1878 a report on the herring fisheries of Scotland could emphasize, as a point of particular importance, that it was the *same* men who fished waters as far apart as the Minch, the Scottish east coast, East Anglia, and Ballantrae Bank.[7] Indeed, considerably earlier than this (in 1844) Hugh Miller seems to have detected this development in its incipient stage where 'the *professional* character of this *class* [the fishers] is found to neutralise in them the *national* character'.[8] And he went on to consider in some detail the psychological influences of the new herring fishery on the quiet rhythm of a fisherman's life when spent exclusively in the locality.

The task set to linguistic geography in the study of the traditional drift-net fishing on the Scottish east coast is therefore not simply the faithful recording and mapping of lexical items. There are at least two factors which any interpretation must recognize: first, the dispersal away from the locality; and, second, new fishing techniques in the developing industry. Hence the task becomes much more the study of what Schuchardt called 'Sachwortgeschichte'—that is, something much more complex than a simple study of 'words and things'. As he put it, 'das und in "Sachen und Wörter" verwandele sich aus einem Additionszeichen in ein Multiplikationszeichen; es entwickle sich eine Sachwortgeschichte'.[9]

---

[7] Frank Buckland, Spencer Walpole, and Archibald Young, *Report on the Herring Fisheries of Scotland* (London, 1878), p. xx.

[8] Hugh Miller, 'Report by the Commissioners for the British Fisheries of their Proceedings 1842' [unsigned], *North British Review*, i, 326–65.

[9] H. Schuchardt, *Schuchardt-Brevier*, ed. L. Spitzer (Halle, 1922), p. 116.

I propose to give an account of the dispersal and the techniques and then to set out the linguistic material.

One aspect of the problem of development away from the locality is a further account in Buckland, Walpole, and Young's 'Report' of 'an otherwise inexplicable dilemma', namely that 'the Fishery Board, on the one hand is annually recording increased takes of herring, while a large number of the fishermen, on the other, are constantly complaining of a failure of the fishing'.[10] The resolution of this dilemma is, in fact, quite crucial for the understanding of the problem of locality and it is worthwhile studying it rather closely.

The authors invite attention, first of all, to the extraordinary expansion of the herring fishery on the Aberdeenshire and Forfarshire coasts from the 1860s onwards. They give figures which indicate that whereas in 1867 the proportion of cured herrings from Aberdeenshire and Forfarshire was about 25 per cent of the total for Scotland, in 1876 it was 47 per cent. Nor, they argue, was this increase wholly to be explained by the capriciousness of the herring shoals which, quite fortuitously, had concentrated themselves in a particular area on the east coast. Wick, Helmsdale, Lybster in the far north, Buckie and Burghead in the western part of the Moray Firth, Anstruther, Eyemouth, Dunbar in the Firth of Forth— in all of these, it was urged with greater or lesser force, the recession might have been due as much to 'the departure of the fishermen themselves to the more remunerative fishing grounds' as to an actual failure in the herring shoals—although it was admitted that 'the superior attractions of Fraserburgh and Peterhead do not account for the whole of the failure and that the herrings visit the districts in fewer numbers than formerly'.

What does seem to be indubitable, however, is that on the east coast (outside the Moray Firth and the Firth of Forth) the herring fishery was taken much further into the offing—sometimes sixty or eighty miles offshore. This was quite new. James Johnson, fishcurer of Montrose, in giving evidence for the Report, said: 'In 1861 commenced the catching of herrings off Montrose. This was the first attempt in Scotland to catch herrings twenty or thirty miles out at sea.' The fishing officer at Aberdeen said that the boats in his district were 'nearly all decked now'. They went fifty or sixty miles off, but 'when he was first a fishery officer, a boat would never have gone out 50 miles'. Finally, James Couper, fishery officer for Fraserburgh, said: 'The boats now go to different grounds from...1861. They used not to go more than 15 miles off. They now go double that distance.

[10] Op. cit., p. xx.

It was not generally known in 1861 that herrings could be caught 30 miles from the shore.'[11]

Nevertheless, in two important areas—The Firth of Forth and the Moray Firth—the innovation of fishing off-shore for herrings did not seem to have taken hold, at least by the time of the 'Report'. For the Firth of Forth there was mention once or twice of the herring fishers as having been 'starved out' (for example, in 1804–5) by a failure within the Firth itself, although it seems to have been known that herrings were in the offing. From another source, 1793 was given as the date at which a large commercial *inshore* fishing within the Firth itself began. By the next year 'adventurers' had increased in number, arriving from many ports complete with barrels and salt. So that in a few years 'it was possible to hang 7800 barrels of red herring at a time in the smoke-houses of Burntisland and 9000 at other parts of the Firth plus Berwick'.[12] This type of fishing was a winter fishing, but had declined by the time of Buckland, Walpole, and Young's 'Report.'

For the Moray Firth the great upsurge of the Scottish herring fishing after the Napoleonic wars and especially in these waters is well known and is usually given as an important *datum*; and it is, of course, vital in any understanding of the situation on the east coast of Scotland. Nevertheless, it is essential to remember (all the more so for our present purpose) that it too was a local, inshore fishery. This was the period of the prodigious fishings on the Guilliam Bank, lying just off Cromarty, about which Hugh Miller wrote, rather memorably, after a night there with the herring fishermen. He saw 'a continuous forest of naked masts and dinghy hulks, that, as the twilight darkened, resembled in the aggregate a flat marshy island in winter, covered with leafless wood'.[13] This was the period of the beginnings of the herring fishery in such well-known Moray Firth ports as Fraserburgh, Peterhead, Banff, Portsoy, Lossiemouth, Nairn, Burghead, Cullen, Macduff, Helmsdale. But, above all, it was the period which revealed those defining characteristics for the Scottish herring fishery which contemporary writers were at some pains to emphasize. 'The Scottish is a land or shore fishery' wrote James Thomson.[14] 'The boats leave the harbours towards evening and the fishermen expect, with favourable wind and weather, to return from

[11] Op. cit., pp. 17, 20, 36.
[12] John Girvin, *A Short Account of the Herring Fishery in The Firth of Forth* (London, 1800), p. 51 n.
[13] Miller, op. cit., p. 349.
[14] James Thomson, *The Value and Importance of the Scottish Fisheries* (London, 1849), p. 51.

4 to 6 o'clock on the following morning.' And ashore: 'A curer who is zealous in his business will always express his satisfaction when he has the fish in salt by the breakfast hour of nine.'

This clear definition of the nature of the Scottish herring fishery had, of course, been achieved only after some centuries of rather impotent rivalry with the Dutch, occasionally (but with no success) imitating their method of buss fishing whereby the vessels kept at sea for some weeks on end, curing and packing on board; and imitating their closely regularized monopoly system of industrial organization. If, however, the Scottish herring fishery had come to the point where it could be defined as a 'land or shore fishery', observers like Thomson were also quick to point out that it could only develop as a fully professional, whole-time fishing and in a direction exactly opposite to what Thomson called the 'cottar system' of Orkney, Shetland, and the Western Isles where a crofter both cultivated the land and fished the sea in a simple subsistence economy. With the same sort of psychological insight into the herring fishers as Hugh Miller, Thomson looked to the day even in the islands 'when the fisheries will altogether be in the hands of men similar in their determination...to fishing pursuit as those on our eastern coast'.[15]

In looking back at the evolution of the Scottish herring fishery, therefore, it is possible to observe one or two well-defined developments. It is first of all an off-shore fishery and a fully professional, whole-time fishery. Unlike the Dutch buss-fishery it is also a 'land or shore fishery'. None of these characteristics, of course, is incompatible with the fishery as operating from a centre removed from the locality of the fisher himself—from Yarmouth, for instance, or Lerwick, or Castlebay—and as one which may occupy the cycle of his entire year.

I turn now to one or two important advances in technique which took place over roughly the same period as the development in organization. The first advance concerned the net itself. R. Hogarth, writing in 1883, spoke of 'an improvement...of recent years...on the drift-net which I cannot explain better than by saying that the net is turned upside down'.[16] To understand this it is necessary to say something of the basic technique in drift-net fishing.

In this type of fishing, the vessel drifts to leeward of a long line of connected nets which extends like a perpendicular wall into the sea. The line of nets is kept relatively taut and straight by the strain imposed on it by the steady drift of the vessel. The nets must also be

15 Op. cit., p. 176.
16 R. Hogarth, 'The Herring Fishery', p. 14. *The Fisheries Exhibition Literature*, Vol. xi *Prize Essays Part IV* (London, 1883).

kept perpendicular, and they must float at a given depth—usually two or three fathoms below the surface. A sufficient number of cork floats is therefore added to the top of the net, and a sufficient weight, in one form or another to the bottom. Since flotation and submersion are thus opposed the net tends to hang perpendicularly.

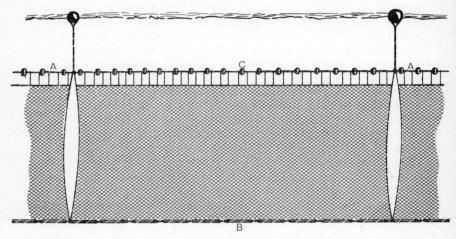

Fig. 1. Diagrammatic representation of a type of drift-net: not to scale

Figure 1[17] shows one means—a rather early means— of realizing these essential points of technique. It will be seen that the individual nets are held together by a connecting rope A (also, of course, made fast to the vessel) and this rope also carries the corks C. But the necessary weight, as counterpoise, is carried in the bottom rope B simply by virtue of its strength and thickness. It is heavier than rope A and is, indeed, often of three or four ply of ropes laid together. (In Berwickshire it was, in fact, called the 'thick rope'.) Sometimes, and especially for fishing near the bottom, stones were used to replace the heavy rope B. These were attached at intervals by short ropes (called 'tower strings' in Berwickshire). Both of these types of net were used quite extensively in Scotland in the nineteenth century. The first was known—especially in the Moray Firth—as the 'corky net', and the second as the 'staned net'.

17 For the illustrations and the map which accompany this essay I am indebted to Mr G. W. Leslie, who is the cartographer on the staff of the Linguistic Survey of Scotland, University of Edinburgh.

These nets were made of hemp; and this of itself was heavier than the cotton twine which was developed in mid-century as a new and lighter and more effective net material. Hemp, however, had the virtue of weight; and it seems that it was not absolutely necessary to weight it with a 'thick rope'. There is an illustration, for instance, given by E. J. March of a Yarmouth lugger riding to her nets *c.* 1860 where the foot of the nets is not roped as in the 'corky net'.[18] Now, the number of cotton nets carried in a vessel tended to increase very greatly, since they were lighter and more compact, and it became

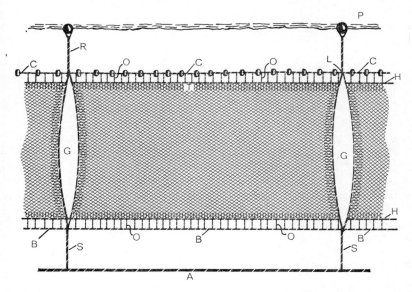

Fig. 2. Diagrammatic representation of a type of drift-net: not to scale

necessary to develop a more substantial rope by which they could be connected and controlled. At this point the net, as Hogarth said, was 'turned upside down'. March's illustration for 1860 shows that the connecting rope was still *above* the nets. The important advance, however, was to a rope set *underneath* the nets to give both control and weight to the lighter cotton twine. It was this rope—very generally called the 'messenger'—which was taken to the newly developed steam capstans for hauling. Formerly the 'thick rope' had been taken to a hand windlass with vertical grooved wheels for the rope.

18 Edgar J. March, *Sailing Drifters* (London, 1952), p. 30.

This type of hand windlass was familiarly known as the 'iron man'.

Figure 2 shows the improved type of drift-net. Various points (some of which correspond to the simpler net shown in Figure 1) can be noted. A is the 'messenger', B the 'sole rope', C the 'cork rope'. O are the 'ossils', and it is to be noted that they are now at top *and* bottom of the net. H is the 'head line' on the edge of the net to which the 'ossils' are attached. G is the 'gavel' of the net, and T 'thick twine' at the edge. I wish also to draw attention to the following points upon which I have not yet adequate distributional information: the nets are supported on the surface of the sea by the buoys P, made fast to the 'cork rope' by the ropes R. The nets are attached to each other by 'lugs' at points L, and to the 'messenger' by the rope S.

The Linguistic Material

Messenger

I begin the presentation of the linguistic material with the word MESSENGER. I use the word as the general term to convey the notion of the connecting and controlling rope for the nets. *Messenger* was given for Berwickshire (Burnmouth and Eyemouth) and the East Neuk of Fife (Crail and St Monans). It appeared again, once, in the Moray Firth at Gamrie[19] but in an area which was otherwise consistently *leader*. *Leader* is used in a very well defined area from Cullen to Peterhead. My information was from Cullen, Banff, Broadsea, Cairnbulg, Peterhead. Immediately south of Peterhead *bush rope* begins at Boddam and extends as far south as Arbroath with no break in the sequence. My information was from Boddam, Skateraw, Stonehaven, Gourdon, Johnshaven, Ferryden, Arbroath. It is to be noted, in addition, that *bush rope* reappears in the far north at Wick and Helmsdale. There was one further word in the investigation, viz. *spring* or *spring back* and, again, this area is well defined. It extends from Avoch to Findochty. My information was from Avoch, Hopeman, Lossiemouth, Buckie, Findochty.

The words for 'messenger', then, show a very clear distribution: *messenger*—The Firth of Forth; *bush rope*—the East Coast and the outer Moray Firth (north); *leader*—the outer Moray Firth (south); *spring*—the inner Moray Firth.[20] Nevertheless, although the distri-

[19] This is the usual fisher designation of what appears as 'Gardenstown' on most maps. It lies on Gamrie Bay.

[20] These terms—'Firth of Forth', 'East Coast', etc.—are areas as here detailed and defined by their usages for this term, *messenger*. They will continue to be used.

16

bution pattern seems clear there are certain difficulties in its correlation with the history of word and thing. R. Hogarth wrote of a *spring-back* which was used for hauling nets on a large type of vessel, similar to the Penzance and St Ives lugger, which West of Scotland fishermen had had built in England. 'The nets in these large boats are nearly all hauled by spring-backs which are hove in by capstans or winches...There is an improved winch or, as fishermen call it "iron man", which can be used without a spring-back...The east coast fishermen regard it as a great improvement.'[21]

In his article Hogarth implied that the *spring-back* was the *top* rope (i.e. before the inversion of the net) and that it was a west coast rather than an east coast term. But he also said, explicitly, that the inverted net was first used in the east and only later adopted in the west. There is a further detailed mention of the term *back-rope* in a request by letter in 1776 from the east coast to the west coast (specifically, from the Commissioners of the Customs at Edinburgh to the Collector and Comptroller of the Customs at Port Glasgow) for information on the herring fishery. The reply from Port Glasgow—John Girvin gives it in his book[22]—was that there was a 'buss fishery' which plied 'from loch to loch in search of herrings', and that the practice was for boats to be sent off from the buss as catchers. If the fishing was scarce each boat had 'two trains of nets 288 yards long and from 11 to 12 yards deep'. This was for fishing in the lochs. But, 'if in deep water (which is generally the case before the herrings set into the lochs) both trains are tied together by the back-rope...and in this case the boat is tied to the leeward end of the train and is allowed to drive with the nets to the leeward'. So that it appears that a *back-rope* is only for use with the drift net in the open sea and not for a stationary or anchored net within the lochs.

For present-day evidence for this item in the west I have relied on some as yet unpublished files of the *Scottish National Dictionary* (kindly made available to me by its editor Mr David Murison)[23] where *spring-back* is given from Ayrshire and specifically for the top rope. Obviously, since my own studies have shown that it occurs in a very well defined area in the inner Moray Firth, the distribution is of considerable interest. Equally obviously, much more evidence for the west coast will be necessary before any sort of interpretation is possible. What can be said, however, is that with the opening of

[21] Hogarth, op. cit., p. 9.   [22] Girvin, op. cit., p. 41.
[23] The Dictionary is still in progress and is published as far as the word *Selkirk* (Vol. viii, part 1). I thank Mr Murison both for giving me access to unpublished material and for much helpful discussion, over the past few years, on the findings of some of my field-work.

the Caledonian Canal there was a very regular west coast fishing by the fleets of the inner Moray Firth—Avoch, Hopeman, Buckie— which also extended to Castlebay (Barra) and Buncrana (Donegal). This is not to say that other fleets from the east did not fish, or had not fished, in the west. But chiefly these went to the Minch. There was a tradition for Buckie, for instance, to fish the lochs of the west coast. This was not so for a port like Peterhead which fished the open Minch; and it may be significant that Buckie is in the *spring back* area and Peterhead is not.

On the technical evidence, if *spring back* was the name for the top connecting rope, it seems that it was simply retained after the new, inverted arrangement of the net. The same was probably true for *bush rope* (='buss rope'). There is, at all events, a *buss rope* shown (as a top rope) in a diagram from the year 1750.[24] Obviously, the *buss rope* was the rope which joined the entire train of nets to the buss itself, and, for nomenclature at least, it made little difference if the rope was above or beneath the nets. *Messenger* is somewhat more difficult to interpret. I have found no particularly early use of it as a special rope in the drift-net fishing, and it may be that it is a mercantile usage. (I have touched on such borrowings, with possible examples, in an earlier article on east coast linguistic problems.)[25] Smythe, for instance, defines it as 'a large cable-laid rope, used to unmoor or heave up the anchor of a ship by the aid of the capstan...by binding a part of the messenger to the cable...with pliant nippers'.[26] It is clear that its use in the herring fishery is almost exactly parallel to this. Possibly the word *leader* is also generally nautical. *Lead* (noun and verb) implies direction in nautical parlance (as also in general parlance). The word is given in its use in the herring fishery in the *Scottish National Dictionary* but without further comment.

Sole Rope

Figure 2 shows the SOLE-ROPE (B) as made fast to the net by the OSSILS (O). Its name implies that it is essentially a rope at the bottom of the net (although not forming part of the actual mesh) and I use the term in this general sense.

The inner Moray Firth again forms an interesting group by using

[24] In [F. Grant] *A Letter to a Member of Parliament concerning the Free British Fisheries; with draughts of a herring-buss and nets, and the harbour and town of Peterhead* (London, 1750).
[25] J. Y. Mather, 'Aspects of the Linguistic Geography of Scotland, II: East Coast Fishing', *Scottish Studies*, x, part 2 (1966), 129–53.
[26] Admiral W. H. Smythe, *The Sailor's Word Book* (London, 1867).

some combination of *back* (='balk') for this rope. Avoch has *grun back*, Hopeman, *back* or *backy*, Buckie, Findochty, and Cullen have *heid back*. (But Lossiemouth has *fit rope*.) The *heid back* of Buckie–Findochty–Cullen seems to point to the retention of the name after the inversion of the net, for Gregor defines *hehd back* as 'the rope that runs along that side of a herring net to which the cork buoys are attached by the *sneeds*'.[27] This presumably means that the corks are on the *sneeds* (='ossils') and not on the *heid back* itself. In fact, in my field-work I have still been able to find one or two very old men who could assert that the top rope of the older types of net—such as the *staned net*, for example—was called the *heid back* and that on this type of net the corks were on the OSSILS.

The outer Moray Firth gave *sole rope*. This seems to be the usage both in the north (Wick and Helmsdale) and in the south (Banff, Gamrie, Broadsea). The usage changes to *fit rope* (='foot rope') at Cairnbulg, and thereafter (proceeding south) the east coast yields a variety of names: *lower raip* at Peterhead, *bottom raip* at Boddam. *Sole rope* reappears at Skateraw and Gourdon and *fit rope* at Stonehaven. Ferryden has *bottom raip*, Arbroath *sunk raip*, Crail *sma raip*, Eyemouth and Burnmouth *thick raip* (but also *sole raip* for both of these places).

It is not easy to explain these varieties of usage, but it may at least be possible to relate them to the drive into the offing in the nineteenth century which has already been examined. This must have entailed a very rapid adaptation to the new type of net with a probably very uneven adaptation of the older nomenclature. For instance, the fact that I could elicit usages in free variation—*thick raip* and *sole raip*—from my informants at Eyemouth and Burnmouth may indicate such a situation, where *thick raip* is reminiscent of the older type of net (Figure 2). Furthermore, the *sma raip* of Crail may also indicate this situation from another point of view where nets, weighted by the strength and thickness of the *thick rope*, needed only a lighter rope (*sma raip*) after the change-over to cotton and after the inversion. There was, however, a type of shallow net used for winter fishing (nine score meshes deep, as against a normal eighteen score) where the *sma raip* consisted of several light ropes bound together, as in the *corky net* already noticed. Such a net, from Fife, is on exhibition at the Fishery Museum at Anstruther.

Cork Rope

This is C in Figure 2. The name is self-explanatory, although in one type of net (already mentioned) the corks can be set on the OSSILS.

[27] Rev. Walter Gregor, *The Dialect of Banffshire* (London, 1866).

19

As might perhaps have been expected, *cork rope* is the commonest designation and the distribution is relatively even over the whole coast line. There are, however, certain exceptions and these occur mainly on the east coast. Thus Boddam has *top raip*, Skateraw *float raip*, Gourdon *top rope*, Arbroath *main raip*. In the outer Moray Firth (north) the usage seems to be simply *the raip* /ðə rep/, at least at Helmsdale. (Wick gave *cork rope*.) Evidently *the raip* has come in from Buckie through the settlement of some fisher families in Helmsdale. In fact, my informant who bore a well-known Buckie fisher name, was a member of such a family. Furthermore, /rep/ is the expected pronunciation of *rope* for the southern, not the northern, shores of the Moray Firth.

All the ports of the outer Moray Firth (south) gave *cork rope* but with an important alternative for Buckie, Findochty, Cullen, and Lossiemouth. This alternative was the word *raipy* /repe/ or *the raip* /ðə rep/. Now, my informant in Buckie, consistently with what has already been noted from Gregor, told me that until about 1890 the corks were set on the OSSILS. Obviously, the top rope which bore no corks could hardly bear the designation *cork rope*. There seems no doubt that it was *this* which was called the /rep/ or /repe/. In addition, my informant told me, this was a single rope, not double. A double rope only became common when it came to bear the corks. The word *raipy*, then, may be an intentional diminutive. (I have not shown this rope as double in Figure 2. When double, only one rope passed *through* the cork. The other passed over it.) Probably the same sort of consideration—the unevenness in the acceptance of a new word for the adaptation of an old thing—can also be applied to the interpretation of the varied usages on the east coast which, as has already been noted, do not employ a compound of the words *cork* and *rope*. It seems at least possible that a *top raip* or *main raip* which now bears the corks, derives from the type of net where the corks were on the OSSILS.

The Edge of the Net

Reference to Figure 2 will show the exact position of this (H). It is not to be confused with the CORK ROPE or SOLE ROPE. It seems that it is not an absolutely universal practice to finish off a net at the edge (to give strength and to resist tearing) with a line seized to the meshes. Alternatively, several strands formed of the net twine itself can be gathered together and seized to form an edge.

For much of the coastline the word distribution is relatively uniform. Thus, from Caithness to Kincardineshire the evidence is for a

20

compound word with *head* as its first element. There is, however, one important exception which will be noticed presently. But, for the pattern in general, Wick and Helmsdale gave *head line*; Avoch, Lossiemouth, and Buckie *head leck*; Findochty and Hopeman *head string*; Gamrie *head towie*; Broadsea, Peterhead, and Boddam *head tow*; Skateraw, Stonehaven, and Gourdon *heed raip*. It is important to notice that in all cases and in spite of the most obvious meaning of the word *head*, these compounds apply to both top *and* bottom of the net.

The exception to this regular usage of *head* over this stretch of coastline is Cairnbulg which has *side tow*. (Again, this refers to both top and bottom of the net.) Mr Murison has suggested to me that this is Scots *side* (='drooping, trailing, hanging down,' ON *síðr*). In fact, this must relate to an important feature in what fishermen usually call the *mounting* or *raiping* of the net. This is the making up of a net into proper, usable, form from the *sheet* (i.e. the simple net—the twine meshes only) by seizing on to it the requisite ropes, ossils, corks, etc. Now, in doing this, and so that the net might be as effective as possible in the meshing of the fish, it is necessary to see that it hangs relatively loosely (i.e. not too flat). It must, as herring fishers often say, have some 'flow'. It must not hang 'ower plain on the raips'. And because this is so the visible effect on the edge of the net, as it hangs on the upper ossils, is that it hangs *side*. That is to say the edge tends to droop. Hence, *side tow*.

South of Kincardineshire, Ferryden gave no return. My informant was unable to give any particular name. Arbroath gave *sma raip* and Fife and Berwickshire *the happing*, i.e. /hapṇ/ for Fife and /hɔpṇ/ for Berwickshire. This, it must be presumed, is *the covering* (cf. the verb *to hap* = 'to cover'). It is commonly said, in this Firth of Forth area, that a net is 'ower plain on the happin' when it has insufficient 'flow'.

There are two observations which might usefully be made on the distributions outlined above: (1) The pattern seems to show a distinct and possibly significant break south of Ferryden: (2) The inner Moray Firth seems to form a significant group by the use of *leck* /lək/ (='lug'; but something will be said of this interpretation under the next item).

The Gable

This is the vertical edge of the net (G). If the word *gable* is used, there are two possible versions—*gavel* /gevl̩/ and, to use Gregor's spelling, *gehl* /gel/. In one or other form this usage extends from Caithness to Kincardineshire (cf. the distribution of the *head* compounds in the previous item). Within this area the *gavel* form appears on the east coast from Broadsea to Stonehaven, again in the outer Moray Firth (north), and again in the inner Moray Firth—at least at Avoch and Lossiemouth. (Hopeman gave *gavel*.) For the outer Moray Firth (south) the form was *gehl*.

South of Kincardineshire there is an abrupt and total change. Ferryden has *end cord* /ɛnd kuərd/, Arbroath *lug*, and Fife and Berwickshire *head back* in the forms /hed bak/ for Fife and /hid bak/ for Berwickshire.

The form *lug* at Arbroath is the first point of interest. In the previous item (THE EDGE OF THE NET) the form *headleck* was given for the inner Moray Firth. This is most probably *head* and *lug*. (See, for example, the entries *Headleck* and *Fitlick* in the *Scottish National Dictionary* where the etymologies *headlug* and *footlug* are given.) The *lug* of a herring net was usually referred to by my informants as the loop at the corners of the net by which it is attached to the next net in the train (Figure 2, L.) It is to be noted, however, that in Berwickshire the word *becket* and not *lug* is used. Now, it may be that both for *head leck* in the inner Moray Firth and *lug* at Arbroath the name of a part has come to designate the whole. This notion is strengthened—at least for *lug* as designating the GABLE of the net—by a statement by Mitchell in his description of what he calls the 'Scotch Method' for nets: 'The ends of each net are strengthened by being attached to a rope (or cords of two or three plies joined together) which ends are termed in certain coasts lugs.'[28] So that the cord itself, we are to understand, runs the entire length of the *gavel* and the *ends* of it are termed *lugs*. This, incidentally, seems to give significance to the term *end cord* of Ferryden. It is fortunate (but of course it is one of the advantages of the geographical method that it tends to elicit this sort of information) that the precise form *lug* has been found to exist at at least one known point and to designate an *edge* of the net (in this case the vertical edge).

The use of the term *head back* in Berwickshire and Fife for the vertical edge of the net appears at first sight to be inappropriate in view of the usages of *head* in the items SOLE ROPE and EDGE OF THE NET which have already been studied. Indeed, it is now clear that the term *head* is variously applied to positions which can unequivocally be defined as top, bottom, or side. Nevertheless, it happens that for GABLE we have what seems to be conclusive historical and documentary evidence to support the evidence gathered in the field.

[28] J. M. Mitchell, *The Herring—Its Natural History and National Importance* (Edinburgh, 1864), p. 92.

In the diagram appended to 'A Letter to a Member of Parliament' (1750) this part of the net is shown and referred to as 'The Head Balk of the Net, being two small Lines about the Thickness of a Quil, to which each Mash at the end of the Net is laced with Threeply Twine'. Now, there is some evidence, in a note which accompanies the diagram, that the term *Head Balk* is a *relative* rather than an absolute term; for the note concludes with a reference to the same part of the net as the *hind Balk*. The precise words are: 'N.B. The hind Balks of the Nets, when fixed for Service, are joined together with short pieces of Twine...' It appears, therefore, that *when the nets are joined together* in a train, edge to edge, the *head balk* of one is joined to what must be termed the *hind balk* of the next. Yet both *head balk* and *hind balk* must also be what is here categorized as GABLE. I have not, in fact, elicited the term *hind balk* in my field-work.

The nomenclature of the diagram would be more convincing and certainly more useful if we knew the precise linguistic background of its author. But the work is unsigned, although Mitchell and Cash attribute it to F. Grant without comment.[29] Mr J. R. Seaton of the Department of Printed Books of the National Library of Scotland has brought to my notice Sir William Fraser's *The Chiefs of Grant* where (i, 512) Francis Grant is given as the third son of Sir Francis Grant, first baronet of Monymusk, and an eminent lord of session (Lord Cullen). Francis Grant, the son, is described as being, among other things, a merchant in Leith and a promoter of the Scotch Fisheries. This accords with the scanty internal evidence in the 'Letter'.

In addition to his diagram of a net, Grant appends a plan of a buss and a plan of Peterhead. There are two copies of the work in the National Library of Scotland. One includes, in addition to the Peterhead plan, plans of the harbours at Campbeltown, Lamlash, Baltasound, Uyeasound, and Fair Isle; and views of Unst, Fetlar, Fair Isle, and Arran. All of this, it need hardly be stressed, would be of great service to herring fishers. It is perhaps worth noting the form *mash* in the passage quoted above. This is the expected form for the East Neuk of Fife—but it may simply be the author's version of English *mesh*. (The form in Berwickshire and in the north of Scotland would be *mask*.) It is also worth recording that he uses the form *bush rope* for MESSENGER.

[29] Sir Arthur Mitchell and C. G. Cash, *A Contribution to the Bibliography of Scottish Topography*, vols. xiv and xv of *Publications of the Scottish Historical Society*, 2nd Series (Edinburgh, 1917).

The Ossils

These are shown at O in Figure 2. They also appear in Figure 1. They are (at the top) short lengths of line from which the net is suspended from the CORK ROPE; and (at the bottom) they are short lengths of line, but rather longer and rather fewer in number than those at the top, which attach the bottom EDGE OF THE NET to the SOLE ROPE. There are, therefore, *top ossils* and *bottom ossils* (OE *nostle*).

There are four fairly well-defined usages. *Ossil* extends, with one or two breaks, from Burnmouth as far as Lossiemouth. The variety *nussel* occurs at Crail, *hussel* at Arbroath, and *russel* at Ferryden. The breaks in the sequence are *hanger* at Gourdon and Johnshaven and (further north) at Cairnbulg. Thereafter (turning into the Moray Firth) *sneed* occurs at Broadsea and Gamrie, before *ossil* again appears at Banff, Findochty, Buckie, and Lossiemouth. *Sneed* then occurs for the inner Moray Firth (Avoch and Hopeman). From another point of view, the Moray Firth (inner and south) can be defined as a *sneed* area extending from Broadsea to Avoch with an *ossil* area intervening in the middle. Finally, the word *daffin* occurs for the outer Moray Firth (north).

At Buckie the form *daffin ossil* occurs, together with *ossil*, and two different types are indicated. The words seem to reflect a particular development in the mounting of the net—a process which has already been described in another connection. Before the rapid advance of the industry—perhaps the drive into the offing on the east coast is a good *datum* here—OSSILS were made by the fishermen themselves. They were formed three-fold from a hank of cotton and affixed to the CORK ROPE with an *ossil knot* which was made (to give a very rough description) by the generally seamanlike practice, which is used in a variety of processes, of passing a few turns of the OSSIL over the CORK ROPE *and* over the thumb of the left hand (which is holding the CORK ROPE)—withdrawing the thumb—passing the end of the OSSIL through the space thus left—and pulling all tight. But this took time. It seems, as the industry progressed, that it became common to buy the OSSILS ready-made. In this case, however, they were twofold, not threefold; and they were made with an eye at one end which made the process of bending-on quicker than with the *ossil knot*. At Peterhead, I was given the word *eye-ossil* for this type.

My information, both from Buckie and Peterhead, was that *daffin ossils* or *eye ossils* were relatively new. Nevertheless, the author of the 'Letter to a Member of Parliament' defines OSSILS as 'small Lines made on Purpose, each 18 Inches long; they are fixed to two Mashes at one end, by an Eye, and to the Spier-rope by the other end'.

24

(Spier-rope is Dutch *speer reep*, i.e. the *top* connecting rope.) Clearly, therefore, *eye-ossils* were not new in the lifetime of any of my informants. Very probably they were simply adaptations in a new, and expanding, situation. In any case, I found that, at St Monans for example, the word *loop* was used to define a two-ply OSSIL which was used at the *winter* fishing. It was weaker and broke more easily and had, therefore, the advantage of not tearing the net in any sort of strain. Obviously, in this connection the historical significance of the inshore fishing of the Firth of Forth, of which some account has been given, is relevant, and it may be that this type of fishing originally and continuously employed this type of OSSIL, and that it is to this which the author of the 'Letter' refers. Certainly, the word *daffin* in the outer Moray Firth (north) seems to refer to this type of fishing. From my field-work, I report the rather remarkable fact that my informant from the island of Stroma (now resident on the mainland after the total exodus from the island of a few years ago) could give me the word *daffin* without knowing the word *ossil* as an alternative. This was a man who had fished for the herring not consistently or particularly commercially, but who had put in a few nets as occasion offered (in fact he fished without a *bush-rope*). For him, *daffin* was the word and there was no other. My informants at Wick and Helmsdale—in common with all other places with different usages—knew, and sometimes used, the word *ossil* while insisting on the common local word. There seems to be little doubt that, at the peak of the drift-net fishing, before the First World War, *ossil* was the dominant form and for this the dispersal, around Britain, of otherwise local fishermen, must be responsible.

The word *sneed* (OE *snōd*) which I have recorded for the Moray Firth (inner and south, i.e. specifically for Avoch, Hopeman, Gamrie, and Broadsea) is also, of course, used, with various dialect reflexes for the *ō*,[30] in all parts of the Scottish east coast, for that part of the traditional small-line or great-line which is attached to the main *balk* of the line and which, eventually, bears the hook. One interesting fact is that, for Avoch, the word when used specifically in this connection (i.e. for small-line or great-line) is generally not *sneed* but *strood* /strud/ or /strëd/. This development of a nasal /n/ to /r/ is common enough in Avoch (e.g. /kri/ *knee*). Hence, not only this pair of doublets but one or two others (not necessarily showing the same phonetic phenomenon) occur in Avoch and are fairly obviously to be related to the Gaelic substratum. The form *sneed* /snid/ might be

[30] For the distribution of these see J. Y. Mather, 'Aspects of the Linguistic Geography of Scotland, III: Fishing Communities of the East Coast', *Scottish Studies*, xiii, part 1 (1969), 1–16.

expected anywhere from Avoch to Stonehaven. The actual occurrence of the word itself extends only to Broadsea, and in any case with a large *ossil* area intervening. There must be a fairly strong argument in favour of the interpretation of this as a new intrusion due to the expanding industry in the Moray Firth. Similarly, it is clear that *ossil* dominates the East Coast, and the Firth of Forth, except for the occurrences of *hanger*.

The thick Twine

To a depth of about five or six meshes the net is given an all-round edging of rather thicker twine (T).

I found the word *selvage* to be in use at two separated places—Helmsdale and Stonehaven. However tenuous this evidence is for any sort of connection between the East Coast and the outer Moray Firth (north), it is to be observed that this is not the first time an indication of this sort has appeared (cf. GABLE, SOLE-ROPE, BUSH-ROPE). Wick gave *thick twine*, and so did Gamrie, Ferryden, and (at least as an alternative term) Burnmouth. Cairnbulg gave *thick cotton*. At Arbroath my informant asserted that there was no name for this particular feature, and that it was to be included under the term *sma raip* which (as has already been pointed out) is the name there for the EDGE OF THE NET.

None of these usages shows a particularly obvious homogeneity in geographical extent. Nevertheless, there are three further terms, and these rather more common, where it is possible to show a relatively continuous usage on a given stretch of coastline. The words are *grofe twine*, *gairdin*, and *twa mash*. The word *grofe twine*, or simply *the grofe*, extends continuously from Avoch to Banff (although with an alternative *boutin* for Avoch and Lossiemouth). At Buckie my informant pointed out that *grofe* referred to the type of twine used and *bord* or *border* to the THICK TWINE. At the same time, he also pointed out that the term *the grofe* was very commonly used to designate the *border* itself. The *Scottish National Dictionary* equates *grofe* with Middle Dutch *grof* (='rough, rude') and Modern Dutch *grof* (='coarse, rough', e.g. of bread or salt). But it also adds: 'The frequency of the word in Ross-shire and Inverness-shire suggests associative influence from Gaelic *garbh*, with similar meanings, thick, rough, stormy, gruff, coarse.' The term *the gairdin* (='the guarding') was used from Broadsea to Skateraw, with a break only at Cairnbulg (*thick cotton*, see above). Fife and Berwickshire were together (once again) in the term *twa mash*, i.e. in the forms /twɔ maʃ/ for Fife and /twe mask/ for Berwickshire.

The historical evidence of the 'Letter to a Member of Parliament' can again be brought to bear—this time for the term *twa mash*. What the key to the diagram refers to as 'the upper edge or two Mashes of the Net' is a *line*, and not an edging of a few meshes deep. This is clear in the diagram and explicit in the key. The words are: 'The upper Edge or two Mashes of the Net, being a Line full twice as big as a Quil, to which each Mash of the upper Edge of the Net is laced with...Twine.' Indeed, the diagram does not show a complete and single *sheet* of net at all, but 'four Pieces of which the net consists'. (The illustration in E. J. March's book shows precisely this.)[31]

One possibility which might seem to emerge from these considerations is that Arbroath, which gave no word, is a relic area which preserves its own name for the line itself (*sma raip*), but has no name (because originally there was no *thing*) for the THICK TWINE. Nevertheless, the situation is probably more subtle than this. Consider the *twaw mash/twae mask* of Fife and Berwickshire, as well as the *two Mashes* of the 'Letter to a Member of Parliament'. What is the precise significance of the term? The answer, I believe, can only come out of a postulation that it refers not to a *thing*, but to a *process*— the process of *raiping* the net and of giving it 'flow'. My informant at Burnmouth spoke of two techniques: (1) *to raip on the third*, and (2) *to raip on the twae mask*. In general, it must be understood that a net will hang quite 'plain' (i.e. without 'flow') if the OSSILS from the CORK ROPE are made fast to the EDGE OF THE NET at a point immediately below; if, in fact, the OSSILS are quite perpendicular. To *raip on the third* is (to describe the technique very roughly) to make fast every third OSSIL rather off the perpendicular and thus to induce a slightly tucked or pleated effect in the net, in other words to induce 'flow'. This was the technique which my informant had constantly practised. But he knew of another—at least by name—and this was *to raip on the twae mask*. It is, perhaps, worth recalling the definition which the author of the 'Letter' gives for OSSIL. (It has already been noticed under this item.) 'Ossils', he says, are 'small Lines...fixed to two Mashes at one end...' I am unable to take the matter any further for the present, but it seems clear that both *on the third* and *on the twae mask* can be interpreted as referring to a *process*. For, as has already been noticed, there is a name for the *thing* itself (THE EDGE OF THE NET). In Burnmouth it is *the hoppin*.

Net furthest away / Net next the Boat

So far as I am aware, these are the only two nets which are expressly designated. The NET FURTHEST AWAY is, obviously, the net

[31] See note 18.

first shot; and the NET NEXT THE BOAT the last. In the following discussion of distributions, where names are given in pairs the first named refers to the net first shot. It is also necessary to note that, in fisher parlance, these names are generally used as substantives, but that they can be used, and often are used, as adjectives qualifying the word *net*.

Trail and *swing* are used in the outer Moray Firth (north), the inner Moray Firth (except Avoch, i.e. specifically in Hopeman, Lossiemouth, Buckie, Findochty) and in Berwickshire. Avoch gave *po en* /po ɛn/ and *buird* /bjurd/. What seems to be a near variant of *trail* and *swing* is *tail* and *swing*, and this is used for the outer Moray Firth (south) and the East Coast as far as Stonehaven. Thereafter (i.e. further south) the usage is *tail* and *buird* /bjurd/ with *tail* and *berd* /berd/ in Fife.

For the NET FURTHEST AWAY, therefore, the distribution shows clearly defined *trail* and *tail* areas and one seemingly isolated instance of *po en*. This last may possibly be *pole end*, i.e. presumably a pole set on a buoy to mark the end of a train of nets, although for Cornwall R. M. Nance (*A Glossary of Cornish Sea-words*, 1963) gives it as: 'The outer end of a net. A wooden pole was formerly used to extend this'. On the other hand, the word may be *poll* (='head, crown'). However interpreted, the expression seems to be in use in East Anglia, but Avoch was the only place in my investigation which gave it as the common, local usage. J. W. de Caux, in a rambling poem which is nevertheless full of East Anglian fishing lore, spoke of the heinousness of running down a drifter's gear:

> ...It is most unfair
> To *take foul berth* or *top a powl end down*
> To sail through nets regardless of all care.[32]

If the word is indeed a borrowing into the terminology of Avoch it is curious that—with a very regular East Anglian fishing from the Moray Firth, and other ports—it has apparently taken hold at no other place.

The *trail*/*tail* distribution is an interesting general type to which— as will be apparent presently— *buird*/*swing* (for the NET NEXT THE BOAT) also conforms. *Tail* appears in a continuous line from Banff to St Monans with *trail* flanking this both to north and south, i.e. in the inner and outer Moray Firth (north) and in Berwickshire. For *buird*/*swing* there is a fairly small area, extending from Stonehaven to St Monans, of *buird* (or *berd*—this must here be classified as a subarea) flanked by an extensive *swing* area to the north and south.

[32] J. W. de Caux, *The Cruise of the 'Bunch of Roses'* (Great Yarmouth, 1887).

Avoch, in this case, is an isolated example of *buird* just as it is also isolated in its use of *po en*.

For the interpretation of the words *trail* and *tail* it is possible that it is unecessary to look much beyond the obvious meaning of the words. Both seem to fit a net which, by definition, is furthest away from the boat. Nevertheless, there is a curious piece of dialect description from the middle of the nineteenth century which might suggest a different interpretation. The anonymous author of the article in *Blackwood's Magazine* to which attention was drawn at the beginning of this essay observed that at least for Fittie (which lies at the mouth of the Dee at the entrance to Aberdeen harbour) the fisher's dialect had this peculiarity: 'The r he scarcely sounds; and his pronunciation is rather labial than guttural.'[33] For example, when buying a hat a fisherman from Fittie will ask for 'a ba ordinary fisher mannie at' and not for 'a bra ordinary fisherman's hat'. It is noteworthy that Fittie lies at the very centre of the *tail* area. The *trail* area—as has already been shown—lies at the extremities.

For the interpretation of the word *swing* there is some indication from informants who at two places—Stonehaven and Burnmouth— were careful to point out that, strictly, the word referred to the *rope* (made fast to the MESSENGER) by which the vessel rode to her nets. Indeed, in some early notes made by William Grant, Stonehaven is referred to as having both *swing* and *buird* for the NET NEXT THE BOAT.[34] In my own field-work my informant for the Downies—a small fishing place to the north of Stonehaven at which fishing is no longer carried on—had no name to give other than *the net next to the boat*. It is noteworthy that north of the Stonehaven area *swing* is the only usage (except, of course, at Avoch) and that south of the Stonehaven area there is a continuous *buird/berd* area, which is eventually flanked, of course, by the *swing* of Berwickshire. Yet it was at Burnmouth that my informant pointed out that, strictly, *swing* did not refer to the net, and that formerly *the beerd net* /ðə bird nɛt/ was perfectly possible. The word *buird/berd* is no doubt to be interpreted as the boards or platform upon which the nets lay as they were hauled.

Conclusion

This essay began by drawing attention to a form of patterning in Scotland which, first, could be described as a simple stratification;

---

[33] Op. cit., p. 297.
[34] The first editor of the *Scottish National Dictionary*. The notes are in its archives.

and, second, could have its linguistic evidence matched, layer by layer, by non-linguistic evidence. It will now be evident that if, in the study of the word geography of the traditional drift-net fishery on the Scottish east coast, Albert Dauzat's 'véritable géologie du langage' is again considered, no simple image is possible—as, for instance, 'les couches successives des mots en grande partie enfouies', as if the words, and their significance, could be shown to be stratified and patiently and systematically exposed. On the contrary, it becomes necessary at all points to determine precisely *what* linguistic geography, as here applied, has succeeded in unearthing.

It is perhaps reasonable to claim that for four words—*side tow*, *lug*, *head balk*, *twae mask*—the geographical method has uncovered certain evidence which further historical investigation might be inclined to place in a wider setting. For instance, *side tow* was found only at one place (Cairnbulg) but was interpreted in such a way as to argue a possibly much wider historical usage. And for *head balk* and *twae mask* which were also found to exist in a limited geographical area, some historical evidence was presented—not, certainly, with an exact provenance, but at least taken from the terminology of a published work intended as propaganda and therefore to be widely and generally understood.

It seems, therefore, that several relic areas have been found to exist. In the assessment of these the argument throughout has been that proper attention should be paid to the non-linguistic evidence, both historical and technical, and a few examples of the probable effects of this and its linguistic consequences have been given. In particular, it is apparent that further careful technical study of various processes in the preparation of the fishing gear, rather than a simple naming of parts, may become more and more rewarding as the processes become better understood in their linguistic usages. The suggested interpretations already given of some of the information gathered in the field will probably be sufficient to show the importance of this.

The material used here has, of course, been very limited. Similarly, the range of the field-work has also been limited. Orkney and Shetland, for instance, have not been included. But probably enough has been said of the linguistic areas which it is the special province of linguistic geography to define. There seems little doubt that the areas inner Moray Firth, outer Moray Firth (north and south), East Coast, and Firth of Forth (Fife and Berwickshire) can be constructed out of the linguistic data, and reinforced by the non-linguistic data. The next most obvious step is to work over more and more relevant material and to extend the range.

It is essential that linguistic geography should not try to claim too much. The fact that certain historical, documentary, evidence has been brought to bear for the interpretation of data collected in the field does not diminish but adds to the geographical method. The aim must be to try to understand a *situation*—the drift-net fishery of the Scottish east coast, for example—not, admittedly, as a totality (which is impossible, and even meaningless) but as a unified structure with all available evidence compacted and brought together. This at least seems possible, and it is all the more important as a basis for comparative studies in a wider area. For example, on the theme which has been discussed here, an area like the entire North Sea basin seems to offer scope for unified studies by scholars from all its coasts. This essay is intended to be a contribution to such studies.

2 Coal-mining Language: a recent Investigation

Peter Wright

My interest in coal-mining language began in the 1950s when I started in mid-term supply teaching in the West Riding.[1] Miners could be recognized as those at village street corners [sɪtɪn ən ðəɪ ʊŋkəz] *sitting on their hunkers* (i.e. haunches, cf. *OED Hunkers*), and in school on non-formal occasions their children's vernacular was equally noticeable. It was astonishing, having laboured with an apparently normal secondary modern class throughout most of the day, to supervise football or cricket matches where the pupils used a different language altogether. Just as puzzling, after a move to a Derbyshire grammar school in another mining district, was constantly to meet *thou* and *thee*, as in [ðaː dɪd ɪt] *Thou did it*, [ðiːl kəp ɪt] *Thee'll cop* (i.e. catch) *it*. The latter usage, very different from Standard English grammar and more typical of the West Country, does occur in some Midland dialects (see *EDD*, s.v. *Thee*, II, 2). Very salutary was the occasion when many of the pupils, told to collect and compare samples of a native's unorthodox grammar, returned with some prize specimens which had just issued from a fellow teacher: after that I was more careful. There were, too, remarkable meetings with audiences of men and women in mining communities, resulting in numerous questions (the attraction being not the speaker but the subject) where the response differed markedly from the polite acceptance similar talks would receive in, say, a residential city suburb. All this suggested that there was great knowledge of mining terms and interest in them waiting to be tapped.

Before starting I had been warned that any attempt to trace mining dialect patterns might well be useless because of the frequent and

[1] My thanks are due to Mr Michael McMahon, lecturer in linguistics at Jordanhill College of Education, for the minute accuracy of his transcriptions from Auchinloch, Dunbartonshire; to National Coal Board publicity officers, pit managers and foremen, officials of the National Union of Mineworkers, and Sheffield and Salford colleagues who helped as contacts for the investigation; and, of course, to the informants themselves, without whose patience and enthusiasm this survey would have been far from easy.

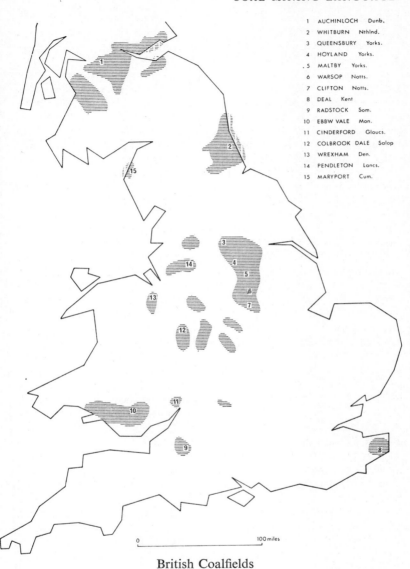

COAL-MINING LANGUAGE

1 AUCHINLOCH Dunb.
2 WHITBURN Nthlnd.
3 QUEENSBURY Yorks.
4 HOYLAND Yorks.
. 5 MALTBY Yorks.
6 WARSOP Notts.
7 CLIFTON Notts.
8 DEAL Kent
9 RADSTOCK Som.
10 EBBW VALE Mon.
11 CINDERFORD Gloucs.
12 COLBROOK DALE Salop
13 WREXHAM Den.
14 PENDLETON Lancs.
15 MARYPORT Cum.

0   100 miles

British Coalfields

33

large-scale exchange of miners and mining words between coalfields, but it is for the reader to judge how far these fears were justified. At one extreme are a few very old collieries like place 12 (the Shropshire collieries of Colbrook Dale were apparently shipping coal down the Severn in the seventeenth century). There are other survivors of larger colliery areas, like place 9, the Kilmerston pit at Radstock, the only one now working on the Somerset coalfield. The Whitburn pit (place 2) has closed, like all those in 'The Forest' (Forest of Dean, including place 11). Linguistic problems certainly start when, as so often, a pit draws many of its workers from other coalfields. For example, Cannock Chase, a deep-mining area which began in a big way about 1850, was manned chiefly from pits in Colbrook Dale and north Staffordshire which had closed; and more recently there have been big migrations from County Durham to the Yorkshire–Derbyshire–Nottinghamshire coalfield, from the Forest of Dean to South Wales, and, in spite of Lord Robens's soothing remarks, many forced moves from the Cumberland and Lancashire pits. The linguistic problem is most acute in relation to the Kent coalfield, the youngest in the country and only sixty years old (mining started in 1908), because it has drawn some of its miners from the fishing industry and the great majority of its workers from all the other coalfields. One official who has worked for the last sixteen years at these mines insists that there is 'no Kent dialect', i.e. no local mining dialect, there. Faced with all this, all one can do is to overhear and question native miners from each area, and assemble the evidence to see what—if anything—it proves.

The remainder of this essay will give an outline description of the present survey, including some account of the localities and informants, and the basic questionnaire which was used. The material was collected, as opportunity arose, during the period 1964–70, from fifteen sections of the English, Scottish, and Welsh coalfields. As informants, elderly and middle-aged natives were preferred, though twice (locs. 7 and 8) younger men were interviewed with the object of determining to what extent age was a significant factor in dialectal usage.

In the list below, each place is preceded by its dialect area identification (D) according to the two maps in A. J. Ellis, *English Dialects: Their Sounds and Homes* (English Dialect Society, 1890), and followed by the initials and ages (at the time of interview) of the chief informants.

1. (D 35) Auchinloch, Dunbartonshire. J. H. (60)
2. (D 32) Whitburn, Nb. M. H. (79), J. T. M. (60)

3. (D 24) Queensbury, Y. H. B. (72)
4. (D 24) Hoyland, Y. R. S. (71)
5. (D 24) Maltby, Y. S. C. (67)
6. (D 27) Warsop, Nt. H. H. (65)
7. (D 27) Clifton, Nt. E. H. (32)
8. (D 9) Deal, K. J. H. (32)
9. (D 4) Radstock, So. V. H. C. (57), F. P. H. (41)
10. (–) Ebbw Vale, Mon. C. S. C. (67)
11. (D 4) Forest of Dean, Gl. E. E. R. (59)
12. (D 14) Colbrook Dale, Sa. G. C. (47)
13. (–) Wrexham, Denbighshire. P. W. (50)
14. (D 22) Pendleton, La. T. D. (60), W. J. (59)
15. (D 31) Maryport, Cu. J. B. W. (55)

Just as important as the results of any dialect survey is the questionnaire which is used, since it reveals how the results have been achieved. Later researchers can, I hope, use, extend or adapt the present one for use in other collieries. Where possible, answers were obtained by overhearing natural conversations, the best method wherever time allows, but the basic tool was the mining questionnaire.

The questionnaire was devised on the lines of the Dieth-Orton one, the master-key to all results in the *Survey of English Dialects*; and was similar in length and approach to the inshore-fishing questionnaire which I used to obtain sets of answers from some fifty places round the British coasts.[2] Answers cited in the present essay, like the fishing ones, were never obtained by a purely postal method: they come from direct conversations and field-work, often conducted in the informants' homes where they could best relax, but also down the pit, in a village hall, on village streets and in a miners' hospital. There was a preliminary questionnaire from which uninteresting items were dropped, while those bringing only sporadically good results were redrafted. The present version, though, like every questionnaire, imperfect, tries to avoid leading questions, the dots prefacing many of the questions meaning simply 'What do you call?' or 'What's your word for?'

Basic Questionnaire

(1)...the place dug straight down in the earth to take out coal? (MINE)

2 See P. Wright, 'Proposal for a Short Questionnaire for use in Fishing Communities', *Transactions of the Yorkshire Dialect Society*, xi, part lxiv (1964), 27–32; 'Fishing Language around England and Wales', *Journal of the Lancashire Dialect Society*, xvii (1968), 2–14.

(2)...the people who work there? (MINERS)

(3)...the rock containing coal that shows above ground? (OUTCROP)

(4)...a mine entered down a sloping passage from the side? (DRIFT-MINE)

(5)...a steel bucket, big enough for two men to stand in, used to make a main shaft? (STEEL BUCKET)

(6)...the part of the mine above ground? (PIT-HEAD)

(7)...those great mounds of useless black material dug up and left near a mine? (SLAG-HEAPS)

(8)...the channel round a shaft lining to catch water draining from the walls? (CHANNEL)

(9)...the iron frame which goes up and down a mine shaft? (CAGE)

(10) How would the men at the pit bottom signal or what would they shout to show they were ready to come up? (HAUL UP!)

(11)...the chief passage in a mine? (MAIN ROAD)

(12)...a sloping passage where loaded tubs pull up the empty ones? (SELF-ACTING INCLINE)

(13)...the places at intervals at the side of a roadway to give cover for miners? (MAN-HOLES)

(14)...making the roadway less narrow? (WIDENING)

(15)...the roads going off the chief passage? (SIDE-ROADS)

(16)...small connecting passages? (CONNECTING PASSAGES)

(17)...a passage that finishes blocked-up? (CUL-DE-SAC)

(18)...for going from the pit bottom to the coal face? (INBY). And the other way? (OUTBY)

(19) How do you say what direction your place will be from the pit bottom? (I'M WORKING UP WEST, etc.)

(20)...the part of a pit allotted to one miner? (STALL)

(21)...the amount of work given to him? (STINT)

(22)...the man in charge at the pit-head? (MANAGER)

(23)...the officials working in the mine? (UNDER-MANAGER, OVER-MAN, DEPUTY, CORPORAL)

(24)...the man controlling the shaft top? (BANKSMAN)

(25)...the man at the pit bottom in charge of loading and unloading cages? (ONSETTER)

(26)...the colliery official who went from house to house in the early morning getting men up for work? (CALLER)

(27)...the man who sees to the pit props? (PIT CARPENTER)

(28)...the man in charge of one working place at the coal face? (STALLMAN)

(29)...the people who work with you? (COMPANIONS)

(30) Several miners work together in a...(TEAM)

(31)...the food you take to work with you as a meal? (LUNCH)

(32) What do you put round above your ankles? (LEG STRAPS)
(33)...this? (Show picture of a PICK)
(34) And this? (Show picture of a TOMMY-BAR)
(35)...a step in the mine floor? (STEP)
(36)...the lowest vein of coal in the mine? (LOWEST VEIN)
(37)...a place where the vein is broken? (FAULT)
(38)...the direction the joints go in coal? (GRAIN)
(39)...making a groove along the bottom of the coal face? (CUTTING UNDERNEATH)
(40)...a small prop of wood or coal to give support while the coal is being cut? (PROP)
(41)...making holes with a machine? (BORING)
(42)...the empty space where coal has been taken out? (WASTE SPACE)
(43)...a timber standing up? (VERTICAL PROP)
(44)...and one going across? (HORIZONTAL PROP)
(45)...a small piece of wood to support the roof? (WEDGE)
(46)...a thick column of stones or coal to support it? (PACK)
(47) What is left of it after it has been sliced? (STOOK)
(48)...a piece taken off it? (SLICE)
(49)...filling a hole ready for firing? (FILLING IT IN)
(50)...when the ground comes up? (FLOOR UPHEAVAL)
(51)...when the roof collapses? (FALL)
(52)...a dangerous piece in a roof which can fall out easily? (POT-HOLE)
(53)...coal which sounds as if it isn't solid? (HOLLOW)
(54)...a trough for carrying water away from the coal face? (SLUICE)
(55)...a small channel feeding water into it? (SMALL CHANNEL)
(56) To take the coal from the face to the shaft it was put into... (TUBS)
(57)...a small one for clearing rubbish? (RUBBISH TUB)
(58)...a label on a tub? (LABEL)
(59)...a number of tubs linked together? (SET)
(60) How do you brake them? (With a HOOK, etc.)
(61) How were the tubs switched to different lines? (By a TURN-TABLE, etc.)
(62) What is dug out of a mine? (COAL)
(63)...the big pieces? (LUMPS)
(64)...the smaller ones? (COBBLES)
(65) What do you put on a fire to keep it in if you are going out for a while? (COAL DUST)
(66)...poor coal? (POOR COAL)
(67)...a soft white substance found in coal seams? (CHALK STONE)
(68)...a gold-coloured vein? (BRASSY COAL)

(69)...stones and other rubbish in a mine? (DEBRIS)

(70)...a sort of fine sand thrown down mines to stop the danger of explosions? (STONE DUST)

(71) What would warn you there was danger of an explosion? (HALO in lamp)

(72)...it where gas keeps coming out of a crack? (ESCAPE OF GAS)

(73)...part of a mine that is no longer worked because of gas? (GAS-FAST)

(74)...the man who would set fire to pockets of gas in the roof? (FIREMAN)

(75)...the channel carrying fresh air into the mine? (INTAKE SHAFT)

(76)...the one carrying out the air? (RETURN SHAFT)

(77) In the airways, what things are there to make air pass right round the mine? (VENTILATION DOORS/CLOTHS)

(78)...the device at the pit-head to put coal onto a conveyor belt? (TIPPLER)

(79) For sorting, the tippler tips the coal through...(SCREENS)

(80)...the heavy substances which drop to the bottom when coal is washed? (DIRT)

(81) Who looked at samples of what a miner had dug to see what he should be paid? (CHECKER)

Selection of Results

The number before an item refers to its numbered question in the questionnaire above. Bracketed numbers after results correspond to the fifteen localities already detailed. * = unrecorded in *OED* and *EDD*.

(1) MINE [maɪn] (11)   [pʊt] *pit* (1–10, 12–15)

(2) MINER [maɪnə] (11, 12)   [məɪnəɾ] (9)   [kəlɪə] *collier* (1, 3–5, 7, 15)   [maɪnə]+older [kəlɪə] (6, 13)   [kəlɪə] if he works at coal-face but otherwise [maɪnə] (10)   [kɒlɪə]+broader dialect [pɪtmən] *pit-man* (2)   [pɪtmən] (8)

(4) DRIFT-MINE [duk] *duck** (1)   [deː-oːl] *day-hole* (2)   [deː-əʊl] (3)   [deː-ɔːl]+modern [fʊtɹɔːd] *foot-road* (4)   [fɒtɹɔːd] (6)   [deɪ-əʊl]+[dɹɪft] (5)   [dɹɪftmaɪn] (7)   [fʊtɹɪdʒ] *foot-ridge* (12)   [maɪn] if slanting down+[lɛvl̩] *level* if entered horizontally (10)   [lɛvl̩] *level* (11, 13)   [diː-aɪ] *day-eye* (14—see *OED Day* sb., 24)

(5) STEEL BUCKET [kɛtl̩] *kettle* (1)   [əpə] *hopper* (3, 4, 11, 13)   [əpʊt] *hoppet* (6)   [kɪbl̩] *kibble* (5, 14)   [skɪp] *skip* (9)   [baʊk] *bowk* (12)   [baʊk]+[kɛp] *kep** (10)

(6) PIT-HEAD [pethɪd] (1)   [pethed] (11, 12)   [pɪttəp] *pit-top* (4, 6, 7, 8)   [pɪthɛd]+[pɪttəp] (10)   [pɪttəp]+[pɪtɪəd] (3)

[baŋk] *bank* (2) [pɪthɛd]+[pɪtbaŋk] (13)   [pɪttəp]+older [pɪtbaŋk] +technical [iːpstɛd] *heap-stead* (5)   older [iːpstɛd]+more modern [pɪtbɹuː] *pit-brow* (14)

(7) SLAG HEAP [beŋ] *bing** (1)   [(pɪt)tɪp] (*pit-*)*tip* (2–4, 6, 8, 10, 11) [pɪtɪl] *pit-hill*+[pɪttɪp] (5)   [bəŋk] *bank* (14)   [dətiːp] *dirt-heap* (7) [dəːtmaɔnt]   *dirt-mount**   (12)   [spɔɪlbaŋk]   *spoil-bank*+[spɔɪliːp] *spoil-heap*+older [dəːttɪp] *dirt-tip* (13)   [tɪp]+older [batʃ] (9–cf. *EDD Bache*)

(11) CHIEF PASSAGE IN MINE [meˑn ɹoːd] *main road* (1)   [meɪn ɹoʊd] (6, 10–12)   [ɹoːd] (7)   [meːn ɹoədweː] *main roadway* (3)   [meən gəːdə ɹoːd] *main girder road* (15)   [geːt] *gate*+[ɹoːdweː]+[pleːn] *plane* (5)

(12) HAULAGE ROAD [kaɤse] *causey**+[hɛdeŋ] *heading** (1)   [dʒɪg] *jig* (12)   [dʒɪg]+[ɹoːp ɹoːd] *rope road* (6)   [dʒɪnɪ] *ginny* (4, 5, 11) [ɪŋklɔɪn] *incline* (9)   [ɪŋklaɪn] (10)   [stiːp] *steep** (8)   [bɹeɪk] *break** (13)   [spɔnɪbɹuː] *spinney-brow** (14)

(13) SAFETY-HOLE [manhol] *man-hole* (1)   [ʁɛfjuːdʒɔːl] *refuge-hole* (2)   [manɔɪl]+older [baɪ-ɔɪl] *by-hole* (3)   [manɔːl] (4)   [manɔːl] +[-ɔɪl] (5)   [manoʊl] (6, 11, 12)   [mænoʊl] (8)   [manhɔːl] (15)

(14) WIDENING THE ROADWAY [tʃiːkɪn] *cheeking**+[bɹʊʃɪn] *brushing** (6)   [tʃiːkɪn] (5, 8)   [bakbɹʊʃen] *back-brushing* (1)   [bakbɹʊʃn̩] (15)   [wɪdnɪn] (4, 11)

(15) SIDE ROAD [duk] *duck**+[hɛdeŋ] *heading* (1)   [ɛdɪn] (10–12) [stɔːlgeɪt] *stall-gate* (6)   [geːt] (3, 5, 13)   [geɪt] (7, 8)   [təˤnəyt] (9–cf. *OED Turn-out* sb., 4)

(16) SMALL CONNECTING PASSAGE [θɹuəɹ] *througher** (1)   [bʊəd] *board* (3, 5)   [bɔəd] (4)   [snɪkɪt] *snicket* (6, 12)   [slɪpɹoːd] *slip-road* +near surface [snɪkət] (7)   [snɪkət geɪt] *snicket gate* (8)   [stɔːlɹɔːd] *stall-road* (10)   [stɔːlɹɔːd]+[ʌpkʌt] *up-cut** (11)   [wɪnɹoːd] *wind-road* (14)   [kɹɔsɛnd] *cross-end** (15)

(17) CUL-DE-SAC [blen hidŋ̍] *blind heading* (1–a term 'deprecated' by the British Standards Institution booklet no. 3618)   [slɪp] *slip* (10)   [stəpɪn] *stopping* (11)   [fastɛnd] *fast-end* (5, 6, 7, 12)

(20) MINER'S WORKING PLACE [ɔɪl] *hole* (3, e.g. 'That's Billy Puck's hole')   [stɪnt] *stint* (7, 8, e.g. 'He's in 14 stint')   [pleːs] *place* (14) [pleːs]+[stɛnt] (1)   [stɔːl] *stall* (5, 6, 11, 12)   [ganənbɔːd] (2–cf. *EDD Gan* v.[1], 3)

(23) DEPUTY [dɛpətɪ] (2–4, 12, 13)   [dɛpətɛ] (7)   [faɪəmən] *fire-man*+[dɛpjətɪ] (10)   [ʃɔt faɪəɹə] *shot firer*+[faɪəmən] (1)   [ɛgzamɪnə] *examiner* (9)   [dəgɪ]* (14–cf. *EDD Doggy* sb.[1])   [dɛbətɪ]+[dəgɪ] (5)

(25) ONSETTER [ɔnsɛtə] (2, 6–7, 11, 12, 14, 15)   [aŋəɹɔn] *hanger-on* (5) [ɪŋəɹɔn] (3)   [aŋəɹɔn]+modern [ɔnsɛtə] (4)   [hɪtʃə] *hitcher* (10)

39

[ɒnsɛtəʳ]+more often [ɪtʃəʳ] (9) [petbətəməʳ] *pit-bottomer* (1) [uːkə] *hooker** (13)

(26) CALLER [nəkəɹɒp] *knocker-up* (4, 6, 14, 15) [nəkəɹʌp] (11, 12) [nəkərəp]+[tʃapərəp] *chapper-up** (1—but cf. *chapper* 'door-knocker' under *EDD Chap* v.²)

(27) PIT-CARPENTER [kɑːpɪntə] (12) [ʃafsmən] *shaftsman* (4, 6, 14, 15) [ʃɑːfsmən] (9) [ɹɪpə] *ripper* (6, 10) [tɪmbəɹə] *timberer** (5, 11) [dʒɔɪnə] *joiner* (7) [dʒeːnə] (1—cf. under *EDD Joiner* the spelling *geinere*)

(28) STALLMAN AND HIS HELPER no words (1) [kɒlɪə] *collier* and [pɒtə] *putter* (2) [kəlɪə] and [əɹɪə] *hurrier* (3) [stɔːlmən] and [tɹamə] *trammer* (4) [stɔːlmən] and [bɒtɪ] *butty* (5) [stɔːlmən]+ older [bɒtɪ] and [deːmən] *dayman* (6) [hjuəʳ] *hewer* and [kaʳtɪnbɔɪ] *carting-boy* (9) [kɒlɪə] and [bʌtɪ] (10) [maɪnə] and [bʌtɪ] (11—also as verb, to *butty* for someone) [kəlɪə] and [deːtələ] *daytaler* (14)

(29) COMPANIONS [nibəz] *neighbours** (1) [maʁəz] *marrows* (2) [marəz] (15) [meːts] *mates* (3, 5, 13, 14) [meɪts] (4, 6, 7, 11) [mɛːts] (12)

(31) LUNCH [piːs] *piece** (1—cf. *EDD Piece-time*) [snap] *snap* in a [snaptɪn] *snap-tin* (4—7, 10, 12, 14) [dʒɔk] *jock* in a [pɪtaŋkətʃ] *pit-handkerchief* (3) [təmɪ] *tommy* in a [təmɪbɒks] *tommy-box* (11) [beːt] *bait* (2) [beːt]+[kɹaʊdɪ] *crowdy* (15) [gɹʌb] *grub* in a [gɹʌbtɪn] *grub-tin* (9) [snap(ɪn)] *snap(ping)* (13)

(35) STEP IN MINE FLOOR [θɹɔː] *throw** (3) [ʌpθɹɔː] *up-throw* (12) [kanʃ] *canch** (6) [ɹaɪz] *rise* (11) [tɹamɪnɹaɪz] *tramming-rise** (5) [dʒɒmpɒp] *jump-up* (7) [ɹoːl] *roll*+[kanʃ]+[kɔːnʃ] (13) [heːtʃ]* (1—cf. *EDD Hatch* sb.⁴) [bɪŋk] *bink* (15)

(38) GRAIN IN COAL [slɪp] *slip* (9—11) [kliːt] *cleat* (6, 12, 15) [gɹeɪn] *grain* (7) [gɹeːn]+[kliːt] (13) [greːn]+[tiθ] *teeth** (1) [kliːt]+[ʃɒt] *shut** (14)

(39) TO CUT UNDERNEATH COAL [hol] *hole*+[hɛok] (1—cf. *EDD Huck* v.³) [hjuː] *hew* (2) [oʊl] (6, 11) [oːl] (5) [kʌt] (7, 10) [oʊl]+[kʌt] (12) [oːl]+[kɒt] (13) [əːl]+[dɪnt] *dint* (4) [hag] *hag* (15) [bɪnʃ] *binch** (9)

(40) SMALL CHOCK [geb] (see *EDD Jib*)+[stɛəl] *stale** (1) [tʃɔk] (8, 11) [tʃɒkə] *chocker**+[spɹag] *sprag* (6) [tʃɒk]+[spɹag] (4) [spɹag]+[klɒg] *clog* (5) [pɒstɪn] *postin** (3) [lid] *lid*+[hɛdtɹɛɪ] *head-tree* (15) [kɒg] *cog** (10)

(42) WASTE AREA [gəbɔɪl] *gob-hole* (3) [gɒb] (4—7, 9, 10, 12, 14) [gɔːf] *goaf* (2) [gɔː-əf] (15; variant of last) [kənde] *cundy* (1) [gɒb]+[weɪst] (11) [wɛːst] (12) [weːst] (13) [gɒb]+[goʊf]+ [weɪst] (8)

(43) VERTICAL PROP [pɹɒp] (8, 11, 13, 14) [lɒŋ pɹɒp] *long prop* (4)

[pɹəp] (15)　[pɹəp]+[lɛg] *leg* (6, 7, 12)　[lɛg] (1, 5)　[aːm] *arm* (10)
[pɒnʃən] *puncheon* (3)　[poːs] *post* under 3 ft.+[tɪmbəʳ] *timber* over
3 ft.+[ʌpɾɔɪt] *upright*+[stɪmpl̩] *stemple* (9)
(44) HORIZONTAL PROP [baː] *bar* (5, 6)　[bɑː] (11–13)　[bəʳ]+
[kɾʏ·n] *crown* (1)　[pɒnʃ(ə)] *punch(er)** (4)　[kələ] *collar* (10)　[flat]
flat (9)
(45) WEDGE [wɛdʒ] (2, 13)　[led] *lid* (1)　[lɪd] (11, 12)　[lid] (3, 15)
[gʌg] *gug** (9)　[pad] *pad* 1 ft.+[lɪd] if 6 inches (7)　[kapɪn] *capping*
(14)　[ɛdtɾɛɪ] *head-tree* (15)
(46) PILLAR [stüp] (*EDD Stoop* sb.[1], 5)+[stʏp]+[pak] *pack* (1)
[pak] (3–5, 11–13, 15)　[pakɪn] *packing* (6, 7)　[pɪlə] of coal+[pak]
of stones (14)
(47) SLICE [kɑt] *cut* (1)　[kɒt] (13)　[lɪft] *lift* (2)　[dʒɛŋk] *jenk** (5)
[dʒaɷ] *jow* (14)
(49) FILL IN CREVICES [gɔb ɪn] (6–cf. *EDD Gob* v.[3])　[stɛm] *stem*
(1, 4, 12–15)　[fɪl ɷp] (3)　[ɹam] *ram* (7, 9)　[stɛm]+[ɹam] (11)
(50) UPHEAVING OF FLOOR [hoveːŋ] *heaving** (1)　[pʌfʌp] *puff-up**
(11)　[pɒkɪn] *pucking* (10)　[flɔəlɪft] *floor-lift** (4, 6, 7, 12, 13)
[flɷəlɪft] (14)　[flɷəlɪft]+[flɷəblɔː] *floor-blow* (5)　[flɔəlɪft]+[flɔə-
bloɷ] (8)　[blɔː] (9)
(52) DEPRESSION IN ROOF [pəʔtɑs] *ʔpot-ash* (1)　[slɪp] *slip* (3)　[slɪp]
+[pətoɷl] *pot-hole* (6)　[pətɔːl] (4, 5, 14)　[stoːn] *stone* (2)　[bad
stjan] *bad stone* (15)　[bad oɷl] *bad hole* (7)　[bad gɹaɷnd] *bad
ground* (12)　[bɛl] *bell**+[wɛlvə] *welver** (11)　[bɛlmoɷld] *bell-
mould* (9)　[slɪp]+[swɪlɪ] (cf. *OED Swally*)+[ɹoːl] *roll* (13)
(53) HOLLOW [bos] *boss* (1)　[ələ] (3, 12, 14)　[dɹɷmɪ] *drummy** (5)
[dɹɷmɛ] (7)　[dɹɷmɪ]+[ələ]+[dɹɔːn] *drawn* (6)　[bagɪ] *baggy* (4,
11, 15)　[nɛʃ] (13–cf. *EDD Nesh* adj., 2)
(54) WATER CHANNEL [kʌʔn̩] *cutting* (1)　[ɹeɪs] *race*+[kɒtɪn]+
[ɹɪkət] *ricket* (5)　[gaːlənd] *garland* (9, 13)　[tʃanl̩] (12, 13)　[gɒlɪ]
gully (14)　Note—also [gɹɪp] *grip* at Wath-on-Dearne, Yorks. West
Riding
(56) TUB [hatʃ] *hatch** (1)　[tʃɔmən] *chumman** (an empty one)+
[tɷb] (2)　[tɒb] (4, 5, 7, 9, 12, 14, 15)　[tʌb] (9, 13)　[(pɪt)tɷb] (6)
[kɔːv] (3–*OED Corf*, 2b)　[dɹam*] (10, 11–cf. *EDD Tram* sb.[1], 8)
(57) TUB FOR DEBRIS [boːgɪ] *bogey* (1)　[dʒɔtɪ] *jotty** (5, 6)　[dʒɔtɛ]
(7)　[mɷktɒb] *muck-tub* (4, 5)　[dɹam]* (10, 13)　[dɔːttʌb] *dirt-tub*
(13)　[dətəpɪt] *dirt-hoppet** (14)　[səplaɪtɒb] *supply-tub* (15)　[dan]
dan (12)　[dɪlɪ] *dilly* (9)　[dəbɪn] *dobbin* (11)
(58) TALLY [talɪ] (9, 12, 13)　[toːkən] *token* (1, 2)　[təːkɪn] (15)
[talɪ]+[kɒt] *cut* (14)　[dəmɪ] *dommy** (3)　'only a number chalked
on' (7, 10)　[mətɪ] *motty** (4–6)
(59) TRAIN OF TUBS [reːtʃ] *reach** (1)　[dʒag] *jag*+[tɹam] *tram* (4)

41

[tɹam] (5) [ɹɒn] *run*+[sɛt] *set* (6) [ɹɒn] (7) [dʒəːnɪ] *journey**
(9, 10, 12, 13) [dʒəːnɪ]+[dʒag] (11) [tʌb] *tub*+a small one [dɹam]
(13) [gaŋ] *gang* (14) [sɛt]+[tram] (15)

(60) BRAKE [snibl̩] *snibble** (1) [kaʊ] *cow* (2) [laʃɪntʃeɪn] *lashing-chain*+[klamkiː] *clam-key* (4) [dɹag] *drag* (5) [klɪvɪ] *clivvis* (6)
[dɹæg] (8) [laʊndʒ] *lounge* (9) [ʃakl̩] *shackle* (10) [spɹag] *sprag*
(11) [ləkə] *locker* (12, 13) [kɒplɪn] *coupling* (14) [bɹtək] (15)

(62) COAL [koːl]+[koːʔ] (1) [kʷoːl] (2) [kəʊl] (3–5) [koʊl] (6, 11,
12) [koːl] (7, 10, 13, 14) [kʊəl] (9) [kʷəl] (15)

(64) SMALL COAL [kəblz] *cobbles* (3, 5, 7, 10, 12) [smɔːlz] *smalls* (13,
14) [kəblz]+[smɔːlz] (6) [nɒts] *nuts* (15) [smaːl kʷoːl] (2)
[dʌfɪ] *duffy* (11—see under *EDD Duff* sb.²)

(65) COAL-DUST [koʔdəst]+[küm] *coom* (1) [dɒf] *duff* (2) [smʊdʒ]
smudge (4) [slak] *slack* (2, 6, 10–15) [slɛk] (3, 5, 7) [gʊmɪn]
gummin* (7)

(66) POOR COAL 'very little poor coal' (1) [bʁəkn̩z] *brokens**+
[splɛnts] *splints* (2) [bagz] *bags* (4) [mʊk] *muck* (5) [mʌðəɹɪn]
mothering* (9) [ɹaʃɪn] *rashing** (10) [kləd] *clod* (11, 13) [ɹʊbɪʃɪ
stɒf] *rubbishy stuff* (12) [bəːgɪ] *burgy* (14) [ɹʊbɪʃ] *rubbish* (15)

(67) CHALK-STONE [baɪndɪn] *binding* (3, 11) [baɪnd] *bind* (4, 5, 12)
[dɔːtband] *dirt-band*+[baɪnd] (6) [baɪnd]+[dətband] (7)

(68) GOLD-COLOURED VEIN [braːs] *brass* (1) [bɹas] (2) [bɹas
lɒmps] *brass lumps* (3) [bɹasəz] *brasses* (4) [kənɪz] *connies** (5)
[bɹasɪ koʊl] *brassy coal* (6) [oʊld koʊl] *old coal* (7) [bɹɑːs] (10)
[bɹasɪ]* (11—only as adj. in *EDD*) [bɹazɪnz] *brazzins** (12) [bras] (15)

(69) DEBRIS [dərt] *dirt*+[dəʔt] (1) [dət] (7, 14) [mʊk] *muck* (3–6, 9,
15) [mʌk] (11, 12) [dəːt]+[mʊk] (13) [ɹɪp] *rip*+[lɪp] *lip** (8)

(72) DISCHARGE OF GAS [gəbɪn] *gobbin** (7) [gas] (9) [bloə]
blower (1, 4, 6, 9, 12) [bloəʳ] (15) [bɛlʃ] *belch* (11)

(77) VENTILATION SCREENS OR DOORS [dʊəz] (3) [ɛədəəz] *air-doors* (4, 5, 12) [vɛntɪleːʃndəəz] (6, 9) [dəəz] permanent+
[bɹatɪsɪz] *brattices* temporary (11) [bɹatɪsklɔθs] *brattice-cloths* (7)
[bɹadɪʃklɔθs] (14) [bɹadɪʃdəəz] *brattice-doors* (15) [tɹapdəəz] *trap-doors* (1) [watəpɹuːf ʃiːts] *waterproof sheets* (3) [əːdlz] *hurdles* (5)

(79) SCREENS [teːblz] *tables* (1) [skʁiːnz] (2) [skɹiːnz] (3–7, 9–14)
[skɹiːz] (15—see *EDD Scree* sb.², 2)

(80) SEDIMENT [slʌɹe] *slurry* (1) [mʊk] *muck* (4, 5) [slʊdʒ] *sludge*
(6) [dət] *dirt* (7) [bɪlɪ] *billy** (10) [slʌdʒ] (11) [dəːt] (12)
[wəʃmʊk] *wash-muck* (15)

(81) SORTER [tʃɛkweːmən] *check-weighman* (1) [tʃɛkwɛɪmən] (3, 8,
14, 15) [wagŋweːmən] *wagon-weighman* (2) [wɛɪə] *weigher* (10)
[tʃɛkə] *checker* (11, 12) [wɛɪə]+[tʃɛkə] (9) [samplə] *sampler* (7)
[klətʃə] *clotcher** (4, 5)

42

MISCELLANEOUS [pɛgɪ] *peggy*+[noɷpə] *noper** 'pick' (the tool–11) [hək] *hack* 'hammer head' (1)   [glɛnɛ] 'lamp' (1, 2–cf. *EDD Glender* 'peep')   [glɛnɛblɛŋk] *glender-blink* 'blindness' (1)

For one notion a bewildering variety of answers may be elicited. This is because, just as in Standard English, each informant has several layers or registers of speech, all helping to break up any neat linguistic pattern, so that to make a completely accurate mining language map would require infinite detail. Thus the label on a tub was [talɪ] *tally* at Cannop and [mətɪ] *motty* at Light Moor, pits only two miles apart in the Forest of Dean. In the West Riding, a ripper may be called *caunchman, dinter, (dummy-)brusher, fettler, kenchman, repairer* or *scourer*; and these terms are themselves rapidly changing with the nationalization of the industry. For *stint*, i.e. the amount of work allotted a miner, the West Riding has [stɪnt] at Maltby, the curious and unrecorded [pəg] *pog* at Kilnhurst and Denaby, and [snɛk] (cf. *EDD Snack* sb.[1]) at Normanton–i.e. from pits within about a ten-mile radius. For 'stallman', the first response at Warsop was [tʃaːdʒmən] *chargeman*, the next [stɔːlmən], and finally the old word [bɒtɪ] *butty* (cf. *EDD Butty* sb.[1], 3). In Somerset, vertical wooden props were according to the same Radstock informant [poːs] *posts*, if under three feet, [tɪmbəʳ] *timber* if longer, [ʌpɾɔɪts] *uprights* in conversation with his friend and in broader dialect [stɪmp|z] (cf. *EDD Stemple*, unrecorded for Somerset and without an *i*-spelling)–in other words, four terms for a single basic idea. One might well wonder why a dialect should make its patterns so complicated. If a word for an idea already exists, why should another word be accepted? Yet it does happen, as in the standard language, where for instance OE *andwlīta* was apparently replaced by the French *face*, and where even today we have *bravery* alongside *courage*.

Sometimes it was impossible to equate answers because the whole idea was expressed differently. Thus, although a miner may often talk of being in a *team* (places 4, 11–14) and sometimes about his *gang* (4) or *pool* (1), he may have no corresponding word because he worked individually (6) or with one boy (3) or just says 'We work together' (7). For the direction of working, answers established that mines were thought of compass-wise from the central shaft but beyond this they were difficult to compare. For example, 'I'm working down the north ducks' (1), 'I's working eighth high side' (2), 'I'm working on t'north side/west board/west ginny' (4), 'I'm working north/up west/down t'south' (6), 'I'm working B panel/I'm going A 10s' (7). Seeking local expressions for a roof collapse, I heard [fɔːl] *fall* (4–7, 15); but also [ðəz bɪn ə wɛɪt ɒn] *There's been a weight on*

43

(i.e. a heavy fall) (4), [ɪts wɛɪtɪn ə bɪt] *It's weighting a bit* (3) and [ɪts ɔn wɛɪt] *It's on weight* (11), i.e. 'It's ready to fall'. There also appeared two extraordinary and up to now unrecorded expressions, namely from place 3 [flɔəz fɔːn ɪn] *The floor's fallen in* (but how can a floor be a roof?); and from place 1 [ɪts fɔːd ɒp] *It's fallen up*, i.e. down. Perversities like these last two must worry the lexicographer and the grammarian and doubtless too the maker of a linguistic atlas.

Considering that mining is an old industry, there is, asterisked in the preceding table of results, a surprising number of hitherto unrecorded words. Yet most of these must have existed, at least in speech, for a long time. Consequently their absence from *OED* and *EDD* means only that the contributors to these dictionaries never noticed them, for even all their combined efforts could not hope to trace every word, with its pronunciations and meanings, then alive in Britain. Secondly, *EDD* records some words in our list and in their current meanings but only from other areas; e.g. *doggy* 'deputy' for Staffordshire and Shropshire only, whereas our survey has collected it in Lancashire and Yorkshire, and *ringer* 'crowbar' only for Cheshire whereas we found it in the West Riding. These could be either dictionary omissions or some proof of word movement between coalfields. On the other hand, many words listed in *EDD* were unused by our informants and rejected by them after gentle pressure or, as a last resort, translation. Words of this type, which seem to have dropped or to be dropping out of existence, are e.g. *stob* and *ruin* 'waste area in a mine', *colley* 'coal-dust', *swad* 'poor coal', and *gird* and *tack* 'small prop of wood or coal'. It would be interesting to know whether they have been heard anywhere recently.

Not only words used but those avoided are significant. Whereas the layman thinks of *miners* going to a *mine*, with very few exceptions the workers themselves are sure they are *colliers* going to their *pit*. This stems apparently from a former need to distinguish themselves from tin-miners, salt-miners, and the like, although before the days of pit-head baths and with the quicker disappearance of other types of miner, the difference was obvious enough. Another example of the avoidance of an official term is that in January 1965 the National Coal Board, according to reports in national newspapers, recommended that slag-heaps should be known as *spoil-heaps*; but the miners we asked, who ought to know, keep referring to them as (*pit-*)*tips*, *pit-hills*, *pit-heaps*, *batches*, *bengs*, *bonks*, *dirt-heaps*, and so on.

Naturally miners, like other workers, remember very clearly the expressions connected with their livelihood. My oldest informant, aged 79, was said to be most absent-minded, but this never showed in his mining explanations; and certainly mining language, in spite of migrations from pit to pit and from area to area, shows little sign yet of becoming one unidentifiable mass. Indeed from time to time it throws up remarkably local features. Such are the Shropshire [bɔŋk] *bank* 'self-acting incline', Leigh (Lancashire) [bɔŋkɪn] *banking* 're-trieving coal from slag-heaps', and Pendleton (Lancashire) [bɔŋk] 'unwind the cage' and [bɔŋksmən] *banksman*. These [ɔ]-pronuncia-tions, as seen in Wright's *English Dialect Grammar* under *Bank*, are typical of Shropshire and Lancashire. Similarly *trub* 'lump of coal' and *clotch* 'disallow coal' appeared for this survey only in York-shire (places 3, 5), *burgy* 'poor coal' only in Lancashire, *dan* 'small tub' only in Shropshire and *shifter* 'man who cleans out the mine ready for the next shift' only in Northumberland, coinciding with the locations of these words according to *EDD*.

Occasionally, however, evidence seems questionable. Compare, for instance, *EDD Brockwell*, Northumberland only, defined as 'lowest workable seam of any district', with the more likely explana-tion, from my Whitburn informants, that it is just the name of their seam. Even less credible, for certain pits near Leeds, is the claim that *Main* means 'colliery'. That this is incorrect is shown by a title like *Worksop Main Colliery Football Club*, and West Riding conversa-tions confirmed, for example, that in *Cadeby Main* and *Denaby Main*, mines without subsidiary shafts, *Main* is in fact the name of a seam.

Perhaps the chief problem in a survey such as this is not so much the filling in of gaps between places as in making sure that answers supplied and apparently fitting a neat pattern are truly relevant. Let us take examples. H. Orton, in his *The Phonology of a South Durham Dialect*, gives for Byers Green *keīker* 'overseer, foreman at pit-head',[3] and twenty miles away at Whitburn I recently heard elderly miners discussing their [keːkə]. Since Byers Green lies within A. J. Ellis's dialect area D 31 and Whitburn in the adjoining D 32, it is tempting to equate these answers, but the Whitburn word is for the man who picked stones off the moving belt, not the foreman. It is, of course, arguable that either the Byers Green or the Whitburn investigator was misled about the local meaning, but this is unlikely when *EDD* itself records the word—and incidentally for quite different areas—rather ambiguously under *Keeker* sb.[3] as 'overseer, especially one appointed to examine the coals as they come out of the mine'. Since *keek* fundamentally means 'to peer', it looks as if the person doing it can be either an overseer or someone with a humbler task, peering for stones on the moving belt. Thus, this word, first collected

[3] H. Orton, *The Phonology of a South Durham Dialect* (London, 1933), 23, 104.

at Byers Green, now emerges at Whitburn, but with a different meaning. Both answers are no doubt correct but would belong to different lexical maps. Another linguistic trap can be the answer for 'cage, iron framework for lowering and raising to the surface tubs and men'. This is usually *cage* but sometimes *chair*, e.g. in the Hoyland (West Riding) order [bɹɪŋ ðat tʃɛə daʊn] *Bring that chair down*, even though their cage has never been shaped like a chair. A Maltby informant states that even technical men will refer by three terms to the same thing in the same conversation, their words being *cage* (most usual), *chair* ('broader dialect') and *lift* ('more educated'). Then, to complicate the picture, come the answers from Clifton (Notts.), which are *cage* for the whole framework and *chair* for each of its two vertically arranged compartments! When first investigating the languages of other industries like textiles, baking, and chemical engineering, I made my share of mistakes through concentrating on words and pronunciations rather than on exact meaning, and I am still not immune from such errors. Probably, therefore, the best advice that can be given here is to check and re-check that answers do mean what one first hoped or thought they meant. This is why drawings, photographs, and the visible presence of the objects in question are such a great help: where we are forced to rely a good deal on ear and background knowledge, we must be particularly careful.

Often where the layman thinks of a particular object only in outline, the industrial worker knows it in greater detail and so uses for it a more complicated word pattern. Thus, whilst most of us think of a conventional door as a door, a window as a window, a flight of stairs as merely stairs, a carpenter thinks of *jambs*, *mullions*, *transoms*, *kites* and so forth. In the same way, although we usually class all underground colliery workers vaguely as *miners*, the miner gives each his rightful place in the occupational word pattern. Some of the many titles have disappeared with the twentieth-century growth of unions and the coming of nationalization, but others are still well-known and in frequent use. The pit-head foreman may be known as the *boss*, *(surface-)gaffer*, *pit-manager* (formal term), *kayker*, *pit-head-man* or by various uncomplimentary titles which would seem out of place here. There was the *knocker-up* or *chapper-up*, who went round from house to house in the early morning rousing men for work, though nowadays when an emergency occurs this can be done by the *lorry-driver* or *odd-job-man*. There are the *banksman* controlling the shaft top and the *puller* 'engine-man'. The hierarchy below ground includes the *under-manager*, ranking above the *overman*, who in turn may supervise six *deputies* or *doggies* (so-called, it seems, because they used to *dog* or follow their men around); and the man at the pit-bottom in charge of loading and unloading the cage is likely to be the *hanger-on, onsetter* (more modern word), *hooker, hitcher*, or quite logically *pit-bottomer*.

Frequently expressions stand out from the word pattern which seem to the linguist remarkable but to the man who uses them just ordinary or technical terms. Note, for example, the Whitburn method of the three shifts [fɔə ʃʊft] *fore shift* (4–11 a.m.), [bak ʃʊft] *back shift* (9.30 a.m.–4 p.m.) and [nɛɪt ʃʊft] *night shift* (2–9 p.m.). In other words, the Whitburn miner has no *evening*, a fact which would slot into the word pattern of many English villages where the evening greeting is 'Good night!' At Maltby two men, including the deputy, would work what was called a [snɪflɪn ʃʊft] *sniffling shift*, smelling for [gɔb stɪŋk] *gob stink* 'the odour given off by the spontaneous heating of coal'; but such terms would hardly appear in the pattern of polite speech.

The outstanding feature of these results is their variety, although they are far from haphazard. They bear little relation to Ellis's dialect areas cited above, but he was scrutinizing general, not mining, language—and before 1890, which is a long time ago.

As for grammatical patterns in mining language, I am very conscious of having left a gap here. Along with stress and intonation, morphology and syntax are surprisingly neglected fields; for example, under the section Accidence in *EDG* they occupy less than forty-two pages, not one-sixteenth of that work. Something could certainly be gleaned from investigating features such as the following:

Place 2 [ə bɪt dɔf] *a bit (of) duff* (i.e. small coal)—omission of *of* typical of the north-east?

[fə tə] *for to* 'in order to'

[ðəz niː pɪtmən gan ɪn ðɛə] *There is* (=are) *no pitmen* (who) *go in there*

Place 3 [ət] *at* 'that' (relative pronoun)

[nɔː amə nə nɔɒt] *no hammer nor naught*, treble negative

Place 5 [tɪl ɪt] *to it*

Place 6 [waɪl] *while* 'until'. [ðɪs ɪə] *this here* 'this' (unrecorded in *EDG*)

[jə dɪdnt ɔːt tə] *you didn't ought to* 'you ought not to'

Place 7 [ɔf əv ɪt] *off of it*—a usage spreading from the south-east?

Place 10 [ə pɛəɪ əv tɪmbə] *a pair of timber* (singular, ='side-props')

Place 14 [mɛːt], past tense 'might'

Such a grammatical survey, difficult as it might well prove, seems much needed.

Changing conditions have meant, sadly, the gradual disappearance of traditional expressions. Men in the cage at the pit bottom and ready to be pulled up used to indicate this by shouting, e.g., *'ing on!* (= 'Hang on!') (3), *Rap off!* (4), *Rap up!* (5), *Rap us up!* (9), *Knock it off!* (12), *Knock it up!* (13). But this shouting was effective only in shallow pits, and much signalling was done by knocking with a lever or hammer and later by bells. Another case is that the *stint*, amount of work allotted a miner, is dying in face of more modern methods and terms for them like the *cycle* of work, perhaps four per shift as at place 15. [stɪnts ɪz fɪnɪʃt] *Stints is* (= are) *finished*, says a Nottinghamshire miner (place 7), though I notice that in spite of his comparative youth—age 32—he uses in conversation the verb *stint*. Old words like *dommy* and *motty* for 'tub label' are still well-known, but only our Maltby informants remembered the *motty-hanger*, who had to fix them. As the mining environment changes, so do its words.

It is in the customs, superstitions and folklore intermingled with miners' language that much of its fascination lies. One feels that one is not just collecting words but learning more important matters impossible to convey without speech, because the word patterns have always to be related to the society using them. For instance, there used to be a checker who would disallow whole tubs for being underweight, a management economy device later stopped by the unions. When old miners speak of this gentleman, known at Hoyland as the *clotcher*, presumably because he clutched away some of their rightful wages, all their intense hatred of him bursts out. Again, the *fireman* in a mine used to crawl forward on hands and knees with a long taper exploding small pockets of gas in the roof; the performer of this dangerous work, now illegal, despite his name, was sometimes not a man but a boy. Many miners did not wash their backs in the belief that it weakened them and made them prone to accidents; and one could hardly blame my Queensbury informant for doing likewise when in his team *the on'y man 'at used to wash 'im* 'the only man who used to wash himself' was killed by a pit fall. In the Rhondda, old colliers were very embarrassed at being seen naked in their pit-head baths. At Maltby, some miners carried lamps fixed to collars round their necks, but those who could not stand the heat caused carried them in their teeth. At Throstle Nest Colliery in the Beeston seam, men in 1920 were paid 2s. 10½d. for loading half a ton of coal and taking it 400 yards along a passage less than three feet high. This type of labour brings out unusual word patterns at any time.

When miners from different areas meet, using different terms for the same idea, there is usually no language barrier because the idea is common to their occupation, and each miner retains his own terms.

However, when they move permanently to other coalfields, confusion over technical terms can sometimes cause accidents. On the South Yorkshire coalfield I met an enthusiastic safety officer compiling for the Coal Board with minutest accuracy a list of local variants in an attempt to reduce accidents. He was listing differences within one small area; and when miners from many regions, bristling with their own technical terms, are transferred wholesale to another area with its own word patterns, difficulties are bound to arise. Small wonder, then, that in 1965 the Kent branch of the National Union of Mine-workers brought out its own *Glossary of Pit Terms*, stating that others not in their list would 'have completely disappeared from use by February, 1966', but that, should they crop up, they would be happy to explain them—to miners!

Coal-miners do not live is such isolated language communities as remote hill farmers or some inshore fishermen, yet they have always been rather a race apart; so that, despite movements of labour be-tween coalfields, their language patterns seem much clearer than those of, say, the transport, catering, or construction industries. Although they do not use particular expressions because they are the 'best', the 'roughest', the 'most beautiful', or the most historically accurate for their area, their words may still fit a general pattern.

Along with farming and inshore fishing, coal-mining seems to me linguistically the most interesting of our industries. But whereas the first two continue on a fairly steady course, more and more pits are closing, and at an ever-increasing rate. At present, mining language is still vigorous and often closely attached to particular areas, and it will be some time before its terms die out altogether from the speech of the older or even younger generation. Nevertheless, the writing is on the wall, and so, in this rapidly changing world, it would well repay the linguist to study coal-mining language while he may still do so.

3 Proverbs and Sayings from Filey

John D. Widdowson

In common with other kinds of traditional lore the proverb is notoriously difficult to define. In its most general sense it may be regarded as an orally transmitted idiomatic utterance which has achieved a relatively stable form. Brunvand defines it as 'the popular *saying* in a relatively *fixed form* which is, or has been, in *oral circulation*'.[1] Other writers refer to various aspects of the proverb in addition to the three essential qualities delineated here by Brunvand. Collins, for example, notes that ' "Proverb" and "maxim", as commonly used, often overlap. Strictly, "maxim" generally applies to a rule for conduct; "proverb" to what, universally, happens or is true.'[2] Champion draws attention to the racial, aphoristic, metaphorical, and allegorical aspects: 'A proverb is in my opinion a racial aphorism which has been, or still is, in common use, conveying advice or counsel, invariably camouflaged figuratively, disguised in metaphor or allegory.'[3] Krappe comments on the didactic and formal elements: 'The two essential features of the proverb are therefore its didacticism for the contents, and its conciseness for the form. That conciseness is often heightened by mnemotechnical devices such as rhyme or alliteration. Such devices are useful but not absolutely necessary.'[4] He adds that 'The proverb strives for no high ideal, difficult of attainment, but merely voices the sum total of everyday experience which has become the common property of a social group and which is after all at the basis of the group morality in a work-a-day world...'[5] The sociological and philosophical implications were also pointed out as long ago as 1914 by Burne: 'But they [proverbs] deserve careful study, because they represent not forgotten ideas surviving in practice, but the actual views of those who use them, their practical philosophy of life, and their principles of action.'[6]

[1] J. H. Brunvand, *The Study of American Folklore* (New York, 1968), p. 38.
[2] V. H. Collins, *A Book of English Proverbs* (London, 1959), p. vii.
[3] S. G. Champion, *Racial Proverbs* (London, 1938), p. xv.
[4] A. H. Krappe, *The Science of Folklore* (London, 1930), p. 143.
[5] Ibid., p. 148.
[6] C. S. Burne, *The Handbook of Folklore* (London, 1914), p. 280.

Like Champion, Burne also noted that 'Racial and national characteristics are revealed in proverbs'.[7]

Such definitions and observations may assist us in delimiting the general connotation of the term 'proverb' and also make us aware of its typical characteristics. It is clear, however, that the term covers such a wide range that most definitions remain unsatisfactory. There is a wealth of sayings and expressions which, while lacking many characteristics of proverbs, are felt to be typical of a given community. Each speech community utilizes a variety of verbal forms which have a specifically local flavour. These may include well-known or 'national' proverbs and proverbial sayings, and a variety of phrases, some of which are proverbial, others merely regarded as peculiarly local and cherished as such. Like other aspects of verbal usage such as vocabulary and pronunciation, these utterances reflect the cultural identity of the group. This identity is inevitably a combination of both national and regional traditions.

Advances in communications, education and the mass media bring wider influences to bear on the traditional usages of each locality. Just as it is now virtually impossible in England to find a so-called 'pure' speaker of a local dialect, uncontaminated by contact with other varieties of English, so also it is inevitable that proverbs and traditional sayings in a given area reflect both general and regional usage in their patterns of distribution. Those proverbs which are drawn from the national stock may still take on a local patterning in pronunciation and lexical variation. The more local sayings have comparatively limited distributional patterns, and although they are well-known in the area concerned they may be quite unheard of in neighbouring regions. In collecting such material one often notices how surprised people are when they discover that a proverb or saying with which they have been familiar all their lives is not known to others who live nearby.

A given community, whether it is a city, town, or village, reflects these patterns in all aspects of its traditional verbal usage. It is therefore not surprising that those diminishing areas which have remained most resistant to the encroachment of more standard usage continue to retain a comparatively high proportion of distinctively local expressions. In those enclaves where the greatest resistance to more standard linguistic forms is to be found, it is often the proverbs and sayings which help to preserve the values and attitudes of an earlier age which are still felt to be relevant today. Such expressions may themselves constitute something of a barrier against encroachment from outside. Not only are they used appositely and with the ease of

[7] Ibid.

51

familiarity in many present-day situations, but also they are quoted and referred to as typical of the attitudes and codes of conduct of those who lived in 'the good old days'. Whatever the modern view of those days may be, the expressions quoted from them echo the continued respect for the modes and standards of behaviour which used to obtain. In spite of the realization that 'times were hard' in those days, the reverence for bygone traditions is tinged with a sincere regret at their passing. It is felt that men are no longer what they used to be, and this gives rise to the time-honoured comment of the older generation upon the shortcomings of the rising generation. One such view was aptly summed up by a fisherman from Filey who told me: 'There used to be wooden ships and iron men; now they're iron ships and wooden men (32)'.[8] This is a typical example of a traditional expression which has a special local significance. Its repetition in similar contexts gives it a characteristically proverbial ring, and it may be expanded by adding further comments on the differences between men in the old days and men today.

A full description of traditional verbal usage in an area necessitates a comprehensive system of classification which includes all aspects of communicative behaviour from gesture and idiolect to the structure and stylistic devices of extended narrative. Such a system would inevitably require segmentation so that each aspect of usage could be studied in depth in building up a full description. While dialect research has been undertaken on quite a large scale in the British Isles no attempt seems to have been made to examine traditional verbal usage in a comprehensive manner or indeed to study in depth many aspects of spoken lore which clearly merit attention. The study of proverbs and sayings is a logical sequel to a dialectal analysis in that it adds a further dimension to a comprehensive description of typical local usage.

The present brief study makes no claim to do more than list a group of sayings from a single area, together with phonetic transcriptions of these citations from everyday conversation. However, where possible, an attempt is made to suggest the meaning of the sayings and also to indicate some of the situational contexts in which they are used. In this way it is hoped to encourage not only the further investigation of distinctive local pronunciations and meanings in other areas but also the description and analysis of their situational contexts and sociolinguistic function. In listing proverbs and sayings it is important to refer them to their context whenever possible so that some tentative approaches may be made towards a description of the

[8] The numbers in parenthesis refer to the list of sayings which concludes this study.

role which they play within a speech community. The role of proverbs as 'impersonal vehicles for human communication' is discussed by Arewa and Dundes[9] who follow up the approach to the study of language in culture advocated by Hymes. They take up in particular Hymes's notion of 'the ethnography of speaking' and insist on setting the material to be studied in its appropriate context.

The classification of proverbs and sayings also presents some difficulty, even in the very restricted corpus of material to be presented here, and it is unwise to insist upon rigid categories, especially in an exploratory study. However, the system of classifying by form rather than content appears to be firmly established and this serves as a useful basis from which to attempt any kind of categorization. The content of proverbs and sayings is so diverse that the kind of structural linguistic approach suggested by Dundes[10] may ultimately be the only satisfactory method of classification. Proverbs and proverbial sayings shade off into traditional usages which clearly have less 'distilled wisdom' inherent in them yet which reflect local attitudes in a similar way. It is through such sayings that older views expressed in traditional ways continue to find a place in local usage despite the radical changes taking place both socially and linguistically in the communities themselves. The aphorism 'to speak like us is to be one of us', so beloved by commentators on language, applies not only to the pronunciation, intonation, and lexicon used by a speech community but also to the hard core of phrases and expressions inherited from the past. It is inevitable that the distinctively local expressions of this kind are declining in dialectal relic areas, and this is reflected in the patterns of usage between the younger and older generations. Similar patterns are of course to be found in any speech community but in the relic areas it is easier to observe the effects which sweeping changes in the social structure are having on the modification and disintegration of the older linguistic patterns.

A further set of distributional patterns is to be found among individual speakers. It is clear that some speakers use proverbial expressions frequently in their everyday conversation, whereas others seem to employ them more sparingly. More specifically, it emerged during the field-work for the present study that some speakers rarely used such expressions, if at all, during extended conversations lasting at times for up to two and a half hours. The use of such expressions was

[9] E. O. Arewa and A. Dundes, 'Proverbs and the Ethnography of Speaking Folklore', *The Ethnography of Communication*, ed. J. J. Gumperz and D. Hymes, *American Anthropologist*, Special Publication (1964), pp. 70–85.

[10] A. Dundes, Review of T. de S. Pool (ed.), *Trends in Content Analysis*, *Midwest Folklore*, xii (1962), pp. 31–8.

also related to the nature of the subject matter concerned. Factual reminiscences of personal experiences, for instance, produced comparatively few proverbial sayings, whereas raconteurs who were telling local legends and anecdotes tended to use such sayings much more freely. There is clearly a need for the investigation of individual usage at this level to determine some of the reasons which lie behind a speaker's choice of words, phrases and more complex linguistic devices.

The material for the present study was collected by means of tape-recordings and personal observation during the years 1959–64 and again in 1969.[11] The recordings were made in the small town of Filey on the East Coast of Yorkshire and also in the neighbouring village of Muston. Filey has many of the features of a dialectal relic area and the local speech is markedly distinct from that of the surrounding Wolds. This is especially true of those aspects of the vocabulary which concern fishing and the sea. Although the town has become a popular holiday resort its economy was originally founded on its fishing industry. Inshore line-fishing has steadily declined, but a handful of fishermen still maintain the tradition in modern versions of the old-style clinker-built boat, the coble. As one fisherman put it, 'The sea tradition dies hard' and so do the words and sayings associated with it.

Environment and occupation often give rise to distinctive local sayings, but many other influences are also at work. The sayings in the present study, for instance, have the common distinguishing feature of social comment. This may either be a general comment on the human condition and the attitudes and behaviour of people, or it may be applied in a more restricted way to individuals or types. Some of the former, such as *Dead men tell no tales* (6), and *(The) weakest go to (the) wall* (31) have a general application and national distribution but their only distinctive local feature is their pronunciation. The same is true of such proverbial comparisons as *as red as fire* (51), *like a cat on hot bricks* (60) and *(as) mad as a hatter* (50). Such expressions as *Man's extremity is God's opportunity* (16) illustrate the continued application of general religious aphorisms to everyday life. This example, however, was used by an old fisherman talking about a shipwreck from which he and his crew narrowly escaped with their lives, and it takes on a more specific significance from its

[11] I should like to express my sincere thanks to all those who helped in so many ways in the collection of this material. I owe a special debt of gratitude to the late Mr Jack Pearson, the late Mr George Sayers and to Mr George Waller, Mr George Burton, and Mr James Brown, without whose help this study would have been impossible.

context. The same is true of other well-known proverbs such as *Time and tide waits for no man* (28). The context in which this was used concerned an explanation of the local tides and it formed part of the elucidation of another proverb relating to tides: *There's always more sea when (the) flood's done* (22). The reference here is to the depth of water inshore when the tide has ceased flowing and is just beginning to ebb. Local fishermen explain that when it is high water and the cobles are coming in to land they try to come in before the tide ebbs, if it is bad weather. They add that there is always more sea (i.e. rougher water) after high water when the tide is beginning to ebb, because the flood and the ebb tides meet and 'they get the double seas'. One man told me: 'The old fishermen used to say, "He doesn't want [i.e. ought not] to come (ashore) yet. He wants to lay off a bit, because there's always more sea when (the) flood's done. If he doesn't come before the high water, he's got to wait an hour or more until it has got away from the cliff. On the flood tide there's only one flow, so if he doesn't come in on that it's no use coming in on the top ebb—better wait a bit until it gets slacker." ' Even a single quotation of this kind at some length illustrates the fact that such proverbial sayings may be used to transmit important factual information learned by experience. A full investigation of each context, which is not possible in the present cursory survey, may well reveal valuable information about how and why such sayings are used.

Familiarity with the sea and ships gives rise to other proverbial sayings which have developed a metaphorical application from a literal source. This is true, for example, of such sayings as *There's great sails on rotten masts* (21), *He has a better tow to tease* (29), *He's no more than (the) ship'll draw* (24), and the comparison *He'll starve like a thole* (70). The first of these is said of a person who has a high opinion of himself but lacks the ability to support his claims. It is used in general pejorative contexts to express disapproval. The literal meaning of the second saying centres on the fact that a captain has a better prize (perhaps a 'salvage case') to tow along—teasing it by means of a tow-rope. Hence it develops the wider meaning that a man has a better proposition in his grasp than he had before. The third saying refers to the fact that a man is 'shallow', like a boat which is unladen and rides high on the water. The disapproval expressed in the context suggests comparison between the shallow draught of a boat and the depth of the ocean. The final saying of the group seems to be derived from the fact that the thole-pin through which the oar is slotted always protrudes from the gunwale in all weathers and is exposed to extreme cold. Further investigation of other contexts might determine whether or not the saying is restricted in its reference to semantic connotations of extreme cold.

Parallel with these proverbial expressions are some common traditional sayings which have little or no proverbial significance but are frequently employed to comment on specific situations with both literal and metaphorical reference in a manner similar to proverbs. These include *He's laid his tide* (122)—literally: he has missed his tide; metaphorically: he has missed his opportunity (cf. 'He has missed the boat'); *He's getten water in* (172)—literally: there is plenty of water in the harbour so he has reached port safely; metaphorically: he has found room to stay in a given place, e.g. chapel; *He's getten brought up* (82), which has the literal meaning 'He's come to anchor' and metaphorically refers to a person who has finished working for a period of time, or who has retired from work and is now taking things easy. *I've lost my berth* (80) literally means that a fishing-place has been lost to a rival boat at the fishing grounds, but metaphorically applies to the loss of a chair or seat to someone else. This is used in humorous contexts such as the taking of a person's chair in the 'top house' (public house) while he is at the bar buying more drinks. *He's always ratching* (140) has the literal meaning that a sailor is always making his boat tack when approaching a destination, and metaphorically it refers to someone who is 'spinning a yarn' or 'telling the tale' by adding to his story and arriving at his aim by a roundabout route. This usage is often euphemistic in that it can imply 'he is telling lies' in a given context, but is felt to be less absolute than an outright accusation. In the contexts in which I have heard it used it seems not to be severely pejorative and is less forceful than the alternative *He was a bigger liar than Tom Pepper* (75) which was used in strong disparagement. *He's trading voyages* (170) is a comment upon someone who is in the habit of calling at many different houses and the analogy was explained as that of a ship which calls at many different ports on a voyage. Further investigation might reveal other possible interpretations such as 'He is selling voyages' with the same success as someone 'taking coals to Newcastle'. *He has two ships at sea* (149) is said in a humorous way of a person who brings a second light into a room where there is already a light. It seems to suggest in a bantering way that the person concerned is so wealthy that he can afford to own two ships. In the old days the saying would refer to candles and oil lamps and the context is one of taking care not to waste money unnecessarily in times of poverty and hardship.

The expressions *He's a little powder-monkey* (137) and *That was (the) first/next salute* (147) refer back to naval jargon common in the days when men were 'copped with a press-gang' (caught by a press-gang) and served some time at sea. The first of these was used in a humorous context with reference to a mischievous young boy. *First salute* and *next salute* were taken over into normal everyday usage to mean simply 'the first thing' and 'the next thing'. For instance, a person speaking about the actions of a third party might say that he did so-and-so and 'that was (the) *first salute*. Enow [presently], *next salute*...', he then did something else.

Even more straightforward usages such as *Sweal it overboard* (162), meaning to throw something overboard with a forceful movement, may not be understood immediately by visitors to the town, but many other sayings are more difficult still for the outsider to interpret. Expressions used by the fishermen in getting their bearings at sea preserve a number of terms no longer in common use. These include such sayings as *Kirk at High Brigg* (120) and *Kirk's coming afore* (121). The first of these denotes a bearing taken between the tower of the parish church and a high point on the rocky headland, known as the Brigg, on the north side of Filey Bay. The second expression simply means that the same church is coming into view ahead and as it is situated on a piece of high ground quite near the cliffs, directly behind the coble landing, it forms a vital landmark for the returning boats. These sayings are always used in contexts appropriate to the navigation of the cobles and they preserve the word *kirk* as a late survival of the more northerly term for church which is still common in Scotland and the border counties. The pronunciation of the word also illustrates a rare feature of the Filey dialect in which the retroflex [ɹ] is replaced by [l]. The same phenomenon occurs very occasionally in such words as *pork* [pɔlk] and seems to have been more common further north on the coast, although it is rapidly disappearing in Filey speech. The normal word used in the Filey dialect is simply *church* [tʃɔtʃ] and *kirk* appears unique in the above contexts.

The pronunciation of everyday phrases concerning fishing may also hinder the outsider from comprehending their meaning immediately. When a hook is deeply embedded above the barb a fisherman might say (*The*) *hook's over* (*the*) *wether* (116), and on those hoped-for occasions when there is a fish on every hook he may say that *They're coming hook on hook* (115). Even if the outsider interprets the pronunciation of *hook* [iək] correctly, he is still left to wrestle with the word *wether*. It is in perhaps minor ways such as these that local speech resists easy penetration from outside.

The weather and the seasons are of course always important to the fisherman and there are many local expressions for them. When the

57

weather is unsettled fishermen may say *It's genny weather* (107) and when the fog comes down they say *It's thick* (167). Humorous tales are told about the philosophical attitude of the old-time fisherman faced with thick fog and the contexts in which the saying is used reflect this phlegmatic outlook on the dangers of the seafaring life. When the clouds are passing the moon very rapidly, indicating a rising storm or bad weather, the old fishermen would say, *The old moon's wading through muck. It's proper bad weather* (17). A saying which is used by fisherman and 'landsailor' alike, and which is found in many parts of the country, refers to the lengthening of the hours of daylight after Old Christmas Day: *Days get a cockstride langer after Old Christmas Day* (5). Here we have an example of how folk-belief and ancient custom may be preserved in sayings still felt to have a relevance today.

Most of the proverbs and sayings recorded from general conversation in a given area are inevitably wide in their application, and although they may be coloured by the surrounding environment they often refer to common situations which could occur almost anywhere. The greatest distinction shown by such expressions when compared with the parallel distribution of traditional sayings elsewhere is their local dialectal form, although many of them may be found with similar or even identical lexical structure in other parts of the country. Although many of the remaining sayings in the present small sample from Filey are of a general nature they are also typified by social comment of various kinds. As with the proverbial sayings already discussed these comments may refer either to people or affairs in general or they may have more specific applications. The saying *Fill thy belly and warm thy hands* (9) is a reference to the generosity of Yorkshire folk, and on the occasion I heard it used it was applied to the old days at Filey when money was scarce. The context suggested very clearly that this saying was true in those days and that 'everybody's house was your own'. It was used as an expression of admiration for old-time hospitality given generously even in the midst of poverty.

These same hard times are also referred to in various sayings which draw attention to the fact that in those days it was customary to serve dumplings or 'pudding' before the main course of a meal. This is regarded humorously as a means of discouraging the eating of meat by encouraging boys and young workers to eat plenty of dumpling or pudding first. In this way the meat, an expensive item, was preserved for use later. This group of sayings has the same basic structure, some examples being more elaborate than others. The same pattern is found elsewhere in Yorkshire and a clear parallel is seen in the custom of eating Yorkshire pudding before the main course which is still common in many areas apart from the East Riding. The context is invariably similar. On local farms, for instance, the waggoner or farm foreman would use a saying of this kind when speaking to the farmhands: 'I used to laugh, you know, when we went in for our dinners, you see. The old waggoner would say, or foreman, "Now then! *Them boys which eats most pudding'll get most beef*!" (138) Why then we used to let into the pudding and then [when] we got our pudding eaten— "Now, my lad! What does thou want?" "Oh, I don't...I don't want much! I've had plenty of pudding!"' A phonetic transcription brings out the local flavour much more clearly: [ɑə ˈjʉustɪ lɛf jə nəu wɛn wə wɛnt ɪn fə wə ˈdinəz jə sii | tɔːd ˈwɐgənə wɒd sɛː | əɪ ˈfoəmən ‖ naə ðɛn | dồɛm bɔiz wɪtʃ iəts mɛəstʔ ˈpɒdɪn l̩ gɛtʔ mɛəstʔ biif ‖ wai ðɛn wɪ ˈjʉustə lɛt ˈintɪtʔ ˈpɒdɪn | ən ðɛn wɨ gɐtʔ wə ˈpɒdɪn ˈeətʔn̩ | nʉu mə lad | wɒtʔ ˈdʉsə wɒntʔ ‖ oː ɐ deəntʔ | a deəntʔ wɒntʔ mɪtʃ ‖ ɑv ad ˈplɛntɪ ə ˈpɒdɪn]. A fisherman who was the father of young and hungry sons might use a similar device to preserve the Sunday joint: 'But (the) old fellow used to say, "Why, *them who doesn't have no dumpling won't get no beef*!" (96) (Of) course, we used to lather into (the) bloody dumpling, like, (and) we got (that) we didn't want no beef. It was a gag in them days, like, to save the beef for dinner another bloody day—cold; make it into a pan-aggie [a kind of hash] or somewhat of that'. [bʉt ɔːd ˈfɛlə ˈjʉustɪ sɛː | wa dɛm wiə ˈdɪznɪ ɛ nɪ ˈdɒmpr̩lɪn wiəŋ gɛtʔ nɪ biif ‖ koːs wɪ ˈjʉustɪ ˈladəɪ ˈɪntɪ ˈblɒdɪ ˈdɒmpr̩lɪn læik ʉn | wɪ gɐtʔ wɪ ˈdɪdn̩tʔ wɒntʔ ne biif ‖ ɪtʔ wəz ə gag ɪ dồɛm dɛəz læikʔ tɪ siəvtʔ biːf fəɪ ˈdɪnəɪ əˈnɒðə ˈblɒdɪ dɛː | kɔːd ‖ mak ɪt ˈintɪv ə pan ˈagii ə ˈsɒmət ə dồat]. Shorter variants include: *Them that eats most dumpling gets most beef* (96) and *Thou has to sup thy soup else thou'll get no beef* (155).

When food was scarce, a number of put-offs were used when children asked what there was to eat. They might be told: *Tunes and buttered haycocks* (171), *Few broth* (99), *Steam pasty* (159), *Toughened dumplings out of (the) pan* (169) or *Naught warmed up* (131) in answer to their questions. There are also a number of adjurations about the keeping up of appearances in the face of poverty. One of these is the proverbial saying *Keep your front doorstep clean; there's more goes by than comes in* (7). This seems to have been said in the serious context of sound advice, but proverbial wisdom can also be expressed in a humorous way as in the saying addressed to a young child: *If thou tumbles, don't stop to get up—roll on*! (30). Adult relationships with children also give rise to many other sayings. A fretful child who is always *genning* (i.e. whining) is the subject of such expressions as *If there's aught in this world I can't stand, it's a genny bairn* (105) and *There's naught worse nor a genny bairn* (106). If a child is *skraiking* [ˈskraikɪn] (screaming) it might be said that *He was screaming into fits* (148). When an old lady complains to a neighbour about a mischievous child who has been chasing her hens with his cap the neighbour says she can do nothing about it because *Bairns is parlous* (2). However, another adult may take direct action by threatening *I'll slap thy chaff* [face] *for thee*! (85) and if the context is one in which the child is crying unnecessarily he may be told *I'll give thee somewhat to gen for*! (104). In the old days, as in many parts of the country, a child would be told to speak only when spoken to when in the company of his elders. He would be told *Thou wants to be seen and not heard* (lad) (23), and a more talkative child would be admonished sharply with *Hold thy noise*! (114). When boys are playing in the street and the game looks as if it might get out of hand they may be told to *Stash it while* (*the*) *game's at* (*the*) *fairest* (158). If the advice to stop the game while it is at its best went unheeded and the boys continued to make mischief the fishermen in the old days would chase them and they had to run fast to escape. Remembering a situation of this kind in his own boyhood one fisherman told me *By! You had to catch your wind with them*! (84).

A longer saying of a composite nature with several variants on a basic theme is often quoted by local people as an example of the unusual nature of the dialect. Such sayings often figure in *blason populaire* when certain distinctive features of local usage are combined into a sentence or a series of phrases and are said to typify the dialect concerned. It is often the case that such sayings have an exaggerated quality and they may be used, and even invented, specifically for the purposes of caricature. However, the examples from Filey are used by local people as tests of the ability of outsiders to understand the local usage and to draw attention to traditional features which are a matter of some pride to those who use them. These sayings are also given a setting in which a child is the centre of attention, and they take the form of strong adjurations that he should smarten himself up. One version of this is *Fasten thy shoon, fond scalp* [silly head], *or else I'll hit thee across the head with this skillet* [pan]! (151). A more complex version sets the saying in a specific street and puts the words into the mouth of an old woman who is scolding a child: *Thou looks like a tramp*! (72) Wipe thy nose—and not on thy sleeve: wipe it on thy snotrag [handkerchief]. When thou's wiped it thou can pull thy socks up, do up thy shoon, stop slodging thy feet— and thy galluses [braces] is trailing! And when thou's done that thou can gan [go] to school. *And don't start genning like that, lest I'll skelp thou over the head with this skillet!* (153). Again the phonetic transcription brings out more clearly the finer details of the passage: [ðω lɔks laik ə tramp ‖ waip ðɩ noəz ən nɔt ən d͡ɔɩ sliəv | waip ɩt ən d͡ɔɩ ˈsnətrag ‖ wɛn ðωz waipt it͡ʔ ˈðωk͡ʔn̩ pɔl ðɩ səks ωp | diˑ ωp ðɩ ˈʃɩvn̩ | stəp ˈslədʒɩn ðɩ fiət | ənd ðɩ ˈgaləsɩz ɩz ˈtrɛilɩn ‖ ən wɛn ðωz diən ðat ˈðωt͡ʔn̩ gan tɩ skiəl | ən diənt͡ʔ staːt͡ʔ ˈgɛnɩn laik͡ʔ d͡ðat͡ʔ lɛs ɑl skɛlp͡ʔ ðʉ ˈʔʉət͡ʔ iəd wɩ ðɩs ˈskɛlɩt]. Clearly such usages are subject to all the modifications of oral transmission and individual invention, and this is true of a similar saying, again addressed to a child, which incorporates an appropriate proverbial saying: *Thou never wants to look gormless, and never look as though thou was brought up in a barrel and never seed naught but what's gone by the bunghole* (110). The proverbial element is so much a part of the complete utterance that it seems best to regard the whole saying as a unit.

Social comments of a more specific nature on individuals and types are a very common feature. It may be said of a wealthy man who has a good job *He's (the) safest card in (the) pack* (3), and a man who always brings home something to show for a day's work is praised in the saying *It's a bare pasture that he gans* [goes] *over without gleaning aught* (20), meaning that he always makes something even out of an unpromising situation. Fools, on the other hand, are the butt of proverbial sayings in all cultures. *As daft as muck* (38) (the context suggests foolish gullibility), *As fond as a turnip* (45) and (*As*) *daft as a scuttle* (39) are examples from Filey usage. Fools are also characterized in the strongly pejorative phrase *fondgotten gocker* (100), which has overtones of illegitimacy. Drunkenness is also commented on in such sayings. Examples include *As drunk as fuzzocks* (41) (said of men drinking ale while sheep-dipping), and *As drunk as a sweep* (43).

A most significant feature of local sayings is their trenchant comments on individual linguistic usage. A person from Filey who adopts more standard pronunciations is said to be 'talking fine' or to have 'a Saturday night voice'. Such speech may be laid on so thickly that *Lord, you could have cutten it with a bloody knife!* (91). The proverb *He's opening gates and shutting yats* (11) is typically used in such contexts and suggests that a man is 'talking fine' at one moment, using the standard word *gate*, and then relapses into his local usage again and says the dialect form *yat* instead. If a man is praising someone who has helped him in some way it may be said in his defence that *He has to shout for (the) stile he climbs over* (25).

61

Physical characteristics also cause social comment. A man who had eaten a great deal was described as (*Blown out*) *like a bursten garden toad* (71), and it is humorously said of a fat man *He'll soon want hooping*! (117). If a person is rather unwell one will hear *He's nobbut dowly* (94) and if he loses weight he is said to be *swealing away to naught* (163). If death seems inevitable people will say (*They'll*) *soon be in* (*the*) *North Riding* (19)—a euphemism which refers to the churchyard over the boundary of the Riding. If a person felt cold he might say *I was turning starved* (157) and if he felt too hot he might be said to be *Sweating like a brock* (58). This latter term was explained as 'cuckoo-spit on grass'.

Although the occupational environment is predominantly that of fishing, the neighbouring farming areas have also contributed to the stock of local sayings. A retired farmer told me that he always remembered one old phrase in particular. It was used to describe the rare moments of leisure which a farmworker might have on a sunny summer's day. He could simply *Lig in* (*the*) *gess* [lie in the grass] *and think of naught* (125). The same man told me a version of the old plough riddle (144) and challenged his listeners to guess its meaning.

It is impossible in such a brief study to refer in detail to more than a few of the sayings listed. However, many of those omitted from the discussion rely simply on the fact that the meaning of one or two words in them is not immediately obvious to an outsider. The specifically local flavour of such sayings endows them with a particular social significance within the speech community and contributes much to their persistence in local tradition.

The list of sayings which follows is grouped under three main headings: I. Proverbs. II. Proverbial comparisons. III. Miscellaneous traditional sayings. The categories are tentative and some expressions in group I might perhaps be listed under group III and vice versa. The choice of headwords in the alphabetical listing is also somewhat arbitrary, but this is of less consequence in a comparatively short list and a number of cross-references are included to facilitate the location of the more elusive items. In the phonetic transcriptions a short pause is marked | and a longer pause is marked ‖.

List of Sayings

I. *Proverbs*

(1) He didn't know *aught* for breakfast time. [ɪ ˈdɪdntʔ nɔː əʊt fə ˈbrɛəkəs tɑəm] He knew nothing.

aught: see 10, 105.

(2) *Bairns* is parlous. [bɛənz ɪz ˈpaːləs] Children are difficult to deal with.

    barrel: see 110.

    beef: see 96, 138, 155.

(3) He's (the) safest *card* in (the) pack. [iːz ˈseəfɪs keəɹd ɪtʃ pɑk]

    church: see 120, 121.

(4) He must have been gotten when all (the) *cocks* was nodding. [ɪ mɒst ə biːn ˈgɒtʃn̩ wɛn ɔəl kɒks wəz ˈnɒdɪn] Said of a fool, implying he was born foolish.

    cursing: see 68.

(5) *Days* get a cockstride langer after Old Christmas Day. [dɛəz gɛɹ ə ˈkɒkstraɪd ˈlaŋgəɹ ˈɛftəɹ ɔəd ˈkɛsməs dɛi]

(6) *Dead* men tell no tales. [diəd mɛn tɛl nɪ tɛilz]

(7) Keep your front *doorstep* clean; there's more goes by than comes in. [kiːp jə frɒntʃ ˈduəstɛp kliin ‖ ðəz muə gɒːz bai ðən kɒmz ɪn]

    doubler: see 18.

    dumpling: see 96, 138, 155, 169.

(8) I'll awand (i.e. vouch, guarantee) he has a deep *dyke* to wade. [al əˈwand iː æz ə diːp dæikʃ tɪ weəd] Said of a person who 'has done some rotten things in his time' and 'can expect a hard time before he has finished'.

    ease: see 164.

    fasten: see 151.

(9) *Fill* thy belly and warm thy hands. [fɪl dɒi ˈbɛlɪ ən waːm dɒi andz] Enjoy the hospitality extended.

(10) He didn't know (the) *first* thing about aught. [ɪ ˈdɪdn̩tʃ nɒu fɒstʃ θɪŋ əˈbʉut æut] He knew nothing.

    game: see 158.

(11) He's opening *gates* and shutting yats. [iːz ˈɒpʃnɪn gɛəts n̩ ˈʃɒtɪn jats] i.e. talking fine and then relapsing into dialect.

    grass: see 125.

    green (i.e. rum): see 93.

    gulley: see 74.

    haycocks: see 171.

    hell: see 47, 66.

    hole: see 92.

(12) They'd believe *horse-turds* is figs. [dɒ̃əd bəˈliːv ˈɒstədz ɪz fɪgz] i.e. they are extremely gullible.

(13) He's *Jack Blunt*. [ɪz dʒækʃ blɒnt] i.e. forthright.

(14) When he shouts, 'Shite!' you have to *jump* on (the) shovel. [wɛn iː ʃʉːts ʃæitʃ ‖ jɒ ɛ tɪ dʒɒmp ən ˈʃɒvl̩] A highly disparaging

reference to someone who abuses his authority and insists on immediate obedience.

know: see 1, 10.
laughing: see 66.
mad: see 50.

(15) (He's) any *man* a guinea. [iːz ˈɔnɪ man ə ˈgɪnɪi] He has plenty of money to give away.

(16) *Man*'s extremity is God's opportunity. [manz ɛkˈstrɛmɪtɪ ɪz gɔdz ɔpəˈtjʉunɪtɪ]

(17) The old *moon*'s wading through muck. (It's proper bad weather.) [tɔːd mʉunz ˈwɛədɪn θrʉu mɔk ‖ ɪts ˈprɔpə bad ˈwɛðəɹ]
name: see 165.
naught: see 165.

(18) You couldn't stir *neither* dish nor doubler. [jɷ ˈkɷdn̩tʔ stɘəɹ ˈneəðəɹ dɪʃ nə ˈdɷbləɹ] There was no room to move.

(19) (They'll) soon be in (the) *North Riding*. [ðəl siən bɪ ɪtʔ nɔːθ ˈraɪdɪn] i.e. buried in the churchyard over the boundary near the town.
own: see 139.
parlous: see 2.
parson: see 97.

(20) It's a bare *pasture* that he gans [goes] over without gleaning aught. [ɪts ə bɛə ˈpastʃəɹ ðət iː ganz ˈaʉəɹ wɪðˈʉutʔ ˈgleənɪn aut] He usually finds something of advantage.
riving: see 166.

(21) There's great *sails* on rotten masts. [ðəz grɛətʔ sɛilz ɔn ˈrɔtʔn̩ masts] i.e. a man may not fulfil his boasts about himself.

(22) There's always more *sea* when (the) flood's done. [ðəz ˈɔələs mɛə sii wɛn fleədz deən]
see: see 111.

(23) Thou wants to be *seen* and not heard, (lad). [ðɷ wants tɪ bɪ siːn ən nɔt iəd lad]

(24) He's no more than (the) *ship*'ll draw. [iːz nɛə mɛəɹ ən ʃɪp l̩ drɔː] He is shallow.
shoon: see 142, 151.

(25) He has to *shout* for (the) stile he climbs over. [iː ɛz tɪ ʃʉutʔ fətʔ staɪl ɪ klɪmz ˈɔvəɹ] He must praise someone who has helped him.
skelp: see 153
skillet: see 151, 153.

(26) She'd *skin* a bloody cat. [ʃɪd skɪn ə ˈblɷdɪ kat]. Said of a very mean person.

(27) He's *solid* from his shoulders up. [iːz ˈsɔlɪd frɛv ɪz ˈʃuːldəz ɒp] i.e. slow-witted.
   soul: see 143.
   starve: see 70, 157.
   stile: see 25.
   swear: see 97.
   tales: see 6.
   tease: see 29.
   tide: see 28, 122.
(28) *Time* and tide waits for no man. [taim ən taɪd wɛits fə nou man]
(29) He has a better *tow* to tease. [iː ɛz ə ˈbɛtə tau tɨ teəz] He has a more attractive prospect.
(30) If thou *tumbles*, don't stop to get up—roll on! [ɪf ða ˈtɒmlz diəntɕ stəp tɪ gɛɹ ɒp ‖ raul ən]
   voyages: see 170.
   walk: see 81.
   walk with: see 44.
(31) (The) *weakest* go to (the) wall. [ˈwiəkɪstɕ gɔː titɕ wɔːl]
   wether (i.e. barb of hook): see 116.
   wick: see 54, 144.
(32) There used to be *wooden* ships and iron men; now they're iron ships and wooden men. [ðɛ̃ə ˈjuːstə bɪ ˈwɒdn̩ ʃɪps ən ˈaɪən mɛn | nɑː dər ˈaɪən ʃɪps ənd ˈwɒdn̩ mɛn]
   ya/yans (i.e. once): see 133.
   yat (i.e. gate): see 11.
   yune (i.e. oven): see 134.

II. *Proverbial comparisons*

(33) (As) *bald* as a badger. [bɔəld əz ə ˈbadʒə]
(34) (As) *black* as darkest night. [blak əz ˈdaːkəstɕ niːt]
(35) (As) *black* as treacle. [blak əz ˈtriːkl̩]
(36) As *clever* as a box of monkeys. [əz ˈklɛvəɹ əz ə bɒks ə ˈmɒŋkɪz] i.e. astute, intelligent.
(37) As *crooked* as a dog's leg. [əz kruukt əz ə dɒgz lɛg] Said of the rigging of a plough.
(38) As *daft* as muck. [əz daft əz mʌk] i.e. foolishly gullible.
(39) (As) *daft* as a scuttle. [daft əz ə ˈskɒtɕl̩]
(40) As *dead* as a coffin nail. [əz diəd əz ə ˈkɒfɪn nɛəl]
(41) As *drunk* as fuzzocks [? asses]. [əz drɒŋk əz ˈfɒzəks] See *EDD Fussock* sb.
(42) As *drunk* as a newt. [əz drɒŋk əz ə niut]
(43) As *drunk* as a sweep. [əz drɒŋk əz ə swɨip]

(44) As *fine* a lot of men as ever you could walk with. [əz fɑin ə lɔt ə mɛn əz ˈɪvə jʉ kɔd wɔːk wɪv]

(45) As *fond* [foolish] as a turnip. [əz fɔnd əz ə ˈtənəp]

(46) As *good* as gold. [əz gɔd əz gɑuld] Said of a person's kind heart.

(47) As *green* as hell. [əz griːn əz ɛl] The comparison here is more of a tag than anything else. See also the similar usages in 55, 66 and 68.

(48) (As) *hard* as brass. [aːd əz bras] Said of dried salted fish.

(49) (As) *ignorant* as pig-shit. [ˈɪgnərənt əz ˈpɪgʃɪtˀ]

(50) (As) *mad* as a hatter. [mad əz ə ˈatəɹ]

(51) As *red* as fire. [əz reɪd əz ˈfɑɪəɹ]

(52) As *red* as sunsets. [əz reɪd əz ˈsɒnsɛts] Said of cheesecakes made of eggs which were 'a bit addle'.

(53) As *sharp* as a box of ferrets. [əz ʃaəp əz ə bɔks ə ˈfɛrɪts] i.e. astute, quick-thinking.

(54) As *wick* [lively] as an eel. [əz wɪk əz ən iil]

(55) Like *all that*. [d͡ɔɪ kɔd ˈkærɪ əm ɔp lɛik əəl dat] Said of women carrying up fishing lines very quickly.

(56) (They leaked) like *baskets*. [dɛ lɛkt læikˀ ˈbaskɪts] Said of leather thigh-boots.

(57) (He was) like hairy *boogie* [? bogey]. [ɪ wəz lɛik ˈɛərɪ ˈbɔgɪ] Said of someone running very fast.

(58) (Sweating) like a *brock* [i.e. cuckoo-spit]. [ˈsweːtɪn laik ə brɔk] Cf. J. Nicholson, *The Folk Speech of East Yorkshire* (London, 1889), p. 22. This work is an excellent reference source for an approach to local speech in a cultural context.

(59) (He was just) like a *cat* in pattens. [ɪ wɒz d͡ʒɒstˀ læik ə kat ɪ ˈpatˀn̩z] i.e. very agitated.

(60) (He was ranting round) like a *cat* on hot bricks. [ɪ wəz ˈrantɪn rʉund læik ə kat ən ɔtˀ brɪks]

(61) (He could swim) like a *duck*. [ɪ kɔd swɪm laik ə dɔk]

(62) (He's) like a bloody *farmer*. [ɪz laik ə ˈblɔdɪ ˈfaəməɹ] Said of a man who is clumsy or inept in a fishing boat.

(63) (She had eyes) like a *ferret*. [ʃɪ ad iːz laik ə ˈfɛrɪtˀ]

(64) (Coming round) like a *flock* of bees. [ˈkɔmɪn rʉund laik ə flɔk ə biiz]

(65) (He was running about) like a blue-arsed *fly*. [ɪ wəz ˈrɒnɪn əˈbʉutˀ lɛik ə ˈbluːaːst flii]

(66) (She's laughing) like *hell*. [ʃɪz ˈlafɪn læik ɛl] (These birds was going round and round) like *hell*. [diːz bədz wəz ˈguɪn ruːnd ən ruːnd læik ɛl]

(67) (He set off) like a *lamplighter*. [ɪ sɛt əf læik ə ˈlampliːtəɹ] Said of a famous local runner.

(68) (He was cursing) like *mad*. [ɪ wəz ˈkɔsɪn laikʔ mad]

(69) (He was) like a little *terrier*. [ɪ wəz laik ə ˈlaətʔļ ˈtɛrɪəɹ] Said of a quick-tempered man who was said to have had 'forty-three fights before breakfast'.

(70) (He'll starve) like a *thole*. [ɪl staːv laik ə θaul] Seems to suggest he will be very cold, like the exposed thole-pin on the gunwale of a boat.

(71) (He was blown out) like a bursten garden *toad* (with beef, like, what he'd eaten). [ɪ wəz bloun uːtʔ læik ə ˈbrɔsņ ˈgæːdņ tuəd wɪ biif læik wət ɪd ˈɪtʔņ]

(72) (Thou looks) like a *tramp*. [ðɷ lɔks lɛik ə tramp]

(73) (She was done up [dressed up]) like a *turkeycock*. [ʃɪ wəz diən ɷp lɛik ə ˈtəɹkɪkək]

(74) (It's) like *water* going down a gulley. [slɛikʔ ˈwatə ˈgoˑɪn duːn ə ˈgɷlii] Said of the way a heavy drinker drinks beer.

(75) (He was) a bigger *liar* than Tom Pepper. [ɪ wəz ə ˈbɪgə ˈlaiəɹ ən tɔm ˈpɛpə]

III. *Miscellaneous traditional sayings*

(76) When *all* come to all. [wɛn ɔːl kɔm tɪ ɔːl] i.e. was cleared up, explained.

(77) He's far *arse-apeak*. [ɪz faəɹ aːsəˈpeək] i.e. wide of the mark. See *OED* and *EDD Apeak* adv., and *OED Peak* adv.

(78) All over the *auction*. [ɔːl ˈɑuətʔ ˈɔkʔʃən] Everywhere.

(79) I'll *awand* [vouch, guarantee] that's where she's gone. [ɑl əˈwand ðats wɛə ʃɪz geən]

(80) I've lost my *berth*. [av lɔstʔ mɪ bəθ] i.e. lost my fishing-place; lost my seat.

(81) He was almost *bet* [beaten] to walk. [ɪ wəz ˈɔːlmɔːstʔ bɛtʔ tɪ wɔːk] i.e. could hardly walk.

(82) He's getten [got] *brought up*. [iːz ˈgɛtʔņ brɑut ɷp] i.e. come to anchor; finished working.

(83) He was proper *bunkested*. [iː wəz ˈprɔpə bɷŋˈkɛstəd] i.e. dumbfounded. Cf. *EDD Bunkas* sb.—a confused crowd.

(84) (By!) You had to *catch* your wind with them. [bai | jɷ ad tɪ katʃ jə wɪnd wɪv əm] i.e. catch your breath.

(85) I'll slap thy *chaff* [face] for thee! [aəl slap ðɪ tʃaf fɔ ðə] See *EDD Chaft* sb.—the jaw, jawbone.

(86) Private *churchyard* of his own, (he had). [ˈpraivətʔ ˈtʃətʃjaːd əv ɪz ɔən iː æd] Said of a fiery-tempered man who was 'always fighting with Dutchmen and Scotchmen at Whitby in herring-time'.

67

(87) *Coming* in brimming. [ˈkɔmɪn ɪ ˈbrɪmɪn] Said of a cow: 'in heat'.

(88) (I was) that *crazed* [angry] I could have choked. [a wəz d̂ðætʔ krɛizd aɪ kɔd ə tʃoʉkt]

(89) Half a pound of *currants*. [əəf ə pɔnd ə ˈkərənz]

(90) (You could) *cut* and come again (as long as you liked). [jɔ kɔd kɔt̂ʔ ņ kɔm əˈgɛn əz lɔŋg əz jə lɛikt] i.e. have more helpings of food.

(91) (Lord, you could have) *cutten it* with a bloody knife. [ləəd jʉ kɔd ə ˈkɔt̂ʔņ ɪt̂ʔ wɪv ə ˈblɔdɪ næif] Said pejoratively of the 'posh' speech of a local man.

(92) It's a *dark hole*. [ɪts ə daək aʉl] Said of a very dark night, or of a ship without lights.

(93) (A) *dash* of green. [daʃ ə griən] Drop of rum.

(94) (He's) nobbut *dowly*. [iːz ˈnɔbət̂ʔ ˈdaʉlɪ] He's not very well. See *EDD Dowly* adj., 3.

(95) Things is only *dowly*. [θɪŋz ɪz ˈɔnlɪ ˈdaʉlɪ] i.e. 'fairly good'. Said of lack of money, food etc.

(96) Them that eats most *dumpling* gets most beef. [dɛm ət ɪts mɛəst̂ʔ ˈdɔmplɪn gɛts mɛəst̂ʔ biif] (But the old fellow used to say) Why, them who doesn't have no *dumpling* won't get no beef. [bʉt ɔːd ˈfɛlə ˈjʉustɪ sɛː | wa dɛm wiə ˈdɪzņt ɛ nɪ ˈdɔmp̂ʔlɪn wiəŋ gɛt̂ʔ nɪ biif]

(97) (It was) *enough* to make a parson swear. [ɪt̂ʔ wəz ɪˈniəf tɪ mak ə ˈpaəsən swiəɹ] Said of a great display of food and drink.

(98) Has he brought thee a *fairing* [present]? [ɛz ɪ braʉt̂ʔ d̂ðə ə ˈfɛɑrɪn] i.e. the customary gift on returning from a voyage.

(99) *Few broth*. [fiu brɔːθ] A put-off used when children ask 'What's for dinner?'

(100) (Thou great) *fondgotten gocker*. [d̂ðʉ grɛːt̂ʔ f̂ɔndˈgɔt̂ʔņ ˈgɔkəɹ] i.e. fool (literally 'foolishly begotten gawker'). In spite of the *OED*'s scepticism, one is hesitant to dismiss entirely the possible influence of ON *gaukr* 'cuckoo'.

(101) (It weren't) a *forced push*. [ɪt̂ʔ waːnt ə fɔːs pɔʃ] i.e. a forced marriage.

(102) (Looks thou, fellow, thou's) gotten (the) fire up to (the) *gallybauk*. [lɔks ð̂ə ˈfɛlə | ð̂ɔz ˈgɔt̂ʔņ ˈfæiəɹ ɔp tɪ ˈgælɪbəək] i.e. heaped as high as 'the cross-beam in a chimney from which the pot-crooks or "reckons" hang' (*EDD*).

(103) (There was) *game alive* (about that). [də wəz geim əˈlaːv əˈbʉut̂ʔ ðat]

(104) I'll give thee somewhat to *gen* [cry] for! [ɑəl gɪ ðɪ ˈsɒmətʃ tɪ gɛn fə]

(105) If there's aught in this world I can't stand, it's a *genny* [crying, fretful] bairn. [ɪf ðəz ɑut ɪn ðɪs wəld aː kɑːnt stand ɪts ə ˈgɛnɪ bɛən]

(106) There's naught worse nor a *genny* bairn. [ðəz nautʃ wəs nəɹ ə ˈgɛnɪ bɛən]

(107) It's *genny* [unsettled] weather. [ɪts ˈgɛnɪ ˈwɛðəɹ]

(108) (He was) that *gobsmacked* [dumbfounded]. [ɪ wəz dætʃ ˈgɒbsmɑkt]

(109) Where's thou *going*? [weəz ðə gain]

(110) Thou never wants to look *gormless*, and never look as though thou was brought up in a barrel and never seed naught but what's gone by the bunghole! [ðɒ ˈnɪvə wants tə liək ˈgɔːmləs ən ˈnɪvə liək əz ðɒː ðɒ wəz braut ɒp ɪn ə ˈbarɪl ən ˈnɪvə siid naut bɒt wats gɒn baitʃ ˈbɒŋuəl]

(111) (You couldn't) see your *hand* afore you. [jə ˈkɒdn̩tʃ siː jəɹ and əˈfoə jə] It was very dark.

(112) (He's) *hearty* in (the) cause. [iːz ˈaːtɪ ɪ kəəz] i.e. helping all he can.

(113) *Hold* on. [əd ɒn] i.e. wait.

(114) *Hold* thy noise! [əd ðɒɪ nɔiz] Be quiet.

(115) (They're coming) *hook* on hook. [ðɪəɹ ˈkɒmɪn iək ən iək] i.e. there is fish on every hook.

(116) (A) *hook* over (the) wether [barb]. [iək ˈɑuəɹtʃ ˈwɛðəɹ] i.e. deeply embedded.

(117) (He'll soon) want *hooping*. [iəl siən want ˈꞍupɪn] Said of a very fat man.

(118) (He was) in a right fair *huff*. [ɪ wəz ɪn ə ræit fɛəɹ ɒf] i.e. very agitated, angry.

(119) Stop thy *kittling* [tickling]. [stəp ði ˈkɪtlɪn]

(120) *Kirk* at High Brigg. [kɛlk ət ai brɪg] A bearing or 'meet' taken between the church and a high point on Filey Brigg when the cobles are coming to land.

(121) (The) *kirk's* coming afore. [kɛlks ˈkɒmɪn əˈfoəɹ] Said when the church is sighted by the returning fishermen.

(122) (He's) *laid* his tide. [ɪz lɛəd ɪz taəd] i.e. missed the tide. But note *OED Lay* vb.[1], I. 5.

(123) (My head's) all of a *lather*. [maˑ iədz əəl əv ə ˈlaðəɹ] i.e. sweating profusely.

(124) *Lawk*-a-mercy! [lɔːk ə ˈmasɨi] Lord have mercy.

(125) *Lig* [lie] in (the) gess [grass] and think of naught. [lɪg ɪ gɛs ən θɪŋk ə naut]

(126) (He was) a little bit *light* in the head. [ɪ wəz ə ˈlaitʃ| bɪtʃ l̵iit ɪt iəd] i.e. slightly deficient mentally.

(127) *Light* on a quarter. [liːt ən ə ˈkwaːtəɹ] Said of a cow: not yielding milk regularly from each teat.

(128) Take the *mense* [freshness, shine etc.] off it. [takʃ ðə mɛns ɔf ɪt]

(129) (He's) *milled* over again. [ɪz mɪld ˈauəɹ əˈgeən] i.e. recovered from an illness.

(130) Thou only just *nabbed* me! There was plenty more mouths watering for me! [ðɷ ˈɔnlɪ dʒɷstʃ nabd mə ‖ ðə wəz ˈplɛntɪ mɛəɹ mɷuðz ˈwatərɪn fə mə] Said to a marriage partner who only just 'caught' a spouse.

(131) *Naught* warmed up. [nautʃ waəmd ɷp] A humorous response or put-off following the question, 'What's for dinner?'

(132) (He was) that *near*. [ɪ wəz ðatʃ niə] i.e. so mean.

(133) *Once* one night. [jans jaː niit] A typical opening line to local tales.

(134) Put it in (the) *oven*. [pɷɹ ɪt ɪ jɷun]

(135) He *plays* war up. [ɪ pleːz waəɹ ɷp] i.e. gets angry.

(136) (He's) *plothered* with mud from head to foot. [ɪz ˈpləðəd wɪ mɷd frəm iəd tɪ fɷt]

(137) He's a little *powder-monkey*. [ɪz ə ˈlaətl̩ ˈpɷudəˈmɷŋkɪ] i.e. mischievous (?).

(138) Them boys which eats most *pudding*'ll get most beef. [dɷ̃ɛm bɔiz wɪtʃ iəts mɛəstʃ ˈpɷdɪn l̩ gɛtʃ mɛəstʃ biif]

(139) Who owns (the) *purse*? [wɛəz ɔːz pɔs]

(140) (He's) always *ratching*. [ɪz ˈɔːləs ˈratʃɪn] i.e. 'spinning a yarn', telling lies.

(141) (I wouldn't let him down) *reason* or none. [ɑə ˈwɷdn̩tʃ lɛt im dɷun ‖ ˈreəzn̩ ə neən] i.e. for any reason.

(142) *Remmon* [move] them shoon. [ˈrɛmən dɷ̃ɛm ʃiən] Often said with strong feeling in reference to the folk-belief that it was bad luck to put shoes on the table.

(143) *Rest* his soul in peace. [rɛst ɪz sɔːl ɪ piəs] Said after referring to a man who is dead.

(144) A *riddle*, a riddle,
 A farmer's fiddle;
 It's wick [alive] at both ends,
 And dead in the middle.   Answer: A man and horses ploughing.
[ə ˈrɪdl̩ ə ˈrɪdl̩
 ə ˈfaəməz ˈfɪdl̩
 ɪts wɪk ətʃ bɔːθ ɛndz
 ən dɛd ɪ ðə ˈmɪdl̩]

(145) (I've) no *rock* for him. [ɐv nɔː rɔk fɔɹ ɪm] i.e. have a low opinion of him.

(146) Half a pound of *saim* [lard]. [ɔɔf ə pɒnd ə sɛim]

(147) (That was the) first *salute.* [dɒ̃at̡ wəz fɔs səˈlʉut] (Enow [presently]) next *salute*...[ɪˈnʉu | nɛks səˈlʉut] i.e. first/next thing which happened, etc.

(148) He was *screaming* into fits. [ɪ wəz ˈskriəmɪn ˈɪntə fɪts]

(149) He has two *ships* at sea. [iˑ ɛz tʉu ʃɪps ət̡ sii] i.e. two lights in one room.

(150) It'll soon *sholl* [slide] on to (the) time. [ɪt ļ seən ʃɔl ən tɪ taəm] The time will soon pass.

(151) Fasten thy *shoon*, thou fond scalp [silly head], or else I'll hit thee across the head with this skillet [pan]. [ˈfasn̩ ðɪ ʃiən dɒ̃ɷ fənd skɔːp əɹ ɛls al ɪt̡ ðɪ əˈkrɔst̡ iəd wɪ ðɪs ˈskɛlɪt]

(152) It *skelled up.* [ɪt̡ skɛld ɷp] It tipped over.

(153) (And don't start genning [crying] like that, lest) I'll *skelp* thou over the head with this skillet [pan]. [ən diənt̡ staːt̡ ˈgɛnɪn laik̡ dɒ̃at̡ lɛs al skɛlp̡ ðʉ ˈɷuət̡ iəd wɪ ðɪs ˈskɛlɪt]

(154) Proper old *slapes* [types, characters]. [ˈprɒpəɹ ɔːd sliəps] Cf. *EDD Slope* sb., 3—an imposter; a defrauder, and *Slape* sb.[1], 6—a fellow who goes from house to house on the chance of getting something to drink.

(155) (Thou has to) sup thy *soup*, else thou'll get no beef! [dɒ̃ɷ ɛz tɪ sɒp dɪ sɷup | ɛs dɔl gɛt̡ neə biif]

(156) (There was) such a *spread.* [ðə wəz saik ə spriəd] i.e. a great display of food, etc.

(157) (I was) turning *starved.* [a wəz ˈtɔnɪn staːvd] i.e. getting cold.

(158) *Stash* [stop] it while (the) game's at (the) fairest. [staʃ ɪt̡ wail gamz ət̡ ˈfɛərɪst]. Said to boys playing in the street.

(159) *Steam pasty.* [stiəm ˈpastə] A put-off said to children who ask what is for dinner.

(160) Get your een [eyes] *stecked* [shut]. [gɛt̡ ðɪ iːn stɛk̡t]

(161) (I was) in a *stew.* [a wəz ɪn ə stiu] i.e. flustered.

(162) *Sweal* it overboard. [swɛəl ɪt ˈaʉəbɔəd] i.e. throw overboard with considerable force.

(163) (He's) *swealing* [wasting] away to naught. [iːz ˈswiəlɪn əˈwɛː tɪ naut] Said of someone who is very ill.

(164) *Take* thy ease. [tak̡ ðɪ iəz] Take it easy.

(165) (I'd) *tell* him his name for naught. [ad tɛl ɪm ɪz niəm fə naut] i.e. tell him what I think of him.

(166) *Tewing* and riving. [ˈtjuːɪn ən ˈraːvɪn] Tossing and turning (e.g. during a sleepless night).

(167) It's thick. [ɪts θɪk] i.e. very foggy.

(168) How ist thou *thwarking*? [ʉustʔ ðə ˈtθwaːkɪn] How are you getting on? Used as a greeting.

(169) *Toughened* dumplings out of (the) pan. [ˈtʊfɪnd ˈdɒmplɪnz uːt ə pan] A put-off used when children ask what is for dinner.

(170) (He's) *trading* voyages. [iːz ˈtrɛːdɪn ˈvɔidʒɪz] i.e. calling at many different houses (?).

(171) *Tunes* and buttered haycocks. [tjʉunz ən ˈbɒtəd ˈɛəkəks] A put-off used when children ask what is for dinner.

(172) (He's) getten *water* in. [iːz ˈɡɛtʔn̩ ˈwatəɹ ɪn] i.e. he has succeeded in getting into a given place, like a ship getting into harbour when there is a sufficient depth of water.

(173) (He's) *well-hefted* with brass. [ɪz wɛlˈɛftɪd wɪ bras] He has plenty of money.

(174) It *wembled* [toppled] over. [itʔ ˈwɛmld ˈɑuəɹ] See *OED Wamble* vb., ii, and *EDD Whemmle* vb. and sb.

(175) *Word* won't pass my lips. [wəd weəntʔ pas maː lɪps] i.e. I shall say nothing; keep the secret.

(176) (It's) going to *wrack* and ruin. [ɪts ˈɡaɪn tɪ rɛk ən ˈrʉuɪn]

4 Dialect and Place-names: the Distributions of Kirk

Martyn F. Wakelin

As the studies of English dialect and place-names proceed further and further with their collections of material, it becomes increasingly obvious that the data collected in each field has much in common with the other. Phonological features such as the occurrence of /a/ < ME *o*, the loss of initial /w/, or the retention of /sk/ in a non-Scandinavian area, names for streams and other natural features, farm-yards and farm-buildings—to name but a very few examples— are illustrated by both dialect and place-names, and it should thus be possible to supplement one body of material by data from the other.[1] As a preliminary to the main subject of this essay, most of the data for which has been provided by the *Survey of English Dialects* and the volumes of the English Place-Name Society (EPNS), two examples explored in a little more detail will bear this out. Both of these relate to the north of England.

(1) Throughout most of the north of England, ME *o* lengthened in the open syllables of disyllabic words gives /uə/ (except that /øː/ occurs in Northumberland and north Durham), but in the southern part of the West Riding of Yorkshire and in central Lancashire it results in /ɒɪ/: cf. *SED coal* (IV.4.5), *overcoat* (VI.14.6), for example. This particular dialectal development accounts for the form of a group of north-west-Midland place-names which comprises a very large number of members, namely those containing the element -*royd* (< OE **rod*, **rodu* 'clearing'), e.g. The Royd, Royds, Broad Royd, Wood Royd, Monkroyd, Mytholmroyd, all in the West

---

[1] The common ground of dialect and onomastic studies has, of course, already been recognized. The volumes of the English Place-Name Society (EPNS) usually include a section of the dialect of the county as illustrated by its place-names, and also gives occasional place-name pronunciations. I myself have used place-name material to amplify the distribution of the dialect words *cree*, *crew*, and *crow*: see M. F. Wakelin, '*Cree, crew* and *crow*: Celtic Words in English Dialect', *Anglia*, lxxxvii (1969), 273–81. A. Mawer's book, *The Place-Names of Northumberland and Durham* (Cambridge, 1920), is an excellent example of a book combining the use of both types of evidence.

Riding.[2] It also accounts for such forms as North Goyts (< OE *gota 'water channel', cf. SED, I, IV.1.1)[3] and Hoyle (< OE, ON hol 'hole, hollow').[4] This is a very local development, occurring nowhere else in the country, and is a good example of the necessity for dialect and place-name studies to be interdependent.

(2) Even more relevant to the present enquiry is the name Cock Flat (PNYNR,[5] p. 68) 'Church field', perhaps land held by the Church of Kirkham. Knowledge of the local dialect makes it clear that this otherwise strange form is due to a northern pronunciation of kirk as [kɔːk] or the like, with the consequent misinterpretation of it as 'cock' instead of 'church'. Cf. SED, I, VIII.5.1.

In this paper I propose to demonstrate what may be achieved with a fairly simple body of dialect and place-name material, namely that relating to the element or word kirk 'church'. This is a useful test-case in that kirk, appearing in only a small area in present-day dialect, can be supplemented by place-name evidence to produce a fuller and more satisfactory picture of its original distribution.

In northern dialects, kirk ~ church is one of a number of 'doublets' showing an initial /k ~ tʃ/ contrast, others being kist ~ chest and kirn ~ churn.[6] In final position, the same contrast emerges in birk ~ birch, sic/sike ~ such and flick ~ flitch, as well as (again) in kirk ~ church. Many of these contrasts were originally produced by the presence of the Scandinavian languages in northern England in the late OE period, and in these cases are due either to the phonetic substitution of ON /k/ for late OE /tʃ/ or to the simple borrowing of the ON cognate forms, namely kirkja (originally borrowed from OE cirice), kista (= OE cist, cest, etc.), kirna (= OE cyren), birki (= OE bierce), slíkr (= OE swylc), flikki (= OE flicce). Cf. also sark 'shirt' (ON serkr = OE serce) and beck 'brook' (ON bekkr = OE bece).

The present-day distribution of /k/ forms in church, as revealed by SED (question VIII.5.1), is shown on the accompanying map, and will be seen to be a very limited one, occurring only in Northumberland, Cumberland, Westmorland, north Lancashire, and the north-west of Yorkshire. It should further be noted that in many localities kirk was given only as a second response, and/or reported to be

[2] See A. H. Smith, The Place-Names of the West Riding of Yorkshire (PNYWR) (Cambridge, 1961–63), vii, 236–7, for a very full list, and 86–7 for full commentary.
[3] Ibid., 86–7, 195.   [4] Ibid., 86–7, 206.
[5] A. H. Smith, The Place-Names of the North Riding of Yorkshire (Cambridge, 1928).
[6] The spellings for these dialectal forms are adopted from EDD. /kaf/ 'chaff' is probably not a relevant example, since initial /k/ here may represent an Anglian unpalatalized form (ME caf < Anglian cæf = WS ceaf).

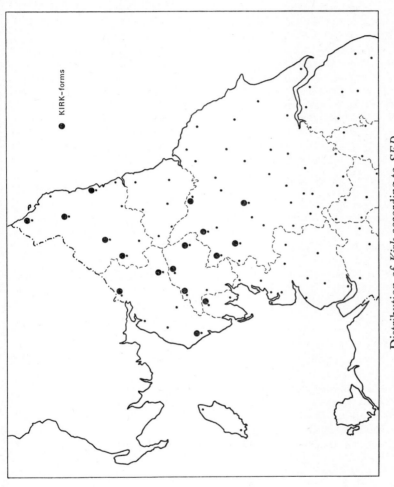

Distribution of *Kirk* according to *SED*

obsolete; at Cumberland locality 1 the *kirk* was the Presbyterian Church (as in Scotland), the Anglican Church being *church*,[7] at Westmorland 2 *kirk* (second response) was said to be 'rare', and at Westmorland 3 it was a 'suggested form'. On the whole, *kirk* appears to have been given with least hesitation in Northumberland. To the examples shown on the map should be added, however, *kirk-hole* 'children's slang for *grave*' at Durham 1 (north Durham) and also the Filey fishermen's use of the word *kirk* (pronounced [kɛlk]) preserved in one or two set phrases cited by Mr Widdowson in his essay in the present volume (see p. 57, above), namely *kirk at High Brigg* (a fishermen's bearing taken between the church and a high point on Filey Brigg) and *kirk's coming afore* (said when the church is sighted by returning fishermen). Contrary to first appearances, this *SED* data more or less agrees with that given in the *English Dialect Dictionary*, which states that *kirk* occurs in Northumberland, Cumberland, Durham, Westmorland, Yorkshire, Lancashire, Derbyshire, Lincolnshire, and ? Devonshire (*sic*). However, on further consultation of the illustrative quotations it is clear that *kirk* was used mainly in place-names in Yorkshire and *only* in place-names in Derbyshire, according to Wright's information, and further that in Lincolnshire it was used dialectally only in the north-east. Devonshire may almost certainly be ruled out altogether, since in the one source quoted, namely Salmon's *West-Country Ballads and Verses* (Edinburgh, 1899), *kirk* perhaps erroneously occurs as an archaic or vaguely dialectal term in the verse:

> So in the kirk at Widdecombe
> They finished evening prayer.

EDD's information is thus seen to be closer to that given in *SED* than appears at first sight, although it still shows a somewhat wider distribution.

On comparison with some of the other initial /k/ forms mentioned above, the present distribution of *kirk* is seen to be relatively limited geographically. *Kirn*, although it shows roughly the same type of pattern, is more extensively attested, occurring in Durham and all down the localities of east Yorkshire as far as the Humber mouth. The words with final /k/ have even wider distributions: *birk* (IV.10.1), it is true, does not extend far into Northumberland, and is almost unattested in Durham, but it does occur in south-west Northumberland, Cumberland, Westmorland, north Lancashire, in the North and East Ridings of Yorkshire, and once or twice in the West Riding and

---

[7] Cf., however, *SED*, VIII.5.5 *churchyard*, where *kirk-yard* is given for this locality.

north Lincolnshire. *Sic, sike* (VIII.9.7) is the regular form all over the north from north Northumberland down to north Lancashire and the North and East Ridings, while *flick* (III.12.3), except in north and south Lancashire, occurs throughout the north, including Yorkshire (except for the east, where the word is *side*), extending into north Lincolnshire.

The fullest distribution of Scandinavian loan-words in English dialect is represented by words such as *beck* (IV.1.1) < ON *bekkr*, which occurs in a broad diagonal belt across the country from Cumberland to Norfolk. Northumberland is excluded, and the western limits of its occurrence in the Midlands are the West Riding and east Nottinghamshire. But most of the other Scandinavian loans show a much smaller distribution. One familiar pattern is that of a broad horizontal band across the country from east Yorkshire to the west coast, its northern and southern boundaries fluctuating quite considerably from word to word. Words showing this distribution are *steg* (< ON *steggr*; IV.6.16) 'gander', *lea* (< ON *lé*; II.9.6) 'scythe', *lait* (< ON *leita*; III.13.18) 'look for', *flay-crow* (< ON *fleyja + crow*; II.3.7) 'scarecrow'. And *birk* (above) more or less falls into this category, except for outlying examples in south-west Northumberland and north Lincolnshire.

The geographical pattern shown by the large number of Scandinavian words mentioned above is obviously due to historical causes—in other words, the pattern may be fairly satisfactorily accounted for. *Kirk*, however, is not such an easy problem, and its distribution is not immediately illuminated when we consider the ME evidence. For the following description of the occurrences of ME *kirk*-forms (as also for much other advice) I am indebted to Professor Angus McIntosh, who has kindly supplied me with a tentative map of them based on his and Professor M. L. Samuels's current research in ME dialectology. This map shows forms of *kirk* extending southwards from south Northumberland, east Cumberland and south and east Westmorland (localized ME material for these counties is sparse), Durham, Yorkshire, and north Lancashire (which all show *kirk* fairly fully, though the rest of Lancashire much less so), the western boundary of the *kirk*-area thereafter running through the centre of Cheshire, north Derbyshire, the eastern county boundary of Nottinghamshire, north Leicestershire, the centre of Rutland, the northeast tip of Northamptonshire, north Cambridgeshire, looping into north Suffolk and then back again to end in north Norfolk (it should be noted, however, that the material for Norfolk is not yet complete). This material accords reasonably well with some of the fuller distributions of ON words in present-day dialect, e.g. *beck* (see above), and with what we know of the Scandinavian settlements in England from historical sources (see below). With the exception of the extreme north, ME *kirk* is predominant throughout northern and eastern England, the western boundary of the area being a roughly diagonal line from the Wirral through the Midlands to Norfolk.

As a final supplement to the dialectal evidence, medieval and modern, we need that of present-day place-names, and as a preliminary to giving this, a very brief statement of the Scandinavian invasions of this country will perhaps be helpful.

Danish attacks on England commenced in earnest about 820, but settlements were not generally made until 865. From then onwards, the Vikings, during the next fifteen years, took possession of most of eastern England, settling in Northumbria in 876, in Mercia in 877 and in East Anglia in 879. An agreement on a territorial division was reached in 886 by King Alfred and Guthrum, King of the East Anglian Danes, in which it was agreed that the boundary between the two jurisdictions should be marked by the Thames estuary as far upstream as the Lea, then turning north and following the Lea to its source. From here the boundary was to run in a straight line to Bedford, thereafter following the Ouse upstream to the point at which it was crossed by Watling Street, i.e. Fenny Stratford. This left Alfred in possession of London but gave Guthrum modern Essex, Norfolk, Suffolk, Cambridgeshire, and parts of Bedfordshire and Hertfordshire. How much further north Guthrum's kingdom extended is not clear, but there were now three separate Scandinavian dominions—Northumbria (Yorkshire), East Anglia and Scandinavian Mercia (which included the 'five boroughs' of Lincoln, Stamford, Leicester, Derby, and Nottingham). During the next forty years, however, the Danish-held lands east of Watling Street were reconquered, although the Kingdom of York remained independent much longer (its final submission was not made until 954). From about 900 onwards, there was a new penetration into the Wirral, the Lancashire coast, Westmorland, Cumberland, and the northern shores of the Solway Firth, this time chiefly by Norwegians from the Norse kingdom established in Dublin. They furthermore succeeded in gaining control of the Danish settlements in Yorkshire until 955.

The period of later raids and political conquest (980–1042) are not of much importance from the present point of view, since the bulk of the Scandinavian place-names were probably given during the earlier periods of invasion.

The influence of the Scandinavian languages on English nomenclature is well-known and needs no discussion. It reveals itself, both in medieval times and today, by the existence of numerous Scandinavian name-elements such as *by* (ON *bær, býr*) 'homestead'; *thorp* (ON *þorp*) 'hamlet', etc.; *lathe* (ON *hlaða*) 'barn'; *scale* (ON *skáli*) 'hut, shed'; *garth* (ON *garðr*) 'enclosure'; *thwaite* (ON *þveit*) 'clearing, meadow'; *beck* (ON *bekkr*) 'brook'; *keld* (ON *kelda*) 'spring'; *ask* (ON *askr*) 'ash-tree'; *stain* (ON *steinn*) 'stone'. All of these, and many others, are common, as are also Scandinavian personal names. A consideration of this quite substantial element in English names supports the historical evidence for Scandinavian conquest and settlement.[8]

Parish-names of Scandinavian origin are spread thickly throughout the North and East Ridings of Yorkshire, in Lincolnshire and Leicestershire, but less densely in Nottinghamshire. In Norfolk they are well represented, while in Suffolk they are well scattered but less numerous. In the West Riding there is a band running from north Lancashire across the county to the North and East Ridings, with another further south, from south Lancashire to Nottinghamshire. Elsewhere in the Danelaw they are rarer or non-existent. The greatest Danish influence is thus seen to be in the three areas of Scandinavian dominion mentioned above, namely Yorkshire, Scandinavian Mercia, and East Anglia. It is less intensive on the borders of these areas. In Northumberland Danish influence is very slight, while in Durham a considerable number of names is found only in the south, near the Tees and the Wear. The area west of Watling Street is almost free of traces of Scandinavian settlement except on the border.

A compact colony of Scandinavians, chiefly Norwegians, in the Wirral is evidenced by place-names, and the same evidence bears witness to the strength and extent of their settlement of the rest of the north-west, along the coastal areas north of the Mersey to Westmorland and Cumberland, and east, beyond the Pennines, into the West and North Ridings of Yorkshire; in Lancashire, south of the Ribble, it is chiefly along the coast, near and north of Liverpool.

Within this area, defined both by historical and place-name evidence, we may now turn more precisely to a consideration of the element *kirk*. Some of its occurrences in English nomenclature may represent a simple substitution of ON *kirkja* for OE *cirice* (e.g. Peakirk, Northamptonshire, which is recorded as *æt Pegecyrcan* 1042–66), and this is especially likely to be the case when the second element of a compound containing *kirk* is English in origin, as in

---

[8] The summary given here is based on that in P. H. Reaney, *The Origin of English Place-Names* (London, 1960), pp. 179 ff., but mention should also be made of E. Ekwall, 'The Scandinavian Element', in the *Introduction to the Survey of English Place-Names*, ed. A. Mawer and F. M. Stenton (Cambridge, 1924), pp. 55–92.

Kirkstead (Lincolnshire), Kirkley (Suffolk). Others are certainly pure Scandinavian names, as Kirkland (Lancashire), where the second element is actually not *land* but ON *lundr* 'grove', Felkirk (Yorkshire West Riding) 'church of boards' (the first element being ON *fjǫl* 'board'). Yet others may be later names, formed after ME *kirk* had become a simple appellative used in forming new names.

Starting in the north, there is a scattering of place-names containing the element *kirk* throughout Northumberland, but not numbering more than half-a-dozen or so examples, while Durham has apparently only one such name, Kirk Merrington, in the south. This accords with the fact stated above that this county and Northumberland are not counties in which place-name (or other) evidence for Scandinavian settlement is strong.[9]

Such evidence is, however, much greater in Cumberland and Westmorland, and is naturally, considering the historical evidence, more of a Norwegian type. A glance at the 'Place-name Elements' sections of the EPNS volumes for these counties will give some idea of the extent of the Scandinavian settlements (see, e.g., ON *á, bekkr, erg, fell, gil, hlaða, skáli*, etc.). In the indexes to the same volumes, place-names containing *kirk* as an element in their present-day form number some forty for Cumberland and some twenty for Westmorland.[10]

In Yorkshire Scandinavian influence on place-names is again very strong, on the whole, more so in the East and North Ridings than in

[9] See A. Mawer, *The Place-Names of Northumberland and Durham* (Cambridge, 1920), p. xix. In the present discussion, my statements are based on the materials provided by the volumes of EPNS where these are available. In other cases they are based either on other books on the place-names of the counties concerned or simply from my own rough observations from maps, lists and so on, including the names listed in *The Concise Oxford Dictionary of English Place-Names*, ed. E. Ekwall (4th edn., Oxford, 1960). One very important fact that must be borne in mind is that the various books on place-names, including those of the EPNS, do not treat all counties equally. Thus, for example, the EPNS volumes have paid more attention to field-names and other minor names as time has gone on, and the vast amount of material assembled in the first six volumes of *PNYWR* (8 vols., 1961–63) is not, therefore, strictly comparable with that in the volumes dealing with the North and East Ridings (1928, 1937). It may well be that some of my statements here will be later proved to be inaccurate to a lesser or greater degree, but short of carrying out a complete survey of the Danelaw area myself, this is to some extent inevitable, although regrettable. In particular, the enormous difference between the hundred examples in Yorkshire and a mere ten in Lancashire seems to be suspect.

[10] A. M. Armstrong, A. Mawer, F. M. Stenton and B. Dickins, *The Place-Names of Cumberland (PNCu)* (Cambridge, 1950–52); A. H. Smith, *The Place-Names of Westmorland (PNWe)* (Cambridge, 1967).

the West Riding. A rough count of the examples of *kirk* in present-day Yorkshire place-names yields over one hundred in all.[11]

Scandinavian place-name elements are also very common in Lancashire, and are probably chiefly of Norwegian origin. I have counted the element *kirk* some ten times in present-day Lancashire place-names.[12]

Derbyshire also has *kirk* some ten times as a place-name element at the present day,[13] nearly all the examples occurring in the east or centre of the county, while Nottinghamshire has about half-a-dozen scattered examples.[14] For Lincolnshire I have counted about a dozen examples, while on the edges of the Danelaw area they tend to be very occasional—one or two in Cheshire, several in Leicestershire, one or two in Warwickshire,[15] Northamptonshire,[16] Cambridgeshire,[17] Norfolk, and Suffolk, and one pure Scandinavian name in north-east Essex,[18] namely Kirby-le-Soken (< ON *kirkjubýr* 'church town'). We may therefore sum up by stating that—according to the rather unequal evidence—*kirk* appears as a place-name element most plentifully in Cumberland, Westmorland, and Yorkshire, that it occurs in much smaller numbers in Lancashire, Derbyshire, Nottinghamshire, Lincolnshire, Leicestershire, and counties to the south-east of these—getting rarer further south—and that it is also attested, although infrequently, in Northumberland and Durham. This pattern is what we should expect, bearing the historical background in mind.

We have now collected evidence regarding *kirk* from (a) present-day northern dialects; (b) ME texts; (c) present-day place-names. This evidence, briefly summarized, presents very widespread geographical distributions for the ME and place-name material, and a very limited one for the present-day dialectal material.

In one sense all this material may be called 'dialectal', in that in all of it *kirk* is regionally restricted (e.g. it is completely absent in London and the south of England) and that it is regionally contrasted with another form—*church*—which is the southern and Standard English

[11] See the Index (for all three Ridings) in *PNYWR*, viii.

[12] E. Ekwall, *The Place-Names of Lancashire* (Manchester, 1922).

[13] K. Cameron, *The Place-Names of Derbyshire* (*PNDb*) (Cambridge, 1959).

[14] J. E. B. Gover, A. Mawer and F. M. Stenton, *The Place-Names of Nottinghamshire* (*PNNt*) (Cambridge, 1940).

[15] Ibid., *The Place-Names of Warwickshire* (Cambridge, 1936).

[16] Ibid., *The Place-Names of Northamptonshire* (*PNNth*) (Cambridge, 1933).

[17] P. H. Reaney, *The Place-Names of Cambridgeshire and the Isle of Ely* (*PNC*) (Cambridge, 1943).

[18] Ibid., *The Place-Names of Essex* (Cambridge, 1935), p. 340.

form. Furthermore, *kirk* in each different body of material can be said to be 'recessive': as time has gone on, northerners have tended to use the word *kirk* as an ordinary component of their vocabulary less and less and to replace it by the Standard English form *church*— to the extent that it is now current only in a comparatively small area in the far north, and even there was often given to the *SED* field-worker only with some qualification. The ME documents reflect this recession in written form, since here too *kirk* appears less and less as time goes on, and *church* more and more. And finally, during the post-medieval period, between the sixteenth and nineteenth centuries, some place-names in written documents can be seen giving up *kirk* forms and adopting *church* forms, as the following examples testify.

Old Church (*PNCu*, pp. 257–8) is perhaps the place known as *New Church* in 1674, *New Kirk* in 1789 and *Newchurch* in 1825, and the comment is added that the whole parish is 'commonly called "*Newkirk* parish"'. (In this case it looks as if the Standard English form was the norm in the seventeenth century, but the traditional local form emerged again in the eighteenth century. Ultimately the Standard English form triumphed in official documents, while the dialectal one was retained in local usage.)[19] In Westmorland, St Paul's Church (*PNWe*, ii, 213) displayed *kirk* forms in 1695 and 1713 (but has apparently adopted *church* since); Church Bank (ibid., i, 58) was *Kirkebanke* in 1574 but *Church Banke* in 1698 (i.e. the traditional form was perhaps given up in the seventeenth century). In the West Riding of Yorkshire, Church Side (Methley; *PNYWR*, ii, 128) was *Kirkside* as late as 1570, and *Church Side* in 1812; Church Fenton (ibid., iv, 63) shows *kirk* forms in 1338, 1365, 1404, and up to 1641 (earlier having been known simply as *Fenton*), and no *church* forms before modern times; the street-name Church Bank in Bradford (ibid., iii, 242) is *Kirkebanke* 1665, but *Church bank* 1674, 1746; Church Wong (a field-name in Tickhill; ibid., i, 57) is *Kirkewong* 1373 but *Church W(h)ong(e)* 1668. In the East Riding of Yorkshire, Church Lane, Beverley (*PNYER*,[20] p. 194) is *Holmkyrklane* 1417, *Kyrkleyn* 1520 and *Kirkelane* 1578 (i.e. there are no early *church* forms); while Church Lane, Kingston-upon-Hull (ibid., p. 211) shows only *kirk* forms until 1415, *church* forms being given from 1546 to 1602. In Derbyshire, Church Broughton (*PNDb*, p. 541) is *Broctun(e)* in Domesday Book and *Broghtone* in 1330, 1577, and 1610, and first shows a prefixed *Chirch(e)-* in 1327, which is also recorded in 1330 and

---

[19] It is frequently the case that local pronunciations preserve the traditional form of a place-name better than the Standard English pronunciations. See G. E. Evans, "Aspects of Oral Tradition', *Folk Life*, vii (1969), 5–14. This is one obvious justification for a complete survey of English place-name pronunciations.

[20] A. H. Smith, *The Place-Names of the East Riding of Yorkshire and York* (Cambridge, 1937).

1626. But side by side with the *church* forms are *kirk* forms recorded from 1383, 1398, 1403, 1454, and up to *c*. 1600. It is, however, the *church* forms which finally prevail. In Nottinghamshire, several Church Farms go back to names with *kirk* forms (*PNNt*, pp. 41, 172, 242), while Church Lane in Sibthorpe (ibid., p. 217) is *Kirkelane* 1336, and Church Meadow Lane in Upton (ibid., p. 179) is (probably) *Kirkemedowe in Upton* 1582, *Kirk meddow* 1654. In Northamptonshire, Churchfield Farm in Benefield (*PNNth*, p. 212) is *ciricfeld c*. 964, *Circafeld* 1125–8, *Chirchefeld* 1189 and up to 1428, then *Kirkefeld* 1202 and *c*. 1250, *Curchefeld* (*sic*) *c*. 1220, but thereafter shows only *church* forms. In Cambridgeshire, Church Croft in Newton (*PNC*, p. 275) is *Kirkecroft* 1385, 1532, but *Church Crofts* 1688; Church Field (Isle of Ely, ibid., p. 264) is *Chirchefeud* 1328, *Kyrkefeld* 1446 (but must have reverted to *church* forms since).

These are only a handful of examples out of what appear to be a very large number. As the editors of *PNNt* put it (p. xxiii), 'in many modern names *kirk* now appears as *church*, *k*- forms usually disappearing after the 14th century'.

Thus, *kirk* is seen to be a recessive dialectal form both in the written and in the spoken language—i.e. in present-day dialectal forms (spoken), and in ME documents and early place-name forms (written). Here, however, some most interesting questions arise. The first and most obvious of these is why the present-day dialectal and place-name distributions are so different, the place-names still showing a fairly full distribution over the whole of the original Scandinavian area, while *kirk* in local dialect is in complete contrast by its apparent retreat to a small area in the far north, its recession being more drastic than that of *kirn* or of *birk*, *flick*, *sic/sike* (see above), not to mention *beck*. And this question has, of course, wider implications since it suggests the more general question—why do dialectal words recede to such a great extent while the same words as elements of place-names (even in their spoken form) remain relatively stable?

Standard English has in general a greater effect on dialect than on place-names, gradually forcing dialectal forms to retire into the edges and corners of an area or into isolated pockets. That it does also have an effect on place-name forms seems to be shown from the examples cited above in which *kirk* was changed to *church* in documents, usually (but note the first example, that of Old Church) reflecting no doubt an earlier change in the spoken language—'earlier' because there is usually a time-lag between a development in the spoken language and its manifestation in written form, especially in place-name forms, which are habitually conservative in their spellings. Leaving aside the fact that there is possibly always a degree of psychological reluctance to change merely one element in a name, for various reasons the effect of Standard English is slower on place-names than it is on ordinary dialect. Proper names, attached to geographical units, are likely to be much more stable than separate dialect words, and there is not the same pressure to change items which may be felt in some way to be 'official', authorized, preserved somewhere in writing. In other words, the status of place-names probably assists in their preservation, while local dialect has no such status at the present day.

The comparatively slight effect of Standard English on place-name forms is contrasted strongly with its effect on dialectal terms, but there is also a contrast between the different effects of Standard English on different dialectal terms. Thus, the question arises (secondly) as to why *kirk* has receded so very drastically as compared with, for example, *beck*. Numerous extremely complex factors may account for such differences, and linguistic geography proves nothing if it is not that 'every word has its own history'. But here, I think, the answer must lie in psychological as well as linguistic facts. There being no Standard English equivalent to *beck*, *beck* is obviously felt as a dialect word, *kirk*, with its Standard English equivalent *church*, as a dialect pronunciation, whatever the type of ON influence may have been, historically speaking (the dialect speaker cannot be expected to be an expert in philology). In these particular cases, the dialect *word* is felt to be acceptable, but not the dialect *pronunciation*, because it has a Standard English equivalent which, being phonetically similar, can easily be substituted. It is hardly conceivable that speakers of local dialect would think it worthwhile to substitute *brook* (the Standard English term) for *beck*, but it is, in my submission, quite conceivable that they would think it not only worthwhile but also very proper to substitute *church* for *kirk*—and perhaps the psychological associations of the notion 'church' have tended to strengthen this trend of thinking. One other factor which may, however, have played a part in the speedy recession of *kirk* is that of familiarity. Unfamiliar, more local, words probably retain local pronunciations the longest, thus perhaps *kirn* (see above), and a possible example from a completely different area is that of *fellies* which, according to the *SED* material (I.9.9), shows a wider distribution of initial /v/ over the south and south-west of England than any of the other initial *f-* words.[21] *Kirk ~ church* express a common notion and occur in everyday collocations— 'go to...', 'at...', and so on, and the church itself is not, for example, like a part of the old wooden

[21] See M. F. Wakelin and M. V. Barry, 'The Voicing of Initial Fricative Consonants in Present-Day Dialectal English', *Leeds Studies in English*, New Series ii: *Studies in Honour of Harold Orton*, ed. S. Ellis (1968), p. 52 and Map 6.

plough, an object which has fallen into disuse and its name with it. The church building is a familiar sight in every English village and matters connected with it are a topic of frequent discussion in small communities, where it is still an institution regarded with a mixture of reverence and affection. A common notion of this sort is likely to change the pronunciation of its name in a Standard English direction rather more readily than some others. Finally, *kirk* has greatly receded since medieval times, probably because of the constant use of *church* by the educated clergy and others in authority, who, whether they were southerners or not (and doubtless they often were), would be very likely to use southern forms both in writing and speech, at least from the Middle Ages onwards.

A third, associated, problem is that of the present-day geographical pattern shown by dialectal *kirk*, and in particular why it occurs throughout Northumberland (but not in Durham) whereas most dialect words of ON origin do not occur here, since, as noted above, neither of these two counties was strongly affected by Scandinavian linguistic influence.

Again, I think the answer must be found in the peculiar ebb and flow of dialectal usage. On the one hand, dialectal forms do spread, on the other hand—a much more familiar picture at the present day— they recede, and perhaps enough has not been made of the first of these. In our paper on the voicing of initial fricative consonants in the west of England, Mr M. V. Barry and I suggested that the pattern was not merely one of recession, but that some forms with initial /v z ð ʒ/ had actually spread during the NE period, and were perhaps still spreading in the nineteenth century.[22] There is every reason to think that Northumberland and Durham underwent very little direct influence from Scandinavian-speaking peoples, but received indirect influence in the form of dialect loans during the ME period and subsequently. Mawer suggested with regard to Durham that the use of the word *beck* in modern times (cf. *SED*, I, IV.1.1, where it is recorded for every locality in Durham) must be due to the influence of Yorkshire custom—where *beck* does occur in place-names it replaces earlier *-burn* (< OE *burna*).[23] *Beck* is an interesting parallel to *kirk*. In Durham, as far as I can ascertain, *kirk* occurs only in Kirk Merrington, which is recorded from *c.* 1125 as *Mærintun, Meringtonas, c.* 1200 *Merrington*; i.e. no *kirk* is mentioned in these early forms. The same is true of most of the Northumberland *kirk*-names: no mention is made of the prefix *kirk* in the early forms of Kirknewton and Kirkwhelpington; Kirkharle is recorded in 1177, but not with

[22] Ibid., 60.   [23] Op. cit., p. xix.

the *kirk* element until *c*. 1250; Kirkhaugh and Kirkheaton both appear for the first time in the thirteenth century and are already complete with the prefix *kirk*. *Kirk* in all these names is thus recorded fairly late (not until the thirteenth century) even when it is recorded at all, and it looks as if by this time the word may have become a simple appellative used in forming place-names, and borrowed from the more 'Scandinavian' regions further south.

At the same time, since the late ME period *kirk*, as we have seen, has been a recessive feature both in speech and (albeit disappearing somewhat more slowly) in writing, and thus the opposite process has been taking place ever since this time. The ME map for Durham is quite full (see above), and the use of the phrase *kirk-hole* (above) suggests that *kirk* was not entirely unknown as a dialect word in this area, even if it now survives only in this one set phrase. The blanks in the far northern part of the map we must thus put down to dialectal disintegration (as in the southern part of the Danelaw), although why Durham should be so exceptionally denuded of dialect forms is not entirely clear. Professor Orton, however, put forward other examples of and reasons for the disintegration of the Byers Green dialect[24]— mainly the enormous rise in the population of the whole area since as far back as 1801, the coal industry in particular being the means of bringing into Durham considerable numbers of workmen and their families from elsewhere (Ireland, Scotland, Wales, Yorkshire, Lancashire, and the Midlands). His examples (mostly of change in the long vowels) show convincingly the dialectal break-down which had taken place in Byers Green in the 1920s, and if such a process was evident even then in this fairly isolated spot ('it was formerly some distance from the beaten track, for it lies in a pocket of land formed by a deep bend of the river'),[25] the inferences to be made with regard to less remote parts of the county are obvious. Also relevant is Professor Orton's comment that: 'In point of vocabulary, too, words of Scandinavian origin seem to be far less common at Byers Green, although possibly many such words here fell out of use because unfamiliar to the families who settled in the village a few decades ago'.[26] (And together with such settlements we should not forget on the other hand the considerable migrations which have taken place *out* of the county to London and elsewhere, especially during periods of depression.) Finally, we are, of course, dealing with the disappearance of a feature which was a loan in the first place, and this too may have something to do with it. Northumberland perhaps retains its

---

[24] H. Orton, *The Phonology of a South Durham Dialect* (London, 1933), Introduction, pp. xiii–xviii.
[25] Ibid., p. xiii.   [26] Ibid., p. xviii.

borrowed *kirk* only on account of the county's greater remoteness (the same is probably true of Cumberland and Westmorland), while the influence of forms from across the Scottish border cannot be entirely discounted, and may be behind some of the dialect and place-name forms in the north of the county (cf. the place-names Ladykirk, Hobkirk, Kirkton, etc.).[27]

[27] In the distribution of dialect vocabulary, the linguistic boundary in the east is apparently often well down in central or south Northumberland, whereas in the west, northern English words tend to spread north into Dumfriesshire. See J. S. Woolley, 'The Linguistic Survey of Scotland and its activities in Cumberland', *Journal of the Lakeland Dialect Society*, xvii (1955), 11. Professor Orton also draws my attention to the fact that Presbyterianism is very strong in Northumberland, but not in Durham, and suggests that Scottish influence disseminated by the Scottish ministers might help to account for the *kirk* forms in Northumberland. I am grateful to Professor Orton for this and other helpful suggestions and advice in connection with this essay.

5 Local Dialect and the Poet :

A Comparison of the Findings in the *Survey of English Dialects* with Dialect in Tennyson's Lincolnshire Poems

Philip M. Tilling

In 1864, some twenty-seven years after he had left Lincolnshire, Alfred, Lord Tennyson published a poem called *Northern Farmer, Old Style*, a dramatic monologue in which a dying farmer rebukes the Lord for calling upon him at such a difficult time. The poem was, according to a note published with it, 'founded on the dying words of a farm-bailiff, as reported to me by my old great-uncle when he was verging upon eighty: "God A'mighty little knows what He's about a-taking me. An' Squire will be mad an' all." I conjectured the man from that one saying.' The poem is especially convincing because Tennyson has taken great care not only in creating the farmer's personality, but also in reproducing the kind of English that he would have used.

Northern Farmer, Old Style (OS) was to be the first of Tennyson's dramatic monologues written in the Lincolnshire dialect. It was written in 1861 and published three years later in 'Enoch Arden and Other Poems'. Over the next twenty-eight years, until Tennyson's death in 1892, a further six Lincolnshire poems were published. The second of these was *Northern Farmer, New Style* (NS) which was begun in 1861, privately printed in 1864 (when it was entitled *Property*) and eventually published in 1869 in 'The Holy Grail'. In 1880 two Lincolnshire poems, *The Northern Cobbler* (NC) and *The Village Wife* (VW) were included in 'Ballads and Other Poems'. In 1885 *The Spinster's Sweet-Arts* (SS) was published in 'Tiresias and Other Poems'; and in 1889 *Owd Roä* (OR) was published in 'Demeter and Other Poems'. The last of the Lincolnshire dialect poems, *The Church-Warden and the Curate* (CWC), was published posthumously in 1892 in 'The Death of Oenone'.[1]

---

[1] The texts that have been used as the basis of this study are those of the Eversley edition of Tennyson's Works (published in nine volumes from 1907–8) which was edited by Hallam, Lord Tennyson. I have also checked the texts against page-proofs of the first published editions of the poems. These were corrected in

In order to convey the sounds of the dialect as accurately as he could, Tennyson developed an elementary phonetic system by which the value of particular letters was changed by the addition of a diaeresis. This was more reliable than a system based on existing combinations of letters which have different phonetic meanings to people who speak different dialects. Even so, his system was not nearly detailed enough to reproduce all the sounds that he required and it caused difficulties which he never managed to resolve. This is seen in the difficulty that Tennyson had with words formerly containing ME $\bar{\imath}$. In OS and NS he used a spelling *oi*, but he was clearly dissatisfied with this for, in a note appended to NC, he suggests a pronunciation *aï* (which he does not define) and leaves the standard spelling. Examination of the page-proofs of the first editions of NC and VW shows Tennyson fluctuating between *oi* and *ii*, before finally retaining the standard spelling. A further difficulty is that Tennyson generally fails to give the reader any guidance on the meaning of his conventions. Hence these poems are virtually inaccessible to a reader who has no previous knowledge of the dialect. This has certainly been responsible for the poems' neglect. With the exception of OS and NS they are seldom included in anthologies and Tennyson scholars have devoted little time to them. Yet, they are important to a complete understanding of Tennyson for they show that throughout the latter half of his life his native Lincolnshire was never far from his mind. It is significant, also, that the first of his Lincolnshire poems was not published until 1864, long after he had left the county. In view of this, and considering the length of time over which the poems were written, it seems reasonable to ask if the language of the poems really does give some indication of the Lincolnshire dialect that Tennyson heard in his youth.

Except for the three years that he spent at Cambridge, Tennyson spent the first twenty-eight years of his life in the neighbourhood of Somersby, a small village in the south Lincolnshire Wolds six miles east-north-east of Horncastle. In 1837 he moved to the south of England where he was to settle permanently, only occasionally revisiting his native county. Since Tennyson spent most of his Lincolnshire years in Somersby, it seems fair to assume that the dialect of the poems is intended to be that of the Somersby region in the early part of the nineteenth century. The only time that Tennyson himself associates the dialect with a particular locality is in a note which pre-

Tennyson's own hand and are now in the possession of the Tennyson Research Centre, the City Library, Lincoln. I would like to express my thanks to the staff of the Tennyson Research Centre for their assistance and for giving me free access to the material in their collection.

89

cedes CWC, in which he says: 'This is written in the dialect which was current in my youth at Spilsby and in the country about it.' Spilsby is about five miles south-east of Somersby.

The dialect of the poems belongs to the area described by A. J. Ellis, in his massive investigation of the phonology of English dialects published in 1889,[2] as the 'Mid Lincolnshire Form' of the 'Border Midland' dialect district. Ellis identifies the 'Border Midland' district with the whole of Lincolnshire and he divides it into southern, central, and northern areas. The division between the northern and central areas is his Transverse Line 6, the southern *hoose* line, north of which ME *ū* remains. This isogloss encloses a fairly small area in the north of the county and lies at least twenty-five miles to the north of Somersby. Three of the localities investigated for the *Survey of English Dialects* are situated in this area. Ellis established the boundary between the 'Mid Lincolnshire Form' and the 'South Lincolnshire Form' some fifteen miles south of Somersby. Four localities investigated for *SED* fall within this area, and data from these relates them to the neighbouring counties to the south and west, rather than to the rest of Lincolnshire.

The work of A. J. Ellis is particularly important to any study of the dialect of Tennyson's Lincolnshire poems, for not only does he discuss their use of dialect material, but his conclusions are based on a discussion which he had with the poet himself.[3] During the course of an interview on 23 March 1881 Tennyson read most of OS and some of NS to Ellis who took notes on his pronunciation and questioned his use of certain unexpected forms. Several of the suggestions made by Ellis were accepted in later editions of the poems and these changes were presumably made as a direct result of the interview. Hence, *yaäl* 'ale' and *yeäd* 'head', which appear in the first edition of OS, appear in later editions as *aäl* OS i.3 (and elsewhere) and *eäd* OS v.2 (and elsewhere). Also *'un*, which appears in OS for 'him' in positions of weak stress, was seen by Tennyson to be a southernism and was changed, though wrongly, it seems, to *'um* OS iii.4 (and elsewhere), rather than to *'im* which is the usual form in all the other dialect poems. On at least one occasion Ellis's comments seem to have led to some rewriting by Tennyson. On hearing him read the following lines:

Why? fur 'e's nobbut a curate, an' weänt nivir git naw 'igher,
An' 'e maäde the bed as 'e liggs on afoor 'e coom'd to the shire.

NS vii.3/4

[2] A. J. Ellis, *On Early English Pronunciation*, part v (London, 1889), p. 302.
[3] I am indebted to Mr S. Ellis of the University of Leeds, who first drew my attention to the remarks of A. J. Ellis on Tennyson's Lincolnshire poems.

Ellis queried the authenticity of the rhyme '*igher/shire* and Tennyson admitted that the two words would probably rhyme only in the speech of the educated. Furthermore, in VW iv.5 and SS iv.3 the word had been spelt *shere* and rhymed with '*ere* 'here' and *theere* 'there' respectively. In later versions of NS the two lines have been changed to:

> Why? fur 'e's nobbut a curate, an' weänt niver git hissen clear,
> An' 'e maäde the bed as 'e ligs on afoor 'e coom'd to the shere.

As a result of his long absence from Lincolnshire and the lack of any direct contact with the speech he was trying to convey, Tennyson lost no opportunity to consult those whom he thought could advise him. Sometimes, unfortunately, the advice was not as sound as it should have been. For example, Ellis observes that Tennyson had adopted the spelling *oo* for words with ME *ū*.[4] This he had been persuaded to do by a friend in order to give the poem, as Ellis says, 'a more antique and northern flavour'. In the first edition of OS the convention had been adopted inconsistently, the *oo* spelling alternating with the Standard English form. In later editions the *oo* spelling was abandoned in these words. Further to this incident, Tennyson is reported by W. F. Rawnsley to have said: 'When I first wrote the *Northern Farmer* I sent it to a solicitor of ours in Lincolnshire. I was afraid I had forgotten the tongue and he altered all my mid-Lincolnshire into North Lincolnshire and I had to put it all back.'[5]

Also important to a study of Tennyson's dialect poems is Joseph Wright's monumental *English Dialect Dictionary*, which was published from 1898 to 1905 and which was compiled from published glossaries, dialect literature, and specially collected unprinted material. A factor of particular interest is that Wright included five of Tennyson's dialect poems (OS, NS, NC, SS, and OR) among his Lincolnshire source-material. The pronunciations that he recorded are listed in the index of *The English Dialect Grammar* which was published in 1905 and included in the final volume of *EDD*. Since the publication of Ellis's material and *EDD* and *EDG*, there has been only one collection of English dialect material that is in any way comparable with them. This is the *Survey of English Dialects*. The field-work for *SED* was carried out from 1950 to 1961; with one exception, the Lincolnshire localities were investigated between 1951 and 1953, that is, roughly one hundred and fourteen years after Tennyson left Somersby. In view of the time difference, is the data

---

[4] Op. cit., p. 304.
[5] Quoted by G. E. Campion, *A Tennyson Dialect Glossary* (Lincoln, 1969), p. 1.

collected for *SED* of any conceivable value to a discussion of Tennyson's Lincolnshire dialect poems? The purpose of *SED* suggests that it is, for, in Orton's words, it was to be 'a systematic and comprehensive national investigation of the oldest existing forms of English used in this country'.[6] With this purpose in mind, great care was taken in selecting the kind of locality to be investigated. Ideally, it lay off the main lines of communication and 'preference was given to agricultural communities that had had a fairly stable' population of about five hundred inhabitants for a century or so'.[7] The informants were also selected with the utmost care. They were generally men over the age of sixty who had been born in the locality and had spent the whole of their lives in it. With a network of three hundred and thirteen comparable localities throughout England, and informants of the same social background who had all answered exactly the same questions, it is possible to draw conclusions from *SED* about the language spoken by men who had learnt their English during the late nineteenth century and had subsequently remained isolated from non-local linguistic influences. Hence, the gap between the publication of Ellis's data and *SED* is perhaps not so great as mere chronology would suggest. The *SED* investigation of Lincolnshire was conducted by a single field-worker, Mr S. Ellis. In all, fifteen localities were investigated: eleven between July 1951 and December 1951, two in July 1952, one in May 1953, and, finally, one in March 1960. Two in particular, Swaby and Old Bolingbroke, are useful to a study of Tennyson's Lincolnshire poems, for Swaby (loc. 7) is situated four miles north-east of Somersby and Old Bolingbroke (loc. 8) five miles south of Somersby. Three other localities are situated near enough for their evidence to be taken into special account. These are, with their distances from Somersby, Tealby (loc. 5) sixteen miles north-west, Wragby (loc. 6) sixteen miles west-north-west, and Scopwick (loc. 9) nineteen miles south-west.

SED, therefore, brings together a large amount of systematically collected data from the Somersby region of central Lincolnshire. This can be applied to a study of Tennyson's use of dialect in his Lincolnshire poems in a variety of ways. Three of these are considered here. Firstly, it can be used to identify the meaning of the orthographic conventions adopted by Tennyson in his attempt to indicate the precise pronunciation of the dialect. Secondly, it can isolate any linguistic features which are suspect and which may be the result of Tennyson's long absence from Lincolnshire and his

6 H. Orton, 'An English Dialect Survey; Linguistic Atlas of England', *Orbis*, ix (1960), 331.

7 H. Orton, *Introduction* to the *Survey of English Dialects* (Leeds, 1962), p. 15.

association with different dialect areas of English. Thirdly, if it supports Tennyson's use of certain forms it can show whether, within the limitations of his primitive phonetic system and the requirements of poetic metre, his material does succeed to a large extent in conveying important aspects of the dialect of central Lincolnshire. With regard to these second and third points, the only material considered in any detail here is that which *SED* suggests is exceptional, either because it is restricted to Lincolnshire or because it is not found in Lincolnshire at all. Dialect forms which have a distribution extending beyond Lincolnshire and which Tennyson uses accurately are not the subject of this present study. Conclusions derived from *SED* have been checked against the earlier material of A. J. Ellis and Wright.

The first problem faced by any reader of the Lincolnshire poems is the precise meaning of the various letter combinations used by Tennyson in his attempts to indicate the sounds that he associated with the speech of central Lincolnshire. The most striking feature of his orthographic system is his employment of *ä*, as in the vowel combinations *aä*, *eä*, and *oä*. Information from *SED* makes it clear that *ä* here represents the second element of a centring diphthong, a characteristic development of certain ME sounds throughout Lincolnshire and parts of Yorkshire to the immediate north. It is to this feature that A. J. Ellis refers when he says: 'The great and peculiar character of the whole district is the marvellous quality of fractured vowels.'[8]

Tennyson's *aä* combination is generally associated with words which have ME *ā*, such as *baäcon* 'bacon' NC xx.2, *maäke* 'make' SS ix.5 (and elsewhere), and *taäble* 'table' SS xv.5. Under BACON III.12.4,[9] MAKE IX.3.6 and (To LAY THE) TABLE V.8.12, *SED* recorded the diphthong [ɛ·ə] in each of these words in all the relevant Lincolnshire localities. Words which in RP share a common development with words with ME *ā* are also usually *aä* in Tennyson and [ɛ·ə] in *SED*. Hence, he writes *waäit* 'wait' NC i.1 (and elsewhere), *claäy* 'clay' SS vi.8 (and elsewhere), and *daäy* 'day' NC xvi.1 (and elsewhere) (cf. the entries in *SED* under CLAY IV.4.2). Tennyson's system is occasionally distorted by inconsistencies, the most common of which are the omission or misplacing of the diaeresis and the retention of the standard spelling. Thus *todaäy* NS iv.1 is recorded beside *to-daay* 'today' CWC vi.5, and *saäy* OS ii.2 (and elsewhere)

---

[8] Op. cit., p. 297.

[9] All key-words quoted from *SED* are followed by the number assigned to them in the *Questionnaire*.

beside *says* NC viii.9 (and elsewhere). With the latter example, however, the different spellings may well be used purposely to denote that the inflected form does not have the vowel sound of the uninflected form *saäy*. The importance of the grammatical context in a consideration of Tennyson's spellings is clearly illustrated by comparing his use of *maäybe* and *mebbe*. Thus, he writes: 'Maäybe she warn't a beauty' NS vi.3 and 'maäybe they'll walk upo' two' OR 17, but 'soom o' thy booöks mebbe worth their weight i' gowd' VW x.4.

Some of Tennyson's apparent inconsistencies are probably intended to point to local dialect differences, as in the spellings *graät* VW vii.6 and *graäter* SS xvii.4, which occur in Tennyson beside *greät* 'great' NC xi.1 (and elsewhere). The *SED* information under GREAT IX.1.6 shows that two developments of ME *ē₂* are recorded in this word in Lincolnshire. One is [ɪ·ə], which is the usual Lincolnshire development of ME isolative *ē₂*, and the other is [ɛ·ə], which parallels the RP development of the vowel in GREAT. The evidence of *SED* is particularly illuminating with regard to Somersby, since at loc. 7 examples of both [ɪ·ə] and [ɛ·ə] are recorded in GREAT, which suggests that the occurrence of both forms in Tennyson accurately reflects the local linguistic situation.

The length of time over which the poems were composed was clearly not in the interests of consistency and failure to check the poems against each other is probably responsible for a number of differences which seem, according to *SED* evidence, not to indicate any local dialect differences. Thus, 'half' in OR and CWC is always *haäfe* (except for one example of *haafe* at CWC v.2 which may be an error), while in NC and VW it is *hafe*. *SED* records [ɛ·ə] under HALF (PAST SEVEN) VII.5.4 throughout north and central Lincolnshire and it seems fair to assume that Tennyson intended both spellings to represent the same pronunciation. A factor of importance in this connection is that both NC and VW were published in the same volume in 1880 and OR and CWC were published within a few years of each other, OR in 1889 and CWC in 1892.

The development of ME isolative *ē₂* is usually represented by *eä* in Tennyson, as in '*eäd* OS v.2 (and elsewhere), *heäd* OR 9, *heäds* OR 25 'head(s)', *heät* 'heat' OR 84, *speäk* 'speak' NS ii.4 (and elsewhere), and *steäls* 'steal' 3 pr. pl. NS xvii.1. Except for single occurrences of [iː] at locs. 7 and 8, *SED* has [ɪ·ə] or [ɪə] in all the relevant Lincolnshire localities under HEAD VI.1.1, (THE) HEAT VI.13.6, SPEAK VI.5.5 and STEAL VIII.7.5 and Tennyson probably intended his *eä* to be identified with one of these. Tennyson also uses his *eä* convention for most of his words with ME *ē₁*, though here there is frequently a fluctuation between an *ee* and an *eä* spelling.

Thus he writes *free* NC xiv.4 (and elsewhere), beside *freeä* OS vii.1 (and elsewhere); *meek* VW ix.3, beside *meeäk* CWC ix. 5; *bees* NS x.4, beside *beeäs* NC iii.5; *keep* NC v.1, beside *keeäps* NC xvi.3, CWC x.6; and *see* OS xvi.4, beside *seeä* NC i.2. Evidence from *SED* under KEEP (HENS) IV.6.2 shows that in loc. 9 there is a mixture of [ɪˈə] and [iː] forms and further information on this point is given by S. Ellis, who writes: 'The regular modern development of ME $\bar{e}_1$ throughout the county is [iː], but there exists considerable confusion between $\bar{e}_1$ and $\bar{e}_2$ forms and many examples were recorded of $\bar{e}_1$ forms with [ɪˈə].'[10] It is certainly possible, therefore, that Tennyson intended two different sounds when he contrasted *ee* with *eä* spellings. This suggestion is supported by Tennyson's own pronunciation of *sweet* NS iii.3 and *seeä'd* 'saw' NS iv.1 in the recording that he made of himself reading a part of NS.[11]

Tennyson also seems to use *ä* to represent the second element of a centring diphthong in words with ME $\bar{o}_2$, which he spells *oä*, as in *boän* 'bone' VW vii.16, *boäth* 'both' NS iii.4 and *coämb* 'comb' VW xii.2. The entries in *SED* under (WISH-)BONE IV.6.22, BOTH VII.2.11, and COMB VI.2.4 show a development to [ɔə] in all the relevant Lincolnshire localities, and it seems probable that this was the pronunciation intended by Tennyson.

Tennyson employs the diaeresis on two further occasions where, confusingly, it serves a different purpose. *ö* added to *oo*, in words with ME $\bar{o}_1$, 'only means', to quote A. J. Ellis, 'that the *oo*...is to be pronounced long...or possibly very long'.[12] Oxley, who includes a phonetic transcription of a part of NS in his study of the dialect of Lindsey,[13] gives *ö* in this context the same value as *ä* and is forced to the conclusion that 'while (the dialect poems) contain forms which, though now obsolete, are perhaps genuine (e.g. [briəd] bread), others seem quite impossible (e.g. [buəks] books)'. In the first edition of OS Tennyson used the spelling *looäk*, but in later editions this was changed to *looök* OS x.1 (and elsewhere) which, as A. J. Ellis notes,[14] brings it into line with the spelling *booök* in VW xi.1 and elsewhere. Ellis derived his interpretation from Tennyson's reading of OS and hence his conclusion must be correct. This agrees with the forms of

10 S. Ellis, 'A Study of the Living Dialects of Lincolnshire Based on an Investigation by Questionnaire' (unpublished M.A. thesis, University of Leeds, 1952), p. 544.
11 *Alfred, Lord Tennyson reads from his own poems*. Produced as a long-playing record by the Tennyson Society from re-recordings of the Edison wax cylinders made by the poet himself in 1890.
12 Op. cit., p. 303.
13 J. E. Oxley, *The Lindsey Dialect* (Leeds, 1940), p. 87.
14 Op. cit., p. 303.

LOOK collected in *SED* under III.13.18, where the vowel is [uː] throughout the relevant Lincolnshire localities, although in locs. 8 and 9 the shortened development [ɔ], which is parallel to the RP development of this word, also occurs. This suggests that the apparent inconsistency between Tennyson's forms *looök* and *look* NC xix.3, and *booök* VW v.2 and *book* VW vii. 13 (and elsewhere) represents a very real distinction present in the dialect. Tennyson also contrasts *booöts* NC iii.3 (and elsewhere) with *boots* SS xv.5, but *SED* records no shortened development of this word under BOOTS VI.14.23, and consequently it is not possible to show that this represents a contrast exactly equivalent to that between *looök* and *look*. The fluctuation between the spellings *ooo* and *ooö* in LOOK in OS and BOOK in VW may be intended as a further distinction in length and could mean, as Ellis suggests, that *ooö* is to be pronounced 'very long', to contrast with *ooo* which could mean simply long.

As has already been mentioned, Tennyson found great difficulty in representing the development of Lincolnshire ME *ī*. In OS and NS he used the combination *oi*, but he found this unsatisfactory and in the later poems he abandoned the convention. To NC he added a note in which he said:

The vowels *aï*, pronounced separately though in the closest conjunction, best render the sound of the long *i* and *y* in this dialect. But since such words as *craïin*, *daïin*, *whaï*, *aï* ("I"), etc. look awkward except in a page of express phonetics, I have thought it better to leave the simple *i* and *y*, and to trust my readers will give them the broader pronunciation.

This information, however, cannot help the reader a great deal, for he can only guess at the meaning of the *ī*. The evidence of *SED* suggests that with words containing ME *ī* the difficulty lies in the nature of the first element of the diphthong, which may be either [a] or [ɑ]. Both are recorded from the relevant Lincolnshire localities, but a comparison of *SED* entries under EYE VI.3.1, ICE VII.6.12, KNIFE I.7.18, and SKY VII.6.1 suggests that the diphthong [ɑˑɪ] is generally associated with A. J. Ellis's southern division of Lincolnshire to the south of loc. 8, while [aˑɪ] occurs in central and northern Lincolnshire. The fact that Somersby is situated close to the boundary between [ɑˑɪ] and [aˑɪ] forms may account for Tennyson's difficulty in notating the sound and his fluctuations between the use of *o* and *a* to describe the first element of the diphthong. Tennyson, like *SED*, probably heard both forms in central Lincolnshire.

The other spelling conventions that Tennyson uses in the dialect poems consist of combinations of letters generally associated with

96

particular sounds in RP. *SED* evidence suggests that this method, as used by Tennyson, seems, on occasion, to conflict with his use of the diaeresis. A comparison of words which in Tennyson have *ai* with their Lincolnshire form as listed by *SED*, suggests that this convention means exactly the same as *aä*, and represents [ɛˑə]. Thus ARM VI.6.8 is [ɛˑəm] in *SED* in all relevant localities (Tennyson has *airm* NC xv.5, *hairm* OR 58/65 and *arm* SS vi.4); and BAIRNS (s.v. CHILDREN) VIII.1.2 is [bɛˑənz] in *SED* (Tennyson has *bairns* SS xii.12, SS xiii.1, *bairn* OR 92 and *barne* OS iv.2, OS vi.1. The retention of the standard spelling in the first two of these may not be intended to have phonetic significance). However, where Tennyson has used different conventions for sounds which, according to *SED* evidence, are exactly the same, one must be careful not to ignore the possibility that he intended a very real distinction to be made. This may be demonstrated by his use of *ey* in *feyther* 'father' NS xiii.3 (and elsewhere), which *SED* evidence would again associate with the pronunciation [ɛˑə] (since three of the relevant Lincolnshire localities have this development, though the two nearest to Somersby have [aː]). *SED* evidence would, therefore, suggest that *aä*, *ai*, and *ey* all represent the same centring diphthong and that *neyther* VW xvii.5 and *naither* VW v.4, OR 2, both of which Tennyson uses as well as *neither* SS x.10, are to be pronounced alike. However, *EDG* records examples of both FATHER and NEITHER from north-west Lincolnshire with a diphthongal development which Wright transcribes [ei]. He also records them from the same area with a pronunciation which he transcribes [eə]. In view of this, Tennyson could well have used *ey* to indicate a development which *SED* evidence suggests is no longer current in central Lincolnshire. This could also apply to Tennyson's use of *ai*, as in (*h*)*airm* and *bairn*(*s*), though here *EDG* has no information.

A. J. Ellis[15] states that Tennyson made no distinction between words in which he used an *aw* spelling and those in which he used *oä*, and that he intended *naw* OS viii.1 (and elsewhere) and *noä* 'no' NS iii.4 (and elsewhere) to have the same sound. This is supported by *SED* evidence which records the centring diphthong [ʊə] under NO VIII.8.13 in all the relevant Lincolnshire localities. However, Tennyson also uses the spelling *aw* in most of his words with ME *ou*, as in *blaws* 3 pr.s. 'blows' NS iv.3, *graw* 'grow' NC xv.6, *knaw* 'know' OS xii.1 (and elsewhere), and *snaw* n. 'snow' VW iv.3 (and elsewhere). Here he is not supported by *SED* which, under GROW IX.3.9, KNOW VII.5.2 and SNOW VII.6.13, records a variety of de-

15 Ibid.

velopments of ME *ou*, [ɔɷ], [ɔ˙ə], and [ɔː], none of which is identified with the development of ME *ō₂* in central Lincolnshire that Tennyson spells *oä*. This is confirmed by the pronunciations in *EDG*, where again a distinction is made between these words and those with ME *ō₂*; a distinction which, if we accept the statement of A. J. Ellis, Tennyson did not recognize.

Similar problems are raised by Tennyson's use of *oo*. In one of his rare footnotes on the pronunciation of his forms, Tennyson says of the word *soon* 'sun' NC i.3, that 'the *oo* (is) short, as in "wood"'. This is probably meant to indicate the close back round vowel [ɷ] which *SED* shows to be the usual development of ME *u* in the north and midlands. Unfortunately, Tennyson's use of *oo* often alternates with other spellings. Where they are the spellings of Standard English, they may simply be the result of carelessness. Thus, in the same poems, he uses *soon* NC i.3 beside *sun* NC viii.6/8, and *soom* VW x.4 beside *some* VW viii.6. Usually, however, variant spellings are associated with different poems, where this kind of inconsistency is less unexpected. Hence, 'another' is *anoother* in NC and CWC, but *another* in VW; 'stuck' p.t. is *stook* in NS, but *stuck* in SS; and 'sunday(s)' is *soondays* in CWC, but *sunday* in NC. There are other examples. The problem is further complicated by Tennyson's frequent use of a *u* spelling for those words with ME *u* which have an *o* spelling in the standard language. Thus, not only does he write *mooney* VW xv.1 and *money* VW vii.17, but he also writes *munney* NS iii.3 (and elsewhere). *SED* under (A LOT OF) MONEY VII.8.7 records [ɷ] in all the relevant Lincolnshire localities and it seems probable that Tennyson intended a single pronunciation. An examination of the transcriptions of Tennyson's reading by A. J. Ellis supports this conclusion. *Coom'd* 'came' NS vii.4, *mun* 'must' OS vi.3, NS vii.2, *thruf* 'through' SS iii.4, and *dosn'* 'doesn't' VW iv.6 were all pronounced with the same vowel sound. Tennyson also used the sound in his pronunciation of *fust* 'first' OS xiv.3 and *woorse* 'worse' NS viii.4, which *SED* evidence shows to be unexpected. According to the *SED* entries for CHURCH VIII.5.1, FIRST VII.2.1, THIRTY VII.1.13, WORSE VI.12.3, and WORST VI.12.5, the usual development in Lincolnshire of the ME *ir/ur* here is the short half-open back round vowel [ə], although a short unrounded central vowel, sometimes with *r*-colouring, is recorded from loc. 7 under CHURCH, THIRTY, and WORSE and from loc. 6 under WORST. Tennyson, however, employs a variety of spellings for these words, all of which imply a pronunciation [ɷ]. Hence he writes: *chooch* OS v.1, *choorch* OS iv.3, *chuch* CWC iii.4, CWC iv.5 'church'; *fust* 'first' CWC ii.5 (and elsewhere); *thutty* 'thirty' OS xii.4, VW vii.13; *woorse* NS viii.4, *wuss* SS xiv.1,

OR 66 'worse'; and *woost* OS iv.1, *wust* VW vii.2 'worst'. This could mean that Tennyson was correct and that a pronunciation which *SED* data associates in these words with Leicestershire was current in Lincolnshire in the early nineteenth century or, alternatively, it could mean that Tennyson did not distinguish between the central vowel [ə], which *SED* records from the Somersby area, and the [ɷ] which was the usual development here of ME *u*. The *SED* distribution is supported by *EDG* which lists no form of CHURCH, FIRST, or WORST for Lincolnshire that suggests an identification with [ɷ]. *SED* evidence further suggests that when followed by an orthographic *r* Tennyson's use of the *oo* convention is ambiguous. Entries under DOOR V.1.8, MORE VII.8.13, and WHAT KIND OF (for SORT) VII.8.16 suggest a centring diphthong [ɷə] for Tennyson's spellings *door-* OR 24, *moor* 'more' OS i.3 (and elsewhere), and *soort* 'sort' OS ii.2, OR 12. This is confirmed by A. J. Ellis's transcriptions of Tennyson's reading and contrasts with the short monophthongal development which seems to be intended for his spellings *choorch* 'church' and *woorse* 'worse'.

These are probably the most confusing of the orthographic conventions used by Tennyson in the Lincolnshire poems, and *SED* is certainly of value in any attempt to determine their phonetic meaning. More interestingly, perhaps, the *SED* data can be used to isolate any features of the dialect of the poems which are definitely not associated with Lincolnshire and which may result from Tennyson's settlement in the south of England. Some of the inaccuracies are confined to single poems, which suggests that Tennyson often recognized them as errors and was careful not to repeat them. Not surprisingly, OS, the first of the dialect poems, contains more material that is suspect than the later poems. Examples are the forms *hond* 'hand' OS iii.3, *lond* 'land' OS iii.4 (and elsewhere), *understond* 'understand' OS vi.3, which contrast with the spellings of the later poems: *'and* 'hand' NS vi.1 (and elsewhere), *'ands* 'hands' NC xiii.2 (and elsewhere), and *land* NS vi.2. *SED* records no examples of HAND and LAND with a rounded vowel in Lincolnshire. A study of the entire *SED* data for HAND VI.7.1 shows that this development is confined to the west-Midland area of England. Campion[16] also believes the spellings *hond* and *lond* to be suspect and it is interesting to observe that the analogous spelling *mon*, which appeared in the page-proofs of the first edition at OS xiv.1, was subsequently changed by Tennyson to *man*. Similarly, examples of *thot* 'that' OS iv.2, OS xv.2/3, which are confined to OS, receive no support from the whole

16 Op. cit., p. 1.

of the east-Midland material of *SED*, and again Tennyson uses the more acceptable spelling *that* in the rest of the poems. Incidentally, *EDD* cites THOT from Lincolnshire, but the only occurrence that is quoted is taken from OS. It is quite possible, therefore, that Wright was here following Tennyson into error. This could also explain other unexpected forms which were thought by Wright to be from Lincolnshire. For example, Tennyson includes three examples of SHE (VW ii.4, VW xvi.12, OR 95) used as object pronoun in the Lincolnshire poems, which he uses beside the expected form HER. The east-Midland material of *SED* records this usage only in Suffolk and Essex, and the *SED* evidence considered in its entirety shows that this form is associated with southern England, where Tennyson could have heard it. *EDD* records a wider, though similar, distribution, but includes a single occurrence from Lincolnshire which, again, is taken from Tennyson. It is interesting to compare *EDD*'s distribution of SHE as object pronoun with that of HE as object pronoun. Their distribution is similar, but there is no occurrence recorded from Lincolnshire and, equally, there is no example of HE used as object pronoun in Tennyson's Lincolnshire poems. On another occasion Wright has misinterpreted Tennyson and this has led him to cite the occurrence of a form which does not, in fact, appear. In OS, weakly stressed forms of the subject pronoun HE appear as *a* and, quoting the line: 'Doctors, they knaws nowt, fur a says what's nawways true' (OS ii.1), Wright includes this an an example of A, an 'unemphatic form' of THEY, a feature which he records from Warwickshire and Shropshire together with this single occurrence from Lincolnshire. A reading of the whole poem, however, shows that there has been a shift in subject and the subject of *says* is here a reduced form of HE, a reduction that occurs no less than twenty-five times throughout OS.

A common source of error in Tennyson seems to result from false analogy; the assumption that words which contain similar sounds in one's own dialect will all contain similar sounds in another. Hence Tennyson is right when he writes *divil's* 'devil's' OS xvi.2, NC xiii.6, *iver* 'ever' NC ii.3 (and elsewhere), *ivry* 'every' OS ii.3 (and elsewhere), *git* 'get' NS vii.3 (and elsewhere), *yis* 'yes' VW i.2 (and elsewhere), and *yit* 'yet' VW ix.6 (and elsewhere), but he is less likely to be right when he writes *kittle* 'kettle' OS xvi.1, *midder* SS viii.8, *midders* OR 31 'meadow(s)', *thim's* 'them's' NS xvi.1, *thin* 'then' NS viii.1, and *whiniver* 'whenever' NS xiii.2, SS v.6. In addition to *kittle*, Tennyson also writes *kettle* SS iii.3 and *SED* evidence under KETTLE V.8.7 makes it clear that this is the correct Lincolnshire form. Forms with [ɪ] are especially common in England south of

Norfolk, and again Tennyson could have heard this pronunciation when he was in the south of England. *EDG* supports the *SED* distribution in not recording the pronunciation in Lincolnshire. The spelling *whiniver* is more credible, for *EDG* records this particular development in central Yorkshire. However, even if we trust Tennyson it must have been rare, for he uses the spelling *whiniver* on two occasions only, whereas he uses the spelling *when* thirty-seven times. *SED* evidence on the nature of the stressed vowel in MEADOW is incomplete, since the word only emerges infrequently at PASTURE II.1.3 and LOW-LYING LAND IV.1.7. Of those which do occur, all have [ɛ], except for one locality in Norfolk and two in Suffolk which have [ɪ]. This conclusion is supported by the evidence of *EDG* which records this development from east Suffolk and, in addition, from west Somerset. The spelling *thim's* 'them is' is used only once by Tennyson and in this respect it contrasts with *them* which he uses twelve times. *SED* records single examples with [ɪ] from Essex under THESE IX.10.5 and THOSE OVER THERE IX.10.6, but *EDG* reports this development from Durham and Yorkshire. *Thin* 'then' is another spelling which Tennyson uses only once and again his use of the spelling *then* thirty times suggests that *thin* should be regarded with suspicion. This is made more likely by an example of *thin* in the page-proofs of the first edition of NC which Tennyson has corrected to *then* NC iii.6. *SED* does not collect examples of THEN, but it is interesting to note than *EDD* records this spelling from Northumberland, Lincolnshire, and Suffolk only, and that the sole Lincolnshire occurrence cited is that in Tennyson.

Tennyson's spelling *plow* 'plough' OS xi.2 (and elsewhere) associates the word wrongly, according to the evidence of *SED*, with other words to which he assigns an *ow* spelling, such as *owt* 'aught' VW vii.19 (and elsewhere), *browt* 'brought' NC xii.4 (and elsewhere), *gowd* 'gold' VW vii.17 (and elsewhere) and *wowd* 'Wold' CWC x.5. A comparison of the *SED* material for ANYTHING (for AUGHT) V.8.16, BROUGHT VIII.1.11, and GOLD VII.7.10 with that of PLOUGH I.8.1 in all the relevant Lincolnshire localities shows that all the former have a diphthongal development [ɔʊ] (with the single exception of an [ɔː] at loc. 5), as opposed to the latter which is always [aʊ].

With regard to Tennyson's spelling *darter* VW ii.6 (and elsewhere) and *darters* VW ii.3 (and elsewhere) 'daughter(s)', it may, on the evidence of *SED*, be possible to suggest the influence of southern English. Certainly, the *ar* spelling does not suggest an identification with either [ɔʊ] or [ɔː], the two forms which *SED* records in Lincolnshire under DAUGHTER VIII.1.4. A pronunciation [aᵊː] is, however,

101

frequent in the south and south-west of England and identification of Tennyson's forms with this seems reasonable. *EDD* records only the spellings *dohter* and *doughter* from Lincolnshire, which seems to support the evidence of *SED*.

In notes appended to OS and OR, Tennyson says of the pronunciation of *four* that the '*ou* [is] as in *hour*' OS x.4 and, again, that the '*ou* [is] as in *house*' OR 17. A comparison of the *SED* material for FOUR VII.1.4, HOUSE V.1.1 and HOUR VII.5.7 in the relevant Lincolnshire localities, and also the forms listed in *EDG*, suggests that this is not a legitimate equation.

Tennyson's use of the verb TO BE is especially interesting, for he commonly uses the form *be* (occasionally *beä*) for all persons of the present tense, but especially for the first person singular and the third persons singular and plural. Alternative forms generally occur in different poems and are associated with different speakers. Tennyson may well have done this intentionally in order to heighten the distinctive personalities of his characters by giving them different, though still locally valid, dialects. Thus, the only speaker to use the standard form I AM, is the church-warden in CWC who says, rather grandly: 'An' saw by the Graäce o' the Lord, Mr. Harry, I ham wot I Ham' CWC ix.6. Elsewhere the form is always I BE, although I AM is used once in the reduced form: *I'm blest* NS xi.3.

The standard form of the third person singular IS is confined to the two earliest poems OS and NS and to OR. This is also true of the forms HE'S, IT'S, SHE'S, THAT'S, and YON'S (but not WHAT'S). The only other occurrence of another form in these poems is a strongly stressed example of *beä* in OS (OS xiv.2). In the other four poems the third singular form is always BE.

The third person plural forms in Tennyson are distributed between IS and BE. IS is confined to NS, except for a single occurrence in OR (OR 80). Elsewhere, the form is BE. Interestingly, *is* in OR is attributed to the wife of the speaker of the poem; he himself uses *be* OR 15.

SED evidence, as listed under IX.7.7 I AM etc. and IX.7.9 WE ARE etc., in no way supports Tennyson's use of BE in Lincolnshire, confining all occurrences to an area of the south and the west Midlands roughly to the west of Watling Street. However, Tennyson is supported in some measure by A. J. Ellis,[17] who says of the first present singular: '*I be*, *I am* are used indifferently, but *I am* seems most common.' *EDD* also quotes A. J. Ellis on this but records no further examples. In fact, *EDD*'s distribution roughly agrees with that of

[17] Op. cit., p. 307.

SED, except that it cites a number of examples from East Anglia. In view of the evidence, it seems likely that Tennyson was using genuine forms of the verb TO BE, but that they were far less common than the frequency of his usage would suggest.

Tennyson's use of *beänt* 1 pr. s., 3 pr. s., 3 pr. pl. and *bean't* 3 pr.s. as the regular negative forms of the present tense of TO BE also conflicts with *SED* evidence which again associates this form with the south and the west Midlands. The only alternative form in Tennyson is a single occurrence of *isn't* NS xi.4. A. J. Ellis says that *beänt* 'may be a southernism',[18] although both he and *EDD* cite examples from the north of Lincolnshire. An additional piece of evidence for the possible authenticity of the form is given by Oxley,[19] who states that one of his informants 'recollects an old inhabitant of Saltfleetby (16 miles east-north-east of Somersby), about 1879, who used the form [biənt] as a negative'.

The data collected by *SED* can be used not only to determine what in Tennyson's Lincolnshire poems is suspect, but also to verify that which at first sight appears unusual, but which a comparison with *SED* may show to be peculiar to Lincolnshire. This is obviously of importance with regard to any judgment on the value of the poems as illustrations of the dialect of early nineteenth-century central Lincolnshire.

One development that *SED* shows to be almost exclusively associated with Lincolnshire, is the development of a long central vowel in words that contain ME *or* plus a following consonant. Tennyson illustrates this development in his spellings *burn* 'born' NC iii.6 (and elsewhere), *curn* 'corn' VW xviii.4, *herse* OR 101, *'erse* VW xiii.6, *'erse's* NS i.1 'horse('s)', *murn* 'morn' NC viii.4, *murnin'* 'morning' NC viii.1, SS vi.1, *thurn* 'thorn' NC iii.4 (and elsewhere), *Thurnaby* 'Thornaby' OS vii.4, OS xiii.4, and *turn* 'torn' NC vii.3. The material collected by *SED* shows that this development is still heard in parts of Lincolnshire, where it co-exists with forms that are clearly the result of RP influence. Under HORSES I.6.5 the *r*-coloured form [əʰː] is recorded from locs. 2, 3, 4, 5, and 7. Elsewhere, the development is [ə]. It is significant, in view of Tennyson's associations with central Lincolnshire, that the development with a central vowel is still common in Swaby (loc. 7), four miles north-east of Somersby. In fact, an examination of the incidental material collected during the *SED* investigation of loc. 7, which has not been included in the published material, shows that this development was heard during conversation with the field-worker in many words which are not

[18] Ibid.   [19] Op. cit., p. 77.

SED key-words. Hence, [ʃəˑɪːt] and [ʃəˑɪt] 'short' were both recorded, [məˑɪʔɹ] 'mortar' and [əv kəˑɪːs] 'of course'. A comparison of the *SED* entries under CORN II.5.1 suggests that this particular development is now frequent only in the Swaby area, though even here the form [kəˑɪn] is recorded only as an alternative pronunciation, and under MORNING VII.3.11 no examples were recorded at all. Thus the occurrence in Tennyson of the spelling *born* OS viii.1 beside *burn* 'born' may possibly be intended to point to the existence of two different developments. Incidentally, single examples of [əˑɪː] were recorded under MORNING VII.3.11 in Worcestershire and Oxfordshire. Otherwise, the only comparable development recorded from an area outside Lincolnshire in the words examined here is confined to two of the Cheshire responses under CORN II.5.1.

Lexical forms probably account for most of the material in the poems that is associated specifically with Lincolnshire. *Squad* NC iv.4, OR 72, which Tennyson uses to mean 'mud', is recorded in *SED* under MUD VII.6.17 only in locs. 5, 8, and 9, all of which localities are situated in the Somersby region. The adjective SQUADDY was also heard at loc. 8. *EDD* records the word in Lincolnshire and Leicestershire only, which implies that the word formerly had a slightly wider distribution, though it is now confined to central Lincolnshire. The example of *bublin'* 'nestling' OR 192 is similar. *SED* records examples from eight localities throughout central and southern Lincolnshire, and also two from Nottinghamshire and one from Derbyshire near the Nottinghamshire border. *EDD*, on the other hand, records examples from Lincolnshire only. Tennyson's use of *clat* to refer to a filthy state, as in: 'wa boäth was i' sich a clat' SS vi.11, gives it a meaning that is confined to Lincolnshire, according to *EDD*. Generally, CLAT refers to a clod of earth and with this meaning it has a wide distribution. The only example from *SED* is a single occurrence of CLATTY, meaning 'muddy', from loc. 9 in the incidental material under MUD VII.6.17.

Tennyson uses a large number of words of Scandinavian origin, such as *a-beälin* 'bealing' (i.e. screaming) OR 89, *beck* 'brook' OR 40 (and elsewhere), and *lig* 'lie' SS x.6 (and elsewhere). However, these have a wide distribution in the north of England and are not especially remarkable. *Unheppen* 'clumsy' VW xvi.4, on the other hand, is a word of Scandinavian origin which a comparison of the evidence of *EDD* and that of *SED* shows to have had a wide distribution in the north of England until recently, but which is now almost restricted to Lincolnshire. Under CLUMSY VI.7.14, *SED* records UNHEPPEN in eleven of its fifteen Lincolnshire localities, but only one in the whole of the northern material. Some of the local words that

104

Tennyson used may have been chosen because they would appeal to the imagination of an audience that did not know them. Hence, *glimmer-gowk* VW vii.6, which he uses for 'owl' is shown by *EDD* to be a Lincolnshire term, but is nowhere recorded in the *SED* material under OWL IV.7.6. Similar interests may also have suggested the choice of *buzzard-clock* which Tennyson uses for 'cockchafer'. *SED* has no information on this word, though, according to *EDD*, it is found only in Lincolnshire.

In view of the conditions under which Tennyson's Lincolnshire poems were written, and the difficulties of interpreting some of his spelling conventions, their linguistic value as records of the speech of central Lincolnshire must be limited. However, where Tennyson is supported by the findings of both *SED* and *EDD*, then the poems can reasonably be used as supplementary evidence.

One general problem which could perhaps be helped by evidence from the dialect poems, is that of the recessive distributions of particular dialect forms. There are several instances in the poems of forms which, though recorded in Lincolnshire in *SED*, are clearly less widespread now than Tennyson's use would suggest. This could imply a genuine change in the linguistic situation of central Lincolnshire during the period between Tennyson's poems and *SED*. ANY, for example, is always spelt *ony* NC xx.3 (and elsewhere) by Tennyson, and *SED* evidence taken by itself would not really support this, for in Lincolnshire under ANY VII.3.16 [ɛnɪ] is recorded throughout, except for two occurrences of [ɔnɪ], one at loc. 1 and the other at loc. 5. Forms with a half-open back round vowel also occur in Leicestershire, Derbyshire, Staffordshire, and Northamptonshire, and are very common in the north. The form *ony* which was associated in ME with the north and Midlands, though still common in the north, is clearly being replaced in the Midlands by the RP form. A comparison of *SED* data and Tennyson suggests that the change in Lincolnshire at least is comparatively recent. Similarly, Tennyson's spelling *pratty* NC viii.1/8, NC xix.2 contrasts with his use of the form *pretty* SS iv. 3 (and elsewhere) and receives no support from the *SED* Lincolnshire material under PRETTY VI.5.18. However, *SED* records an occurrence with [a] from Welwick in the extreme south-east of Yorkshire across the Humber from Lincolnshire, which could mean that a form which has now almost vanished from this area was formerly sufficiently widespread for Tennyson to have heard it. His use of both spellings would suggest, in this case, that both pronunciations could be heard in the Somersby region.

There are many occurrences in Tennyson of forms which *SED* material would suggest, on the evidence of its fifteen localities, have disappeared from Lincolnshire. However, a check with the earlier evidence of *EDD* suggests that this is again the result of the time difference between the two. Examples of this are: *atween* 'between' VW vii.8, *fuzz* 'furze' (i.e. gorse) OS x.2, *mow'ds* 'moulds' (i.e. earth) VW xv.5, *mind* (i.e. remember) SS vi.1, *mays* 3 pr. s. 'makes' NS x.3, *maäin* 'main' (i.e. very) NC i.2, NC ii.3, and *ivin* 'ivy' OR 26.

SED evidence under BETWEEN IX.2.11 shows that the form ATWEEN is still widely used, particularly in the north. Elsewhere there are scattered occurrences throughout the country, but TWEEN, which is the regular form in the east-Midland area (including Lincolnshire) and much of the south, could represent either ATWEEN or BETWEEN. In any case, with the statement by *EDD* that ATWEEN is 'in general dialect use in Scotland, Ireland and England', it seems fair to accept Tennyson's usage. Entries under GORSE IV.10.11 in *SED* suggest that FURZE is essentially a southern word with very scattered occurrences in the north and the west Midlands and with no occurrences at all in the northern half of the east-Midland area. However, the entries under BILL-HOOK IV.2.6 suggest a different distribution, for here FUR-BILL, which probably derives its first element from FURZE in the way that the synonymous GORSE-HOOK is derived from GORSE, occurs throughout Nottinghamshire and Lincolnshire. In fact, according to *SED* evidence this word is confined exclusively to these counties, though this is not necessarily accurate since it may elsewhere refer to an implement specifically used for cutting FURZE or GORSE, in which case it would not be needed in *SED* under BILL-HOOK IV.2.6. The conclusion seems to be that FURZE was once recorded throughout Lincolnshire, but since the time of Tennyson it has been replaced by GORSE and has been retained only as the first element of FUR-BILL, in which form, presumably, all association with the word FURZE has been lost.

No examples of MOULDS, meaning 'earth', have been recorded in Lincolnshire under EARTH VIII.5.8, although examples have been recorded from Northamptonshire, Norfolk, Suffolk, and London in the east Midlands, and Herefordshire, Gloucestershire, and Monmouthshire in the west Midlands. In the north, single occurrences have been recorded from Yorkshire and the Isle of Man. *EDD*, however, suggests that the distribution in the north of England was formerly more extensive and Tennyson's use of the word is probably authentic. The example of *mind* (meaning 'remember'), which Tennyson also uses in the inflected forms *minds* CWC vi.3, CWC vii.1 and *minded* NC viii.1/3, is exactly parallel, except that *SED* shows that, although not recorded in Lincolnshire, the word still has a wide distribution. *EDD* indicates a much wider distribution including Lincolnshire and Tennyson's use of it is doubtless genuine. This is also probably true of *mays* a variant of the third present singular inflected form of the verb MAKE. According to the entries in *SED* under MAKES IX.3.6, this form is confined to central Lancashire and the extreme West Riding of Yorkshire in the north, and central Derbyshire and north Staffordshire in the west Midlands. *EDD* records this form throughout the north-west and also in Lincolnshire, Leicestershire and Nottinghamshire in the north of the east-Midland area. Tennyson probably heard the form in Lincolnshire, but the fact that he used it only once, in contrast to *maäke*, which he uses three times as an infinitive and six times as the inflected present tense *maäkes*, suggests that it was uncommon. *Maäin* 'main' used as an intensifier has, according to the evidence of *SED* under VERY VIII.3.2, a very limited distribution and is confined to Wiltshire, Hampshire, and Berkshire. This contrasts rather sharply with the evidence of *EDD* which shows a distribution embracing most of the north country, the east Midlands, and the south and south-west. Similarly, *ivin* 'ivy', which Tennyson uses on two occasions, does not occur in the *SED* entries under IVY IV.10.10, although *EDD* gives it a fairly widespread distribution that includes Lincolnshire.

Finally, the occurrence of a particular form in Tennyson's Lincolnshire poems may suggest an explanation for some of the unexpected forms in *SED*. Under AFRAID VIII.8.2, for example, forms of AFRAID are recorded in the incidental material for locs. 2 and 7 with a diphthongal development [ʋ˙ə], and not the expected [ɛ˙ə] which occurs elsewhere in Lincolnshire. Tennyson does not use AFRAID at all, but he uses *afear'd* VW ix.3, SS vi.5, *afeärd* OR 86 (2x) 'afeared' which *SED* does not record from Lincolnshire. However, *EDD* states that AFEARD is 'in general dialect use throughout Scotland, Ireland and England' and cites an example from Lincolnshire. In the light of this, it seems possible that the [ʋ˙ə] forms recorded by *SED* were influenced by the diphthong of the synonymous AFEARED, an expression which both Tennyson and *EDD* associate with Lincolnshire, but which *SED* suggests is no longer used.

A close study of the circumstances in which the poems were composed and a comparison of the phonetic conventions and dialect material with evidence provided by A. J. Ellis and Wright and by the later *SED*, lead one to the conclusion that the poems, though they contain much that seems to be genuine, cannot really be said to give an entirely reliable impression of the Lincolnshire dialect heard by Tennyson in his youth. His attempts to indicate the quality of particular sounds by use of a diaeresis and by unusual letter combinations were not consistently applied and Tennyson clearly found it difficult to describe some of the sounds that he heard. His failure to provide an adequate key to his phonetic conventions has meant that his intentions are not always clear and this probably accounts for the poems' neglect. However, if treated with caution, they do contain dialect information that is of undoubted value, particularly when used in conjunction with later scholarly surveys. When other sources suggest that Tennyson's use of dialect is reliable, the poems can justifiably be used to corroborate these other sources. Tennyson's distinctions between *greät* and *graät* and *looök* and *look*, for example, agree with distinctions recorded by *SED* and are likely, therefore, to be genuine. In certain circumstances, where evidence from elsewhere suggests that Tennyson is accurate, his poems may also be used to provide information on changes that have since taken place in the distribution of particular forms and on occasion they may even help to explain certain difficulties in *SED*. The Lincolnshire poems are, therefore, of some value as linguistic source material, though it is as literature that they remain chiefly interesting. It is a pity that these poems, which show an aspect of Tennyson not revealed elsewhere, should be largely inaccessible to the general reader because of an unsuccessful attempt by the poet to indicate the precise nature of the sounds of his native dialect.

6 The Scotch-Irish Dialect Boundaries in Ulster

Robert J. Gregg

The experts—and laymen—have long been aware that, linguistically considered, the province of Ulster is divided into three parts: the Ulster Anglo-Irish (UAI), the Scotch-Irish (SI), and the Gaelic-speaking. Professor Heinrich Wagner's *Linguistic Atlas and Survey of Irish Dialects* (1958) has provided us with the location and approximate limits of the scattered fragments of the dwindling Ulster Gaeltacht. As late as 1960, however, the boundaries separating the other two language types had never been fixed with any degree of precision in spite of their strikingly contrasted features.

With this objective of boundary-drawing in mind the present writer undertook a detailed survey of the SI dialects between 1960–63. It was felt than an accurate delimitation of the speech area concerned was a necessary preliminary to any future work in this field, and further, that Ulster, where three language types are in sharp confrontation, was the perfect arena for trying out experimental discovery procedures for boundary mapping. Apart from its intrinsic interest the enterprise was also intended to provide information for the various Irish dialectology surveys as well as the linguistic surveys of Scotland and England and—more remotely—to make some contribution to the understanding of North American English dialect features, especially for certain parts of New England, Pennsylvania, the Ohio Valley, and the Southern Highlands where, according to Dr Hans Kurath and his colleagues, Scotch-Irish settlements as far back as the eighteenth century contributed to local speechways. The same claim could be made for more recent times in Eastern Canada, especially the Ottawa Valley and neighbouring areas where mass migratory movements from Ulster have introduced a strong Scotch-Irish element, markedly in contrast with the surrounding typical Ontario speech patterns. It should be emphasized, however, that as used in North America the term 'Scotch-Irish' has a rather wide frame of reference, including all types of Ulster speech, which stand in sharp contrast with the well-known southern Irish brogue. In this paper, Scotch-Irish (SI) is restricted to the rural Ulster dialects of an

109

archaic broad Scots type, stemming mainly from south-west Scotland. SI is set off against Gaelic and Ulster Anglo-Irish (UAI),[1] the latter being based on north and west Midland English dialects as spoken during the Plantation period in the seventeenth century. Within the SI districts the towns have developed their own version of Standard English which may be called Scotch-Irish Urban (SIU),[2] important because it is also the second language of educated SI dialect speakers and because, when SI forms drop out, they tend to be replaced by SIU equivalents.

Even a casual observer from outside will notice that all the dialects of English spoken in Ulster have features that contribute to what might be called their 'Irishness'. The task of the boundary seeker is to try to recognize these features and then to ignore them, aiming rather to collect the data that will polarize the systematic differences between the dialect groups. Thus no capital can be made of the universal frictionless continuant [ɹ][3] occurring even in word- and syllable-final position, so different from the Scottish trilled or flapped [R] and linking up rather with the [ɹ] of other parts of Ireland and North America —doubtless a common Elizabethan or Jacobean English colonial legacy of the sixteenth and seventeenth centuries; nor of the ubiquitous Ulster 'light' [l] which contrasts rather with the laterals of most English and Scottish dialects in Great Britain, and probably derives— all over Ireland—from the Gaelic substratum; nor of the front-central rounded /ü/ found everywhere in Ulster, whose allophones constitute one phoneme vis-à-vis the two English phonemes /u/ and /ɷ/. Here we have, of course, a parallel with Scottish speech in general, but the monophonemic /ü/ belongs just as much in UAI as in SI, and in standard speech of all types as well as in all the dialects. This central /ü/ also belongs to the Gaelic of Ulster, apart from west Donegal which, like the southern varieties of Irish, has /u/.[4]

[1] G. B. Adams, *An Introduction to the Study of Ulster Dialects* (Proceedings of the Royal Irish Academy, Dublin, 1948), pp. 9–23, gives a description of UAI phonology.

[2] R. J. Gregg, 'Scotch-Irish Urban Speech in Ulster'/*SIUSU*, *Ulster Dialects* (Ulster Folk Museum, Belfast, 1964), pp. 163–91, describes SIU. D. Abercrombie, 'The Way People Speak', *The Listener* (6 September 1951), and T. Hill, 'Institutional Linguistics', *Orbis*, vii, no. 2 (1958), 441–55, discuss the concept of standard language, specifically Standard English.

[3] See pp. 134–5 for explanation of symbols.

[4] Emrys Evans, 'Some East Ulster Features in Inishowen Irish'/*EUFII*, *Studia Celtica*, iv (1969), 81, and 'The Irish Dialect of Urris, Inishowen, Co. Donegal'/*IDU*, *Lochlann*, iv, Supplement to *Norsk Tidsskrift for Sprogvidenskap* (Oslo, 1970), p. 20 and p. 25. Also S. Ó Searcaigh, *Foghraidheacht Ghaedhilge an*

In fact even with the limited data provided by Séamus Ó Searcaigh,[5] and by Nils Holmer's two studies of County Antrim Gaelic[6] coupled with the information gleaned during joint field research the writer made with Dr Emrys Evans in the Fanad peninsula and Inishowen in County Donegal,[7] it becomes quite clear that there is a very close link in general between the Ulster Gaelic phonological material on the one hand and that of all the Ulster dialects of English on the other.[8]

Suprasegmental features such as pitch patterns, and the realizations of juncture would bear out these widespread areal linguistic or substratum manifestations. In the same way syntax is a useless yardstick, as even superficially very distinctive dialectal expressions turn out on closer examination to have an identical underlying syntactic structure, e.g. [ˌtɑːmz ˈöt we ðə ˈdʌg, ˈsnoːkən əböt ðə ˈʃʌxs, ˈlʌkən fəɹ ə ˈbɹɔːk] corresponds word for word—even without any transformational differences at the surface level—to the standard utterance that translates it: 'Tom's out with the dog, poking about the ditches, looking for a badger'. This underlying identity of patterning in all the dialects of English surely explains why so many dialect grammars stop short at the end of the phonology section, and why Wright's *English Dialect Grammar* in particular has 655 pages of phonology as compared to 41 pages devoted to the rest of the grammar. There is, in short, little of interest to be found at the grammatical, specifically morphological and syntactic, level when we are searching for polarized contrasts.

Thus neither the phonological material at the raw phonetic level nor the grammatical structures could be relied on in drawing up a questionnaire which would serve as the basic tool in the whole enquiry and provide suitable data to permit the clear separation of the dialect groups concerned. From various quarters the suggestion came that questions should be asked with the purpose of eliciting contrastive lexical items as had been the case with the Leeds survey and the first and second postal enquiry booklets of the Linguistic Survey of Scotland, but the results obtained from over a period of three months—mainly in Donegal—were disappointing, as the isoglosses failed to bundle and simply confirmed the well-known concept that every word has its own history—and, we could add,

---

Tuaiscirt/FGT (Belfast, 1925), § 31, and N. M. Holmer, *The Irish Language in Rathlin Island, Co. Antrim/ILRI* (Dublin, 1942), pp. 123–4.

[5] Throughout Ó Searcaigh, *FGT*.

[6] N. M. Holmer, *On some Relics of the Irish Dialect Spoken in the Glens of Antrim/IDGA* (Uppsala, 1940), and *ILRI*.

[7] Evans, *EUFII* and *IDU*.   [8] Gregg, *SIUSU*.

geography.[9] What did emerge, however, from these preliminary investigations was that in many cases where a given question did not elicit a variety of unrelated lexical forms but rather variations of what was historically the same form, a clear-cut bundle of isoglosses did show up separating the typically Scottish historical-phonological developments from the equally typical north-west-Midland English forms reflected in the UAI dialects.

Following up this promising clue, it was easy to produce a questionnaire based mainly on items pinpointing these divergent historical-phonological reflexes of older English forms, relying for the most part on contrastive changes in the vowel and diphthong nuclei. The English consonants, as is widely known, exhibit much less systematic regional variation, the main contrastive situation among the Ulster dialects of English being the preservation of ME voiceless velar fricative /x/ versus its loss, i.e. /Ø/, or replacement by /f/ in such forms as *daughter, night, laugh, high*, etc.

To cope with the predictable variability among the SI dialects themselves, it was felt necessary to set up a model with regard to which phonological segments could be judged as to whether or not they were representatives of normal Scottish developments, or their known variants—particularly among the south-west group of Scottish dialects spoken in Ayrshire, Galloway and adjacent areas from which settlement history shows the Scottish planters to have migrated to Ulster from the early seventeenth century onwards. This model was established on the basis of the writer's experience gained with the well-preserved east Antrim SI dialects during a period of over thirty years of investigation and study, with their synchronic and diachronic phonology and their lexicon as the main focus of attention.[10] The model was, of course, subject to revision and amendment throughout the survey and later, when the results were under scrutiny.

The main concern of the project was to trace the spread of specifically Scottish forms, but naturally in what ultimately proved to be the neighbourhood of the dialect border equally specific UAI forms began to appear and thus gradually a contrasting model for UAI was built up whose 'Englishness' was for the most part immediately apparent, although some checking had to be done among the field records at Leeds, supplemented by special private investigations

[9] K. Jaberg, *Sprachgeographie/SG* (Aarau, 1908), and Y. Malkiel, 'Each Word has a History of its Own'/*EWHO*, *Glossa*, i (Burnaby, B. C., 1967).

[10] R. J. Gregg, 'Notes on the Phonology of a Co. Antrim Scotch-Irish Dialect, Part I, Synchronic'/*NPSID 1*, *Orbis*, vii, no. 2 (1958) and ibid., 'Part II, Diachronic'/*NPSID 2*, *Orbis*, viii, no. 2 (1959).

in parts of the English Midlands, to establish firmly the identity of certain English dialectal terms such as [ˈɛːLDəɹ] 'udder', [ˈɛːdəsəz] 'after-grass', [sTRit] 'farmyard',[11] etc., which had penetrated deep into the SI areas, and markedly non-standard phonological forms such as [sTROː] *straw*, [θoː] *thaw*, [joː] *ewe*, which take the place of SI [sTREː], [θəü] and [jəü], once we cross the dialect border. These and other similar forms did point back to the north and west Midlands thus confirming the story told by the Plantation historians, namely that Chester was the main port of embarkation for the English settlers who came not only from Cheshire but the wider hinterland.

It is an interesting fact that SI speakers—knowing that the UAI speech of their neighbours generally approximates much more closely to Standard English than their own Scottish type of dialect does—tend to assume that UAI always uses 'correct' standard forms. For example, when asked about their name for a female sheep they often responded: 'We ca' 'er a *yow* [jəü], but it should be a *yoe* [joː], should it no'?' Likewise, through some original taboo or avoidance of imagined coarseness, a cow's udder is frequently referred to by SI speakers as her *elder* [ˈɛːLDəɹ], the UAI word, rather than her *bag* [baːg], the older, traditional SI term. The UAI dialect term (widely used in Ulster) for 'farmyard', namely *street* [sTRit], has come to replace the original Scottish term everywhere in the SI part of the Laggan district in Donegal, though Antrim SI has preserved the Scottish *cassey* [ˈkaːse] and Down SI mostly *close* [kloːs] in this sense.

The confrontation of SI and Gaelic, of course, presented no problems of separation in general as here we are dealing with one of the major historical linguistic boundaries between varieties of Indo-European speech in Europe, a boundary which has been moving slowly but steadily westward in the British Isles for the last millennium and a half and whose contemporary position the writer was able to confirm with some accuracy as far as the northern Donegal sector was concerned.[12] The only problem that arose occasionally with Gaelic forms was the question whether a given item such as [ˈgɛːlək] 'earwig', [ˈgɹiśəx] 'embers', etc., had been borrowed into SI or UAI *in situ* from Ulster Gaelic or represented an earlier borrowing from Scots Gaelic imported by the seventeenth century settlers. The complete disappearance of east Ulster Gaelic in the last thirty or forty years has made the task of tracing the history of such borrowings much more difficult, although O'Searcaigh's phonetic studies, Holmer's two monographs, Sommerfelt's work, and the

11 Now in use only in the Isle of Man. See *SED*, I, I.1.3.
12 M. W. Heslinga, *The Irish Border as a Cultural Divide* (Leiden, 1962).

113

more recent researches of Dr Emrys Evans on Fanad, Glenvar, and Inishowen Irish[13] have made valuable contributions to the reconstruction of east Ulster Gaelic in general. The SI/Gaelic boundary in Donegal was thus easily determined, and the line established on the basis of the writer's survey is confirmed by Professor Heinrich Wagner's *Linguistic Atlas*[14] as well as by the data worked out on the basis of the 1911 general census figures by G. B. Adams.[15] At one point (Termon, Co. Donegal) a bilingual informant (Mr James O'Donnell, b. 1887) was found, who spoke Gaelic as his mother tongue, and as his second—now habitual—language, the Donegal version of SI. With him the boundaries ran together in one person.

In these ways the nature of the border separating SI from the other types of Ulster speech varies considerably, ranging from a major interlingual boundary with Gaelic in Donegal to a confrontation with a widely divergent type of English, namely UAI, an Irish derivative based on English Midland dialects, now in complementary distribution with SI throughout the province outside the Gaeltacht.

The scope of this SI boundary survey may be judged on the basis of some statistics. With the help of many well-informed local people, 125 informants were finally selected and interviewed: 34 in Donegal, 4 in the north-east corner of Londonderry, 23 in Antrim, and 64 in Down.[16] The density of coverage was purposely varied for a variety of reasons. Co. Antrim—well-known to the writer as his native county —was sampled round the perimeter of the SI heartland, at points about 10 miles apart. Four points in Co. Londonderry were enough to link Antrim with Donegal. The latter county—unexplored territory—was given a more thorough survey. Co. Down was covered with a micromesh, not only for the sake of pinpointing the dialect boundary, but for the theoretical purpose of seeing what extra information would come up, for example, from checking the speech of *every* farmer within the transition zone in the South Ards peninsula, thus closing in the mesh to points one or two miles apart. The

13 Ó Searcaigh, *FGT*; Holmer, *IDGA* and *ILRI*; A. Sommerfelt, 'South Armagh Irish', *Norsk Tidsskrift for Sprogvidenskap*, ii (Oslo, 1929); and Evans, *EUFII* and *IDU*.

14 Heinrich Wagner, *Linguistic Atlas and Survey of Irish Dialects* (Dublin, 1958–).

15 G. B. Adams, 'The Last Language Census in Northern Ireland', *Ulster Dialects* (Belfast, 1964), pp. 111–45; also in personal communications with the writer.

16 R. J. Gregg, 'The Boundaries of the Scotch-Irish Dialects in Ulster' (Ph.D. dissertation, University of Edinburgh, 1963, to be published by the Institute of Irish Studies, Belfast). The majority were in the age group 60–80 years of age. Only three were under 50, and only three over 90. The oldest (97) and the youngest (25) had perfect control of their SI dialects.

experiment was well worth while, for the micromesh certainly revealed linguistic facts and patterns that would otherwise have been missed, e.g. the detailed distribution of SI variant forms for *above*—[əˈbĭn] and [əˈbin], for *dog*—[dʌg] and [dəüg], and for *farm*—[fɛːɹm] and [fɔːɹm], as well as, e.g., the enormous phonetic variability in the forms of *ant*. This Co. Down micromesh investigation is probably one of the closest surveys ever to be carried out, certainly the closest in the British Isles.[17] The materials were collected during a period of over a year and a half, the distance covered within Ulster was about 25,000 miles, and the final form of the questionnaire included 683 items.

To return to the elaboration of the historical-phonological questionnaire previously mentioned as a necessary tool of investigation, the basic assumption was that the sets of vowels which are found nowadays in both SI and UAI represent two distinctive and divergent lines of development of the underlying ME vowel system. Indeed, the very fact that the two main source areas from which settlers came to Ulster in the seventeenth century were located at relatively distant points in the continuum of English dialects on the island of Great Britain means that we find quite sharply contrasted developments in the two vowel systems.

The history of any range of phenomena can be considered diachronically from either the past or the present, the first method being more familiar to us. I feel, however, that as a matter of principle, historical dialectology should be dialect-oriented[18] and should take the contemporary state of the dialect as its starting point, mapping the present on to the past rather than vice versa. The current synchronic state is, after all, what is available for complete investigation: all past states are either more or less imperfectly or incompletely recorded or in some cases even quite unknown. Only for the present situation can we work out a coherent, viable, phonological system that can be thoroughly checked by unrestricted additional enquiries, and it is only on the basis of such systematized materials that we can fully understand the function and development of phonological units, and discover the ordered succession of rules added to and internalized into the grammar throughout the recorded history—where such exists.[19]

[17] In about a quarter of Co. Down 64 informants were interviewed, i.e. the coverage was at the density of over 250 for the whole country. Cf. the density of 6 informants for the whole of Co. Durham under the English survey. Down had an area of 609,439 acres and a population of 267,013 in 1967. In the same year the figures for Durham are 649,431 acres, and 1,547,050 population.

[18] Gregg, *NPSID 2*, 400–1.

[19] R. D. King, *Historical Linguistics and Generative Grammar/HLGG* (Engle-

115

The same considerations naturally apply to the other levels of grammatical analysis as well: to morphology and syntax and, of course, to the lexical and semantic levels. We are in any case always scientifically obligated to seek 'un système où tout se tient', and the only systems completely accessible to us are the current ones, whether we wish objectively to collect so-called empirical data or subjectively to probe grammaticalness by introspective methods. On the basis of such arguments the final questionnaire was worked out, as already noted, on the results of a detailed study in great depth of an east Antrim SI dialect, namely that of the Glenoe district spoken natively as a second language by the writer and as their first language by many of his relatives. Being located geographically close to Larne, one of the ports of entry for incoming Scots throughout the whole settlement period, the Glenoe dialect (G)[20] has incorporated south-western Scottish innovations that came into force during the seventeenth century and perhaps even later. In this way G is more 'up-to-date', i.e. represents a less archaic type of Scots than, say, the SI of Donegal or the Mid Ards. The lists in the questionnaire, then, represent groupings of items to be elicited, items incorporating in the dialectal forms of Standard English words, as well as occasionally in purely dialect words, first the consonantal phoneme /x/, and then in turn all the vocalic phonemes of G and similar SI dialects,[21] which means the dominant forms of Antrim, north-east Londonderry and north-east Down SI dialectal speech. The order is thus:

List 1	/x/	List 8	/ɔ/
2	/ī/	9	/i/
3	/ǣ/	10	/e/
4	/ɛ/	11	/o/
5	/ü/	12	/əi/ and /ae/
6	/ʌ/	13	/əü/
7	/a/	14	(morphology)

wood Cliffs, N.J., 1969), especially Chap. 3, Chap. 4, and Chap. 7, for languages with a written record. The experts on unwritten, aboriginal American, Australian or African languages have to rely on the detailed internal analysis, along with the comparative study of purely synchronic materials in order to establish proto-languages and interlinguistic relationships. A. J. Aitken, 'Lowland Scots c. 1350–1370' (MS, Edinburgh, no date), was able, on the other hand, to reconstruct a workable phonology for Lowland Scots in the second half of the fourteenth century on the basis of written documents.

[20] Gregg, *NPSID 1* and *NPSID 2*. See also Phonemic Systems p. 135 below.

[21] Actually, all except /ae/, which proved to be so marginal and unproductive in providing contrasts with UAI that only a couple of dialect forms with this nucleus were appended to List 12. See Tabulated Summary of Phonological Rules (pp. 136–7) and Final Questionnaire (pp. 137–9).

These phonemes are linked back by phonological rules to earlier English forms which have given rise to a contrasting phonemic system in UAI.

Another reason endorsing the use of G as a model is that, according to Catford's schematic analysis,[22] G is a ten-vowel dialect, compared with which the Mid Ards/Donegal and north Antrim SI have nine-vowel systems, in other words they under-differentiate as compared with the G type, having neutralizations in the phonological space[23] occupied by /i/ and /e/ respectively.

A detailed consideration of the questions—section by section—and an evaluation of the results obtained will now be embarked upon. For purposes of reference the full questionnaire is appended at the end of the paper, preceded by a tabulated summary of the relationships between SI, UAI, and earlier English.[24]

As stated above, the phonological rule by which ME voiceless velar fricative /x/ remained in SI, whereas in UAI the ME /x/ > /∅/ or /f/, proved to be the main general consonantal feature useful in separating the dialects. Consequently the first subgroup of questions in List 1 sought to elicit informants' reflexes for items such as DAUGHTER, EIGHT, ENOUGH, FIGHT, NIGHT, TOUGH, TROUGH, etc., all of which occur in Standard English and therefore have UAI as well as SI reflexes as shown in this tabulation:

[22] J. C. Catford, 'Vowel-systems of Scots Dialects', *Transactions of the Philological Society* (1957). It is interesting that the SI dialects do not match precisely any of the vowel-systems actually described by Catford in phonetic terms. Structurally, of course, G is a 10-vowel system, consisting of Catford's Basic 8 vowels + AY (where $A = /ɔ/$ as in *cot* [kɔːt], distinct from *coat* [koːt] and *cat* [kɑːt], and $Y = /ɪ/$ as in *boot* [bɪt] distinct from *bit* [bæt]). Still, G differs from Catford's example of AY (north Kirkcudbright), but is very close to his A (Lanarkshire) which—with the *boot/bit* (/ɪ/ versus /æ/) distinction added—would be structurally identical and phonetically very similar to G. The north Antrim/Londonderry sub-dialects have one type of 9-vowel system while the Mid Ards/west Strangford and Donegal subdialects have another. There is a neutralization in the first group of /ɪ/ and /i/ as in *boot* [bit], *beet* [bit], and in the second group of /i/ and /e/, as in *boot* [beːt], *beat* or *bait* [beːt]. The link between G and Catford's Lanarkshire type is historically valid, for his map (p. 110) shows this 9-vowel system as covering Renfrew and most of north and central Ayrshire—well-known sources of the Scots settlers who came to Ulster in the seventeenth century. The expansion of G, etc. to a 10-vowel system and the various neutralizations elsewhere may represent archaic developments within the Scots dialects themselves or may be the result of substratum or other local innovations that took place within Ulster.

[23] W. G. Moulton, 'Dialect Geography and the Concept of Phonological Space', *Word*, xviii (1962), 23–32, and King, *HLGG*, pp. 191–202.

[24] See pp. 136–9.

SI		UAI
[ˈdɔːxTəɹ]	*versus*	[ˈdɒTəɹ]
[ɛːxt]	*versus*	[eːt]
[əˈńʌx], [əˈnʌx]	*versus*	[əˈnöf]
[fɛːxt]	*versus*	[fəit]
[næxt]	*versus*	[nəit]
[tśʌx], [t́ʌx], [tʌx]	*versus*	[töf]

It should be noted that the SI forms frequently exhibit a special vocalism: [ɛː] in EIGHT and FIGHT; [æ] in NIGHT; [jʌ] < ME *ọ* + velar, in ENOUGH and TOUGH where the yod either combines with the preceding alveolar to produce palatalization or affrication, or becomes zero.

The second subgroup of List 1 elicited purely dialectal words with /x/ which have no obvious current equivalent in Standard English, some being of ON or Gaelic origin. It is interesting to note that many of these—even when of Scottish provenance—have spread to the UAI dialects and are in fact found all over Ulster and undoubtedly beyond (hence being useless as boundary markers), e.g. [DRix] 'dreary', etc., [ˈgɹiśəx] 'embers', [ˈlɑːxTəɹ] 'brood of chickens', etc., [skɹeːx] 'shout', [śʌx] 'ditch', [ˈspɹɑːxəl] 'sprawl', etc. A few of these have even crept into the standard speech of many educated Ulster folk who are quite familiar with such forms as [śʌx], [skɹeːx], [ˈspɹɑːxəl] and who—strangely enough—tend in many cases (even in the city of Belfast) to use /x/ rather than /f/ in the word TROUGH. Incidentally UAI speakers have generally no difficulty in producing the voiceless velar fricative as it is of fairly frequent occurrence in Ulster place-names and family names: *Doagh* [dɔːx], *Donaghadee* [ˌdönəxəˈdiː], *Aghalee* [ˌaxəˈliː], *Ahoghill* [əˈhɒxəl], *Dogherty* [ˈdɒxəɹte], *Gallagher* [ˈgaləxəɹ].

At the phonetic level an important regional variation was noticed in parts of Co. Donegal where /x/ was represented by /h/ (or even /ɦ/) thus DAUGHTER [ˈdəhTəɹ], HIGH [hih], LAUGH [lah], TOUGH [töh], as well as [ˈlahTəɹ] 'brood of chickens', etc., [ləh] 'lough', [śöh] 'ditch', etc. This phenomenon is of interest to substratum theorists as the same phonological shift—[x] > [h] > [ɦ]—occurs in some types of Donegal Gaelic.[25] Further, from the point of view of general phonetics, the shift [x] > [h] > [ɦ] helps to reinforce the theory of phonetic change by a series of simple steps.[26] A final step in this case would be [ɦ] > [Ø].

List 2 of the questionnaire plunged straight into the investigation

25 Evans, *EUFII*, 86–7, and *IDU*, 57–8.
26 King, *HLGG*, pp. 105–19.

of the vowel systems with an inventory of items that elicited the various reflexes of ME $\bar{\varrho}$, which seems to have been represented by $\bar{u}$ in Early Scots (ES) and Middle Scots (MS), the direct ancestor of the SI dialects. Mid Antrim, the heartland of the SI dialects, usually proved to have a lowered front-central, unrounded vowel here, viz. /ï/, phonetically close to the vowel in Standard Southern British (SSB) *bit* [bɪt], but somewhat retracted. In fact, a vowel of this type corresponds to SSB /ɪ/ in the Standard English (SIU. See p. 110 above) spoken in the urban areas within the SI dialect zones, e.g. *bit* [bïd], etc. This vowel is phonetically close to Russian ы as in сын [sïn] but is generally a shade more open. It has also parallels in Gaelic.[27] Other SI reflexes were /i/ and /e/. UAI generally had /ü/ and /ö/ in these words, /ü/ corresponding to both SSB /u/ and /ɔ/, and /ö/—a short centralized type of [o]—being the equivalent of SSB /ʌ/ thus:

	SI (1)	SI (2)	SI (3)	UAI
ABOVE	[əˈbïn]	[əˈbeːn]	[əˈbin]	[əˈböv]
DONE	[dïn]	[deːn]	[din]	[dön]
GOOD	[gïd]	[geːd]	[gid]	[güd]
SCHOOL	[skïl]	[skeːl]	[skil]	[skül]
SHOES	[śïn]	[śeːn]	[śin]	[śüːz]

The forms with /ï/—SI (1)—are characteristic not only of mid Antrim as stated, but also the North Ards and a number of other points in Co. Down. A similar reflex occurs in present-day Ayrshire and other parts of south-west Scotland. The /e/-forms—SI (2)—belong to north Antrim and three points in north-east Londonderry. On the other hand reflexes with /i/—SI (3)—were found among all SI speakers in Co. Donegal, in the Mid Ards peninsula and at many points in the area west of Strangford Lough in Co. Down. Contrary to appearances this feature does not link up SI with north-east Scots as described, for example, by Eugen Dieth in *A Grammar of the Buchan Dialect* (1932). There also, ME $\bar{\varrho}$ or MS $\bar{u}$ > /i/ in general, but Buchan has a special development after velars so that GOOD is [gwid], SCHOOL is [skwil] with a /w/-glide never found in SI.[28] In any case the settlement history clearly points to south-west Scotland as the source of the overwhelming majority of Scottish settlers in seventeenth-century Ulster, and the Linguistic Survey of Scotland investigators subsequently found these reflexes with /i/ (including GOOD /gid/, SCHOOL /skil/ without the /w/-glide) in rather remote

[27] Evans, *EUFII*, 82, and *IDU*, 16, etc.
[28] E. Dieth, *A Grammar of the Buchan Dialect* (Zürich, 1932), pp. 8–9.

relic areas—Wanlockhead and Leadhills—on the borders of Dumfries and Lanarkshire, thus substantiating the theory that these /i/-forms were once current in the south-west of Scotland and represent an archaism in SI. The present distribution bears out this theory if we assume that /ĭ/ is an innovation spreading from the usual ports of entry in Antrim and Down for the incoming Scots, from the early seventeenth century onwards, completely replacing the /i/-forms in Co. Antrim and the North Ards but leaving the /i/-forms unchanged in the Mid Ards and frequently west of Strangford Lough where the influx of new immigrants may have fallen off soon after the first settlement period. For the same reason /i/-forms survive unaltered in the Laggan district of Donegal where the settlement of 1610 did not subsequently receive any notable reinforcement from Scotland. It should be observed that the change postulated here from /i/ to /ĭ/ was not a regular, internal, phonological change in the SI areas concerned, but rather the result of the spread of a set of new forms incorporating an innovation that may actually have had its origins somewhere in eastern Scotland, and the simple substitution of the new /ĭ/ for the older /i/ in a restricted subset of words—not a random subset, however, but the subset that had ME ọ̄/MS ū̃. In other words the earlier south-western Scots dialects and their seventeenth-century Ulster offshoots had a neutralization in the phonological space occupied by the /i/-reflexes of ME ọ̄/MS ū̃ as well as by the /i/-reflexes from other sources, but this neutralization was later reversed by the adoption of the /ĭ/-forms introduced from another—perhaps more prestigious—Scots dialect. A restricted area in north Antrim and northeast Londonderry has developed a new neutralization by which /ĭ/ > /e/, thus: DONE [deːn] and SCHOOL [skeːl] become homophonous with *Dane* and *scale*. In areas with /ĭ/, an [eː] allophone has developed in open syllables and before /v/ and /r/ (the latter being a frictionless continuant), thus DO [deː], SHOE [śeː], MOVE [meːv], FLOOR [fleːɹ]. The vowel before /r/ in some areas is retracted, e.g. [flëːɹ] FLOOR.

Some specifically dialectal words with the same vowel nuclei as those described appear in List 2, e.g. [lĭf] 'palm of hand'— from ON *lōfi*—[ˈfjʌge] or [ˈfÍʌge] 'left-handed', [śʌx] 'ditch', the latter two exhibiting the change to [jʌ] mentioned above (p. 118).

A morphological feature of interest occurs in the alternate developments for the plural of SHOE [śeː] which with different speakers was [śeːz] or [śĭn]. The long vowel in [śeːz] marks the morpheme boundary which is lost in [śĭn] with the older /-n/ plural allomorph. The solid morpheme SOON also cropped up as [śĭn] as well as [sĭn]. The shortening of a vowel with an underlying length feature occurred also in the general SI dialectal plural for EYE [iː], namely [in].

List 3 covered items of diverse origins which characteristically exhibit a short, half open (or lower), somewhat retracted vowel /ǽ/ or /ĕ/, the SI dialect speakers' usual equivalent for the vowel in SSB *bit* [bɪt] (SI [bæt] or [bĕt]). The SSB forms show a variety of developments in these words, e.g. the /aɪ/ diphthong in BLIND, CLIMB, etc.; /ɷ/ in BULL; /ʌ/ in DOZEN, NUT, SON, SUMMER, SUN, ASUNDER, etc.; /ɪ/ in BRIDGE, BUILD, etc.; and /ɛ/ in CHEST, RED, TREMBLE, etc.

The SI dialects as a group tended to have the vowel /ǽ/ (or /ĕ/, especially in Donegal)—in all the items in this list, with occasional special consonantal reflexes, thus: [blæn], [klæm]; [bæl]; ['dæzən], [næt], [sæn], ['sæməɹ], [sæn], ['sæNəRe]; [bɹæg], [bæg]; [kæst], [ɹæd], ['TRæml̩].

The UAI dialects had reflexes closer to SSB: [bləin(d)], [kləim]; [bül] or [böl]; ['dözən], [nöt], [sön], ['söməɹ], [sön], [ə'söNDəɹ]; [bɹüdź], [bïld]; [tśɛst], [ɹɛːd], ['TRɛmbl̩]. The /g/ in SI [bræg], and the /k/ in [kæst] represent typical Scottish consonantism over against the English affricates, as does the /Ø/ *versus* /b/ or /d/ in the contrasting forms of TREMBLE, BLIND, and ASUNDER. Interdental [T], [D], [N], [L], and the flapped [R] associated with them are a non-contrastive, universal, feature of the Ulster dialects and undoubtedly derive phonetically from the Gaelic substratum. They are allophonically distributed variants of /t/, /d/, /n/, /l/, and /r/ respectively, although their use may be an oristic signal, marking the absence of a morpheme boundary, for example: BOULDER ['boːLDəɹ]—a solid morpheme—versus BOLDER ['boːldəɹ] from BOLD+the comparative morpheme [-əɹ].[29]

List 4 brings together forms that generally have [ɛ] in SI over against UAI /a/ or /e/, as well as occasionally /ĭ/, /i/, or /əi/, e.g.

AFTER ['ɛːfTəɹ], APPLE ['ɛːpl̩], BLADE [blɛːd], FATHER ['fɛːðəɹ], FLAT [flɛːt], GRASS [gɹɛːs], HALTER ['hɛːLTəɹ], HAMMER ['hɛːməɹ], HASP [hɛːsp], LADDER ['lɛːðəɹ], MASTER ['mɛːsTəɹ], SACK [sɛːk], SATURDAY ['sɛːTəɹde], SHAFT [śɛːft], TRAVEL ['TRɛːvl̩], ARM [ɛːɹm], CART [kɛːɹt], MARRIED TO ['mɛːɹet ˌəːn], NARROW ['nɛːɹə], BRANCH [bɹɛːnś], HAUNCH [hɛːnś], DINNER ['dɛːNəɹ], KINDLING ['kɛːnələn], EITHER ['ɛːðəɹ].

For these words the UAI dialects had mostly /aː/: ['afTəɹ], ['apl̩], ['faːðəɹ], [flat], [gɹas], ['haməɹ], [hasp], ['laːdəɹ], ['masTəɹ], [sak], ['saTəɹde], [śaft], ['TRaːvl̩], [aːɹm], [kaːɹt], ['maːɹed ˌtüː], ['naːɹə],

29 Gregg, *NPSID 1*, 405.

[bɹanś], but various other vowels in the other items: [bleːd], [ˈhɒLTəɹ], [hɒnś], [ˈdïNəɹ], [ˈkïnələn], [ˈiːðəɹ], or [ˈəiðəɹ]. Among the consonantal differences we note that SI has /ð/ instead of /d/ in LADDER, and BLADDER. The allophonic interdentals cropped up in both dialect groups in AFTER, GANDER, HALTER, MANNER, MASTER, MATTER PLASTER, SATURDAY, TRAVEL, PARTRIDGE, DINNER. SI has /v/ in MARBLES [ˈmɛːɹvəlz]–UAI [ˈmɑːɹlez] (i.e. the game of marbles). The SI form of STANCHION is either [ˈstɛːnśəl] or [ˈstɛːnśəɹ]. Note also that this SSB cluster [-ntʃ] is represented by [-nś] in both Ulster dialect groups, just as [-ndʒ] is represented by [-nź].

As already seen, the diphthongization process that produced SSB /aɪ/ (mainly from ME ī) did not always affect the same items in SI as in UAI or the standard language. Hence forms like BRIGHT, FIGHT, HEIGHT, etc., did not have a diphthong in SI but did have /əi/ in UAI. SI, of course, has its own system of diphthongs of the /əi/ and /ɑe/ type from ME ī and other sources and with characteristic phonemic and subphonemic groupings.[30]

On the other hand, ME ū has not been diphthongized at all in SI any more than in the Scots dialects generally, and an SI pure vowel is thus in contrast with the diphthong /əü/[31] appearing in all the UAI dialects (the UAI equivalent of SSB /aɒ/) in many words such as the major subset of List 5. The ME ū has of course been changed in SI, having been fronted and in certain contexts allophonically shortened and opened as also in south-western Scots generally, thus:

ALLOW [əˈlü]	BROWN [bɹön]	DOUBT [döt]
ABOUT [əˈböt]	HOUSE [hös]	MOUTH [möθ]
DROUGHT [DRöθ]	RUST [ɹöst]	SUCK [sök]
ROUND [ɹön]	THOUSAND [ˈθüːzən]	POWDER [ˈpöðəɹ]
COW [küː]		THUMB [θöm]

The more open allophone [ö] occurred in closed monosyllables except before voiced fricatives, as well as in dissyllables except before /z/. Directly before /r/ there was a long lowered allophone, a somewhat centred [öː], as in OUR [öːɹ], but dissyllabic words such as FLOUR or FLOWER, POWER, SHOWER, SOUR with [-əɹ] as the final syllable had [üː] thus: [ˈflüːəɹ], [ˈpüːəɹ], [ˈśüːəɹ], [ˈsüːəɹ]. HOUR [ˈüːəɹ] was therefore in contrast with OUR [öːɹ]. Further, when OUR

---

30 Gregg, ibid., 400, 404–5; also *NPSID 2*, 416–18, and *SIUSU*, pp. 173–4.

31 A diphthong of this Ulster type—/əü/—is characteristic of the Ottawa Valley dialect. It has no allophonic variants and is in sharp contrast with the usual Canadian diphthong /aw/ with its allophones [aɒ], and either [əu] or [ʌu], occurring in other parts of Ontario as well as the rest of the country, e.g. *out loud*: Ottawa Valley [ˌəüt ˈləüd]; other Canadian [ˌəut ˈlaɒd] or [ˌʌut ˈlaɒd].

occurred with weak stress it was reduced to [wəɹ]. The word COW [küː] often had the old umlaut plural [kɑe] in SI, especially in a collective sense, referring to a farmer's whole herd. The regularly-formed plural with [-z], i.e. [küːz], often cropped up as a second form when a specific number of cows was mentioned: TWO COWS [ˌtwɔː ˈküːz].

PLOUGH had various SI forms: [pĺüː], [plüː], [pjüː], with palatalized [ĺ], ordinary 'light' [l], or a simple yod with the lateral element deleted. These forms lacked the expected final /x/. UAI of course had only [pləü].

HOUSE [hös] usually formed the plural [ˈhösəz], but in north Antrim [ˈhözəz] and occasionally [ˈhüːzəz]. UAI had [ˈhəüzəz]. Not all the items in List 5 had a diphthong—[əü]—in UAI. Some had contrastive SI consonantal developments as compared with UAI, e.g. BLUE [bĺüː] or [bjüː], LUKE (WARM) [lüː], FULL [füː], PULL [püː], COULTER [ˈkötəɹ], SHOULDER [ˈśöðəɹ] were SI forms contrasting with UAI [blüː], [ˈlökˌwɑːɹm], [föl] or [fül], [pöl] or [pül], [ˈkoːLtəɹ], [ˈśəüLdəɹ] or [ˈśoːLdəɹ]. DROUGHT had a special SI consonantal development, giving [dRöθ] versus UAI [dRəüt].[32] Some items with a French background such as *foison(less)* [ˈföźən(ləs)][33] 'tasteless' and *foutre* [ˈfötəɹ] 'clumsy person' had /ü/ in SI, but as often happens with dialect words that have no etymological equivalent in the standard language, the latter word, [ˈfötəɹ], proved to have widespread if not completely universal currency throughout the whole province. Some few items in this list had suffered earlier vowel shortening in the English dialects (though not in Scots) and appeared therefore with /ö/ in UAI, e.g. the SI forms PLUM [plöm], SUCK [sök], THUMB [θöm] contrasted with UAI [plöm], [sök], [θöm].

List 6 consists of words of various origins that had /ʌ/ in SI versus mainly /ĭ/ in UAI, the SI /ʌ/ occurring in many cases in the sequence /wʌ/ or /ʍʌ/:

QUILT [kwʌlt]	SWITCH [swʌtś]	WHIP [ʍʌp]
WHISKEY [ˈʍʌske]	WILL [wʌl]	WIND [wʌn]
WINTER [ˈwʌntəɹ]	WITCH [wʌtś]	WRIST [ɹʌst]

(though the latter word has now lost its *w*!) All these had UAI [ĭ]. Some forms with SI /ʌ/ such as FOUND [fʌn], GROUND [gɹʌn], MOUNTAIN [ˈmʌnʔn̩], POUND [pʌn] (especially in the monetary sense) had [əü] in UAI. STEADY and STITHY both appeared as [ˈstʌde] in

---

[32] For *drought*, Northern American speech often has /drawθ/ (U.S. [dɹaɒθ]; Canadian [dɹəuθ] or [dɹʌuθ]) which would suggest a blend of these Ulster forms or of their originals in the Scots and Midland English dialects.

[33] Also [ˈfʌźən(ləs)], e.g. in G.

SI. CINDERS gave SI ['ˈśANǝɪz] *versus* UAI ['ˈsïNDǝɪz]. The SI ['ˈmʌne] for MANY was in contrast with UAI ['ˈmɛne] or ['ˈmane].

List 7 elicited SI forms with the vowel /ɑ/ which had developed historically from various sources. The first subset consists of words in which SI /ɑ/ represented earlier short *o* and which had reflexes with [ɒ] in UAI. In CROP [kɹɑːp], DROP [DRɑːp], HOB [hɑːb], JOB [dźɑːb], LOFT [lɑːft], OFF [ɑːf], TOM [tɑːm], BOTTLE (of hay, etc.) ['ˈbɑːtl̩], FOND [fɑːnd], MUST [mɑːn], PORRIDGE ['ˈpɑːɹɪtś] we see that the triggering environment of the phonological change ME *o* > SI /ɑ/ seems to be a following, or occasionally a preceding, labial (the dialectal equivalent of the auxiliary MUST represents the altered form of *mon). In all these cases UAI had /ɒ/, but for MUST had [möst].

A second subset shows the result of another conditional phono-logical change in SI, viz. ME *o* > SI /ɑ/ followed by the velar nasal, as in LONG [lɑːŋ], SONG [sɑːŋ], THRONG (crowded) [θRɑːŋ], etc. THONG usually gave SI [ʍɑːŋ] and STRONG always gave [sTRɔːŋ] with [ɔː] instead of [ɑː]. UAI has [ɒ] in all of these.

A third subset illustrates the historical-phonological rule that ME *e* > SI /ɑ/ in the environment of a preceding /w/ or /ʍ/, as in SWELL [swɑːl], TWELVE [twɑːl], WEATHER ['ˈwɑːðǝɹ], WEB [wɑːb], WEDDING ['ˈwɑːdn̩], WELL n. [wɑːl], WET adj. [wɑːt], WHELM 'overturn' ['ˈʍɑːm]],[34] WREN [ɹɑːn], WRESTLE ['ˈɹɑːs]].[35] Note the loss of /v/ in TWELVE and the influence of the now silent *w* in the WR- clusters, i.e. *wre* > /wrɑ/ > /rɑ/, with *e* > /ɑ/ before the /w/ was deleted. WELL adv. is [wil] and WET vb. is [wit] in SI. A frequent form of QUIT was [kwɛt] and from this an underlying form [kwɑːt] had developed by the application of the rule just described. The usual SI version of WADE was [wɑːd] versus UAI [weːd], and the SI dialectal *wale* 'select' had three forms [wɛːl], [wɑːl], and [weːl], which reflect divergent de-velopments of an older alternation between an underlying short or long vowel. The second version shows the same development as the other words with [wɑː].

The words in List 8 were intended to focus on forms with /ɔ/ in SI dialects, although some of them turned out to have /ɑ/ with or without a labialized off-glide (thus: [ɑw]) in many of the items elicited.

The first subset includes words which had ME *al* for which SI had reflexes with [ɔː], [ɑw], [ɑː] or [aː]. The *l* has been deleted, thus for

---

[34] Note the metathesis here: /lm/ > /ml/, which means that /l/ becomes syllabic.

[35] The popular form of this word both in Canada and the U.S. is ['ˈɹæsl̩], often actually spelled *rassle* in newspaper sports reports.

Antrim and Down SI, ALL, FALL, WALL gave [ɔː], [fɔː], [wɔː]; [ɑʷ], [fɑʷ], [wɑʷ]; or [ɑː], [fɑː], [wɑː], whereas the generally more archaic Donegal forms were [aː], [faː], [waː]. However, even the dialects that had developed [ɔː] had [ɑː] in items where ME *al* was followed by another consonant, hence: BEHOLDEN [beˈhɑːdn̩], *dwalm* 'sick turn' [dwɑːm], SALT [sɑːt], SCALD (in the sense 'tea') [skɑːd]. In a further subset ME *a* was followed by *w* or preceded by *w* or *wh*, a combination that produced all the above reflexes in the various SI areas, e.g. BLOW [blɔː], [blɑʷ], [blɑː], CROW n./vb. [kɹɔː], etc., ROW (a series) [ɹɔː], etc., SOW vb. [sɔː], etc., as well as TWO [twɔː], etc., WHO [ʍɔː], etc. The words AWAY [əˈwɔː], etc., and WHERE [ʍɔːɹ], etc., fitted in here, pointing back to older *w(h)a*–sequences. Donegal SI had /a/ in all these forms as well as items like DRAW [DRaː], etc. HAW [haː], HAWK [haːk],[36] JACKDAW [ˌdʑɛkˈdaː], JAW [dʑaː], etc. The words BORROW [ˈbɔːɹə] and TASSLE [ˈtɔːsl] frequently turned up with /ɔ/[37] in SI.

The UAI dialects have preserved the lateral in the first and second subsets: ALL [Dːl], etc., SCALD [skɒld], etc. With *l*+voiceless consonant, [ɔ] occurred, as in SALT [sɔlt]. The *l* has been deleted in UAI WALK [wɒːk], TALK [tɒːk]. In Donegal it was discovered that this set of words (with original *-lk*): STALK [staːk], TALK [taːk], and BALK ('beam') [baːk], were in phonemic contrast with original *l*-less forms such as STACK [staːḱ], TACK [taːḱ], and BACK [baːḱ], having plain /k/ *versus* the palatalized /ḱ/.

List 9 produced SI forms with /i/ in contrast with a wide variety of vowels in the UAI reflexes. SI had [i(ː)] in BRIAR [ˈbriːəɹ], DIE [diː], EYE [iː], FLY n./vb. [fliː], HIGH [hix], LIE n./vb. [liː] over against the UAI diphthong /əi/ in [ˈbɹəiəɹ], [dəi], [əi], [fləi], [həi], [ləi]; although in Donegal SI [diː] means 'do' and DIE is pronounced [dəi], apparently a borrowing from UAI to avoid homophonic clash. It was noted that in EYES—[in]—the SI dialects had the archaic plural marker /-n/ along with the short allophone [i], and yet in DIED [diːd] the normal past tense/past participle marker /-d/ does not produce this shortening. DIED [diːd] is thus in minimal contrast with DEAD [did] which is a solid morpheme, and therefore has the normal short allophone which occurs in all closed syllables except those with a a final voiced fricative or [ɹ]. The contrast was with UAI /ɛ/ in another subset where SI has BREAST [bɹist], DEVIL [dil], FRIEND [fɹin], MEADOW [ˈmidə], THREAD [θRid], WET vb. [wit], BREAD [bɹid],

---

[36] In Donegal SI *hawk* [haːk] is in minimal contrast with *hack* [haːḱ]. See next paragraph.

[37] In *tassle* [ˈtɔːsl] the /ɔ/ may reflect the influence of the vowel in *toss*.

DEAD [did], DEAF [dif],[38] DEAFEN [diːv], HEAD [hid], LEAD n. [lid], MARE [miːɹ], PEAR [piːɹ], WELL adv. [wil], etc.

In a few instances SI had the reflex [i(ː)] developed through lengthening from an earlier short *i* which is represented by [ɪ̈] in UAI, e.g. DRIP [DRip], KING [kiŋ], LIVE [liːv], SWIM [swim], WIDOW [ˈwidə].

That the older, underlying form of this SI vowel is always long, and that the clipped allophone is a relatively recent innovation, is borne out by the preservation at a few points in the most conservative part of the SI area (viz. the Mid Ards) of forms like [kiːk] (peep) and [ˈkɹiːpe] (three-legged stool) with [iː], in contrast with the forms [kik] and [ˈkɹipe] in which the shortening rule applies, and which were found everywhere else, even in other similar items in the dialect of the same Mid Ards speakers who had [kiːk], etc. The sporadic survival of this archaic [iː] has, of course, also been attested by the Linguistic Survey of Scotland. It is noteworthy that semantically the words concerned tend to have a strong affective connotation.

List 10 brings together words that have /e/ in SI in contrast with UAI /o/, /ɒ/, /ɛ/, depending on their origin and development. The first subset show contrastive reflexes of OE *ā*, SI having /e/ in BONE [beːn] CLOTHES [kleːz], FROM [fɹeː], or [feː] (with deletion of [ɹ]), HOME [heːm], MOST [meːst], NO adj. [neː], STONE [steːn], STRAW [stREː] as against UAI /o/ and /ɒ/ in [boːn], [kloːz], [fɹɒːm], [hoːm], [moːst], [noː], [stoːn], [stRɒː]. A morphophonemic shortening rule for SI by which [eː] > [ɪ], marks the morpheme boundary in the compound form NOTHING [ˈnɪθən] *versus* UAI [ˈnɒθən]. The close vowel /e/ does not occur before /r/ in SI; hence MORE [mɛːɹ] and SORE [sɛːɹ] have [ɛː] in contrast with UAI [oː] in [moːɹ], [soːɹ]. The numeral ONE has a special development: UAI [wɑːn] *versus* SI [jæn] instead of the expected [eːn]. The latter reflex does, however, occasionally crop up in Donegal, and in all SI districts in ALONE [əˈleːn]. The [eː] also appears in OWN adj. [eːn]. Another small subset contrasts SI [eː] with UAI [ɛ] in SEVEN [ˈseːvən], ELEVEN [əˈleːvən] *versus* UAI [ˈsɛvən], [əˈlɛvən]. A third, larger, subset of words in this list with orthographic *ea* proved unhelpful in separating the dialects, as UAI tended to have the archaic [eː] in the same items as SI and perhaps in an even wider range, many of these occurring in the popular speech of Belfast. Thus: BEAK [beːk] (in the vulgar phrase [ˈʃʌt jəɹ ˈbeːk] 'Shut up!'), BEAST [beːst], CREATURE [ˈkɹeːtər], EASTER [ˈeːstəɹ], NEAT [neːt], TEA [teː] tend to crop up in all Ulster dialects

---

[38] The form /dif/ crops up sporadically in the U.S. and Canada for *deaf*, even in educated speech.

whether of English or Scottish background, although a special detailed study might reveal that, apart from the group used in common, each dialect type has a special group of its own items not shared by the other type.[39]

A few special lexical items characteristic of SI proved to be useless as boundary markers. For example [heːn] 'use sparingly', [weːnz] 'children'—although UAI has often preserved the older simple plural form [ˈtšĭLDəɹ]—have for the most part spread beyond SI areas.

Because of the development of OE $\bar{a}$ > SI /e/ instead of > /o/ as in UAI, the phoneme /o/ has a relatively low frequency in SI. List 11 brought together some items with SI /o/ from various sources, which contrasted with /ɒ/ or /ə/ in UAI. Some special SI lexical items were also included, such as [ˈgoːpən] 'a double handful', [hoːk] 'poke; search blindly', [ˈloːnən] 'lane', [snoːk] 'poke with snout', [θoːl] 'bear; stand; put up with', [skoːb] 'scrape off with the teeth and eat thin shreds of'—an apple, turnip, etc. These, however, tended not to be limited geographically to the Scottish-settled areas. Before [ɹ] SI had [oː] in CORD [koːɹd], CORN [koːɹn], MORNING [ˈmoːɹnən], SHORT [šoːɹt], SORT [soːɹt], where UAI had [ɔː];[40] and also in the words NOT [noː] (emphatic) and ROCK which was frequently [ɹoːk] *versus* UAI [nɒt] and [ɹɒk]. The word DOG had at least three variant forms in SI, viz. [doːg], [dʌg], and [dəüg], over against UAI [dɒːg].

List 12 was intended to throw light on the complex situation that has arisen in the Ulster dialects with regard to the occurrence and distribution of diphthongs of the [əi], [aι], or [ɑe] type from various ME sources.

[39] J. Wilson, *Lowland Scotch* (London, 1915), has drawn up such a list (p. 39) of items with /e/ for the Strathearne dialect of Perthshire which he later contrasts with the list for the central Ayrshire dialect in his book *The Dialect of Robert Burns as Spoken in Central Ayrshire* (London, 1923). The latter list is almost identical with the comparable items for the SI dialect of G, which again underlines the kinship of SI with south-western Scots, specifically Ayrshire and hinterland.

[40] As in the case of words with orthographic *ea*, a special overall survey of the English-speaking world would be profitable for the words which in various regions preserve a traditional opposition between /ə/ and /o/ in the environment of a following /r/, e.g. *horse* /hərs/ versus *hoarse* /hors/, which has been widely neutralized in the standard speech of British as well as American type. For the present situation in Ulster speech, see Gregg *SIUSU*, pp. 170–1. The /ə/ *versus* /o/ opposition is maintained in some parts of the U.S. and is indicated in dictionaries, even the latest, such as Webster's *Third New International Dictionary*. Daniel Jones, *The Pronunciation of English* (Cambridge, 1963), p. 40, points to the west of England as an area where the opposition is preserved. It is, of course, well preserved in Scotland, but note that in the Scottish dialects as in SI, the range of /o/ + /r/ is wider than in the standard forms of speech.

The UAI group had generally only the narrow type of diphthong—[əi]—almost exclusively (as in SSB) representing a reflex of ME *ī*. In the same items SI has developed two reflexes in allophonic distribution: (1) the same narrow type—[əi]—as in UAI, which may be considered as the main member of this diphthongal phoneme; (2) a broad diphthong [ae] (or in Donegal [aɪ]) which occurs in open syllables or in hiatus (except when flanked by [w-] and [-əɹ]), as well as before voiced fricatives. Thus contrasts emerged between SI [ae] and UAI [əi] in words like:

	SI		UAI
BUY; BY	[bae]	*versus*	[bəi]
DYE	[dae]	*versus*	[dəi]
LIE (recline)	[lae]	*versus*	[ləi]
MY	[mae]	*versus*	[məi]
PIE	[pae]	*versus*	[pəi]
RYE	[ɹae]	*versus*	[ɹəi]
TIE	[tae]	*versus*	[təi]
DIAL	[ˈdaeəl]	*versus*	[ˈdəiəl]
FRIAR	[ˈfɹaeəɹ]	*versus*	[ˈfɹəiəɹ]
DIVE	[daev]	*versus*	[dəiv]
PRIZE	[pɹaez]	*versus*	[pɹəiz]
SCYTHE	[saeð]	*versus*	[səið]

But note that there was no contrast with items like:

	SI	UAI
WIRE	[ˈwəiəɹ]	[ˈwəiəɹ]
CHOIR	[ˈkwəiəɹ] and	[ˈkwəiəɹ]

To complicate the situation SI has preserved one of these diphthongs, namely [əi], in a small set of monosyllabic words that had a ME diphthong of the *ei/ai* type. As a result SI /əi/ and /ae/ must in the final analysis be recognized as separate phonemes as demonstrated by the following minimal pairs:

/əi/	ay; always	*versus*	/ae/	aye; yes
/bəi/	bay	*versus*	/bae/	buy
/gəi/	very	*versus*	/gae/	guy
/məi/	May (month)	*versus*	/mae/	my
/pəi/	pay	*versus*	/pae/	pie
/stəi/	stay	*versus*	/stae/	sty (for pigs)

A similar contrast occurs with the word MINE: /məin/ *mine* (coal, etc.) *versus* /maen/ *mine* (possessive). All these latter forms would be in contrast with UAI which has no such diphthongal phonemic opposition but has /e/ in place of SI /əi/ in the first column and /əi/ instead of SI /ɑe/ in the second.

To round off this complicated picture, SI has [i(ː)] in a few items where UAI has [əi], thus:

	SI		UAI
EYE	[iː]	*versus*	[əi]
DIE	[diː]	*versus*	[dəi]
LIE ('fib')	[liː]	*versus*	[ləi]
HIGH	[hix]	*versus*	[həi]

and where SI has /əi/ < ME *ei/ai*, UAI has /e/, as shown by the following contrasts:[41]

	SI		UAI
BRAY	[bɹəi]	*versus*	[bɹeː]
CLAY	[kləi]	*versus*	[kleː]
HAY	[həi]	*versus*	[heː]
REINS	[ɹəinz]	*versus*	[ɹeːnz]
WAY/WEIGH	[wəi]	*versus*	[weː]
WHEY	[ʍəi]	*versus*	[ʍeː]
NEIGHBOUR	['nəibəɹ]	*versus*	['neːbəɹ]

The SI lexical form [kwəi] 'heifer' and the adverb [əi] 'always' tended to spread outside the SI districts, and the general, archaic pronunciation [bəil] for BOIL n. was widely preserved in dialectal speech in all districts of the province.

The other frequently-occurring diphthong /əü/ belonged to both dialects in a subset of the List 13 items, derived mainly from ME *-ald* < OE *-ald* where the standard English spelling has *-old*. Thus BOLD, COLD, HOLD, OLD, SOLD, TOLD have [əü] as the vocalic nucleus in both dialect groups, though SI has the special distinction of regularly deleting the final [d] as well. From other sources both dialects had [əü] in BOWL, SOUL, CHEW but SI alone had [əü] in EWE [jəü], FOUR ['fəüəɹ], POLE [pəül], ROLL [ɹəül], BESTOW [be'stəü], GROW [gɹəü], OVER ['əüəɹ], THAW [θəü], TOW n. [təü], where UAI had [oː] as follows:

[joː],[42] [foːɹ], [poːl], [ɹoːl], [be'stoː], [gɹoː], ['oːvəɹ], [θoː], [toː].
SI LOOSE [ləüs] and LOOSEN [ləüz] contrast with UAI [lüs] and ['lüsən].

Dialectal lexical items such as [kəüp] 'overturn', [gəül] 'howl' were found to be very widespread, occurring in both dialect groups,

---

41 See also comments on SI tabulation /əi/ *versus* /ɑe/.

42 The form /jo/ for *ewe* also occurs sporadically in Canada, especially in Ontario.

129

while [gəüp] 'throb' (with pain), [ləün] 'calm', [ləüp] 'leap' (specifically for the Salmon Loup, i.e. Salmon Leap–a place name[43]) tended to be restricted to the SI areas.

The diphthong /əe/ proved to be of relatively rare occurrence in dialectal words. Some forms like [ˈmɔele] 'hornless' (cow)–from Gaelic sources–cropped up almost everywhere, but [stɔex] 'stench' was specifically SI, though not very widely known.

The final list, List 14, attempted to check contrastive morphological patterns involving verb forms and negatives thus:

	SI		UAI
	SI		**UAI**
DO	[deː]	*vs.*	[düː]
DON'T	[ˈdɪne]	*vs.*	[doːnt]
DOES	[dɪz]	*vs.*	[döz] or [dɔːz]
DOESN'T	[ˈdɪzne]	*vs.*	[ˈdözn̩t]
(he made me) DO IT	[dɪt]	*vs.*	[ˈdüːət]
FROM	[feː]	*vs.*	[fɹɒːm]
FROM IT	[fɪt]	*vs.*	[ˈfɹɒmət]
WITH	[weː]	*vs.*	[wï̈θ]
WITH IT	[wɪt]	*vs.*	[ˈwï̈θət]
HAVE	[heː]	*vs.*	[haːv]
HAVEN'T	[ˈhɪne]	*vs.*	[ˈhaːvn̩t]
HAVE TO	[ˈhɪte]	*vs.*	[ˈhaftə]
HAS	[hɪz]	*vs.*	[haːz]
HASN'T	[ˈhɪzne]	*vs.*	[ˈhaːzn̩t]
HAD HAD	[hədəˈhɪn]	*vs.*	[hədəˈhaːd]
MUST	[maːn]	*vs.*	[möst]
MUST'NT	[ˈmaːne]	*vs.*	[ˈmösn̩t]
CAN	[kaːn]	*vs.*	[kaːn]
CAN'T	[ˈkaːne]	*vs.*	[kant]
GIVE	[giː]	*vs.*	[gï̈v]
GAVE	[gin]	*vs.*	[gï̈v] or [geːv]
GIVEN	[gin]	*vs.*	[gï̈v] or [ˈgï̈vən]
HIT	[æ̈t]	*vs.*	[hï̈t]
HIT (past)	[hʌt]	*vs.*	[hï̈t]
LET (past)	[lɔːt]	*vs.*	[lɛt]
SAT	[sʌt]	*vs.*	[sat]
SET (past)	[sɔːt]	*vs.*	[sɛt]
IS/ARE THERE?	[ˈæ̈ɹ₁ˌðeː]	*vs.*	[ˈï̈z ðəɹ]
WAS/WERE THERE?	[ˈwʌɹ₁ˌðeː]	*vs.*	[ˈwöz ðəɹ]
I'LL NOT BE ABLE TO...	[ˌɪal ˈnoː kən]	*vs.*	[ˌɪəil ˈnɒt be ˈeːdl̩ tə]

[43] All Ulster dialects, SI and UAI, have /lɛp/ for *leap* (in a general sense), presumably a back formation from *lept* /lɛpt/.

In the area of morphology in general the best criteria proved to be the SI negatives in [-ne], contrasting with UAI [nɒt] or [n̩t], in addition to the archaic SI plurals: EYES [in], SHOES [śĭn], etc., COWS [kɑe] discussed above (pp. 120, 123), and the various plurals of HOUSE (p. 123). Verb forms such as DO [deː], DID, DONE [dĭn], GIVE [giː], GAVE, GIVEN [gin], or [giːd], etc., HAVE [heː], MUST [mɑːn] proved to be reliable markers of SI dialect *versus* [düː], [dön], [gĭv], [gïv], or [geːv], [haːv], [möst] for UAI, as was the syntactic use of CAN as infinitive[44] in phrases like [ˌɑːl ˈnoː kən ˈstəi] *versus* [əil ˈnɒt be ˈeːbḷ tə ˈsteː] 'I'll not be able to stay'. The contracted forms of preposition + pronoun were also distinctively SI, e.g.

FROM [feː]+IT [ǟt] > FROM IT [fɪt]
WITH [weː]+IT [ǟt] > WITH IT [wɪt].

When the task of collecting and scrutinizing the materials provided by the informants was completed, the phonologically relevant parts of all the responses were tabulated in the numerical order of the Questionnaire, county by county. From these tabulations ninety items were selected so as to cover all the Lists, 1–14, in a representative way. These items were then plotted on a series of base maps which made it immediately apparent that in the majority of cases the SI phonological features discussed above and listed in the Tabulated Summary (pp. 136–7) stood in sharp contrast with corresponding characteristic UAI features in such a way as to give a clear boundary between the two dialect groups. Further, the demarcation lines in item after item fell between the same points on the map—in other words the isoglosses bundled in a very consistent manner. As the main purpose of the research was to map the extent of Scottish-type dialect features in Ulster, a careful statistical examination had to be made of the distribution of each item in its function as an SI boundary marker and then a further statistical estimate made for the classification of each informant as an SI speaker[45] or as a non-SI speaker.

Each map, of course, once again bore out the truth of the contention that every word has its own history—and geography,[46] for even a well-preserved Scottish feature like the voiceless, velar fricative /x/ was missing in the word *daughter* with 4 out of the 89 informants classified as SI speakers; in the word *eight* it was missing with 9 (the influence of the schools could have been a factor here); in the word *enough*, with 3; in the word *fight*, with only 2; whereas in the word

---

[44] G. S. Ščur, 'On the Non-finite Forms of the Verb *can* in Scottish', *Acta Linguistica Hafniensia*, xi, no. 2 (Copenhagen, 1968), 212.

[45] Actually 89 out of the total of 125 were so classified.

[46] Jaberg, *SG*, and Malkiel, *EWHO*.

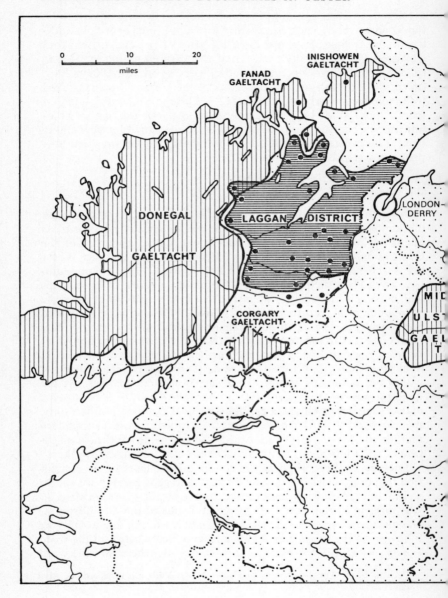

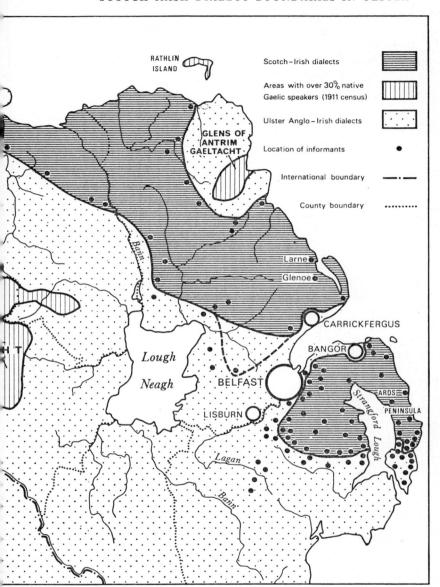

Boundaries of the Scotch-Irish Dialects

tough all the SI informants had the /x/ and 6 of the non-SI speakers as well, and in the word *trough* likewise not only all the SI group but even 34 out of 36 of the non-SI used the /x/. The /x/ in *trough* was thus virtually universal, hence useless as a boundary marker as compared with most of the other words with /x/.

A careful study of the ninety maps showed that thirty-six items were not useful criteria for boundary drawing because of atypical distribution (cf. *trough* above); because some SI forms were not in contrast with a clearly recognizable UAI equivalent; because the morphological items were often obsolescent; because of incomplete coverage. The rest of the maps, which showed very little variation, provided the basis for a generalized Final Boundary map (above), which separated all the points producing consistently SI forms from those that did not. Deviations either way—either SI forms missing inside the boundary or present outside it—never amounted on any map to more than 10 out of a population of 125. From the point of view of the 125 informants likewise it turned out that 49 of them had no deviations; up to 115 had only 5 or fewer; another 8 had up to 12 or fewer and only 2 came anywhere near a point where their classification was tentative or doubtful. In this way then the Final Boundary was authenticated both from the point of view of the items investigated and from that of the dialect of the informants viewed as a coherent whole.

It should be emphasized, in conclusion, that the Final Boundary drawn represents the maximal extent of the SI dialects at the time of the investigation and among the oldest speakers available. On the few occasions when it was possible to check the speech of the three generations it was observed that the younger and the youngest had lost many of the characteristic SI forms, especially along the fringes of the SI dialect zones. Only in the heart of the SI areas was the dialect well preserved among the youngest speakers. In other words the SI dialect boundary is and will be receding from the position marked in the Final Boundary Map and the ultimate extinction of the dialect may be envisaged, probably within the next two or three generations.

Explanation of Symbols used in Phonological Notations

T
D
N
L   interdental allophones of /t/, /d/, /n/, /l/.

R   used instead of IPA [ɾ], i.e. an alveolar flap, the allophone of the /r/ phoneme that is associated with the above inter-dentals, as well as with /θ/ and /ð/.

ɹ   the main member of the /r/ phoneme, which is an alveolar frictionless continuant.

t }
d }   palatalized alveolar [t] and [d].

ś }
ź }   palatalized alveolar [s] and [z], often the equivalent of SSB [ʃ] and [ʒ].

tś }
dź }   palatalized affricates, alternating with [t́] and [d́] or used as the equivalent of SSB [tʃ] and [dʒ].

l   in all positions (and in all Ulster dialects of English) a 'light', i.e. front resonance type of alveolar lateral.

ĺ   the palatalized version of the same.

ń   palatalized alveolar [n].

Phonemic Systems of Ulster Dialects (Vowels)

	SI (1)	SI (2)	SI (3)	SIU	UAI	Antrim Gaelic
BEET	i	i	⎧ i	i	i	i
BOOT	ï	⎧ e	⎩ i	ü	ü	ï
BAIT	e	⎩ e	e	e	e	e
BIT	ӓ	ӓ	ӛ	ï	ï	ӓ
BET	ɛ	ɛ	ɛ	ɛ	ɛ̦	ɛ
BAT	ɑ	ɑ	a	a	a	ɑ
POT	ɔ	ɔ	ɔ	ɔ	ɒ	ɔ
BOAT	o	o	o	o	o	o
BUT	ʌ	ʌ	ö	ʌ	ö	ö/ʌ?
ABOUT	ü	ü	ü	əü	əü	ü

SI (1) represents the main Co. Antrim SI dialect, as well as north Ards and part of the area west of Strangford Lough in Co. Down. SI (2) covers the north Antrim and north-east Londonderry sub-dialect. SI (3) includes the SI Laggan dialect of Donegal, along with the Mid Ards, part of the area west of Strangford Lough and the Magilligan subdialect in north-east Derry. Antrim Gaelic is added for purposes of comparison. The inventory, based on the investigations of N. M. Holmer (see Notes 4 and 6, above), represents the Gaelic of the Glens of Antrim as well as that of Rathlin Island.

135

The phonemic symbols have been chosen in such a way as to give some idea of the underlying phonetic features of the vowel. Diphthongs are intentionally excluded from these basic systems, as is also all consideration of the suprasegmental feature of length.

Tabulated Summary of Phonological Rules

List	SI		ME	UAI
(1)	/x/	→	/x/	← /f/, /Ø/
(2)	/ï/	→	ǭ	← /ü/
	/jʌ/	→	ǭ+$\begin{cases} k \\ g \\ h \end{cases}$	← /ü/, /ö/, etc.
(3)	/ä(n)/	→	i(nd)	← /əi(nd)/
	/ä/	→	u	← /ü/, /ö/
	/ä(g)/	→	i(g)	← /ï(dź)/
(4)	/ɛ/	→	a	← /a/, /e/, etc.
(5)	/ü/	→	ū	← /əü/, /o/
(6)	/(w)ʌ/	→	(w)i	← /(w)ï/
	/ʌ(n)/	→	u(nd)	← /əü(nd)/
(7)	/ɑ/	→	o$\begin{cases} p \\ b \\ m \end{cases}$	← /ɒ/, /ə/
	/ɑ(ŋ)/	→	a(ng)	← /ɒ(ŋ)/
	/(w)ɑ/	→	(w)e	← /(w)ɛ/
(8)	/ə(Ø)/	→	a(l)	← /ɒ(l)/
	/ɑ(ØC)/	→	a(lC)	← /ɒ(lC)/, /ə(lC)/
	/ə(Ø)/	→	a(w)	← /ɒ(Ø)/
(9)	/i/	→	ẹ̄, ẹ̄	← /e/, /ɛ/, etc.
(10)	/e/	→	ā	← /o/
(11)	/o/	→	o	← /ɒ/

136

List	SI		ME		UAI
(12)	/əi/	→	ẹi, ai	←	/e/
	/əi/, /ae/	→	ī	←	/əi/
(13)	/əü(l)/	→	a(ld)	←	/o(ld)/, /əü(ld)/
	/əü(ØC)/	→	o(lC)	←	/o(lC)/
	/əü/	→	ōw	←	/o/, /ü/

Final Phonological Questionnaire

List 1(1–47)

BOUGHT BRIGHT BROUGHT COUGH DAUGHTER DOUGH DRAUGHT EIGHT
ENOUGH FIGHT FOUGHT HEIGHT HIGH LAUGH LIGHT MIGHT NEIGH
NIGHT OUGHT (pron.) RIGHT ROUGH SIGH SIGHT SOUGH STRAIGHT
THOUGHT TIGHT TOUGH TROUGH WEIGHT WRIGHT WROUGHT *baghle*
brugh dight dreegh, forfoghen greeshagh hough laghter laigh paghle pegh
scraigh sheugh spleughan spraghle styaghie weght

List 2 (48–96)

ABOVE AFTERNOON BEHOVE BLOOD BOARD BOOT BROTHER *cloot* COOL
CUD DONE FLOOR (DOOR) FOOL FOOT GOOD GOOSE *groop* GUM HOOD
JUST (adv.) *loof* MOON MOORS MOTHER MOVE OTHER POOR PUT ROOD
ROOST ROOTS SCHOOL SHOE, SHOE (*a horse*), *SHOES SHOOT SOON SOOT
SPOON STOOL TO TOO TOOTH ENOUGH HOOK *flyuggy* NOOK PLOUGH
sheugh TOUGH

List 3 (97–123)

BEHIND BLIND CLIMB FIND BULL DOZEN DUN (*the colour*) NUT SON
STUBBLE SUMMER SUN TUP ('*ram*') ASUNDER TRUNDLE RUN *SUCH *a*
BRIDGE BUILD RIDGE RIDGE TILES *trig* ('*neat*') CHEST RED TOGETHER
TREMBLE VETCH

List 4 (124–180)

AFTER AFTERGRASS APPLE AXLE BLADDER BLADE BRASS CRADLE FAMILY
FATHER FLAT GANDER GATHER GLAD GLASS GRASS HALTER HAMMER
hames HASP JACKDAW LADDER MAGPIE MANNER MASTER MATTER
PANE PLASTER RATHER SACK SATURDAY SHAFT TRAVEL WASH ARM
CARRY CART FARM GARDEN HARM HARVEST MARBLES MARCH (DYKE)
*MARRIED TO NARROW PART PARTRIDGE SHARP STARVING TART (adj.)
YARD BRANCH HAUNCH STANCHION DINNER KINDLING EITHER NEITHER

137

List 5 (181–260)

ALLOW BOW (v.) BROW (*riverbank*) COW *COWS FLOUR HOUR HOW
NOW POWER SHOWER SOUR SOW (n.) THOUSAND BLUE LUKEWARM
PLOUGH FULL PULL COULTER SHOULDER POWDER ABOUT ACCOUNT
BROWN COARSE COUNCIL COUNT COUNTY COURSE COURT CROWN DIS-
COURSE DOUBT DOWN DROUGHT DROWN *drook* DUCK[1] ('*dodge*') DUCK[2]
('*drench*') DUCK (n.) *foisonless foutre* GOWN HOUSE *HOUSES LOUD LOUSE
MOUSE MOUTH OUR (*stressed*) OUR (*weak*) OUT OWL PLUM POACHER
POISON POUCH POUR POWDER PROUD ROUND RUST SCOWL SHROUD
SNOUT SOUND (n.) SORREL SOUTH SPOUT SPROUT *stoon* STOUT SUCK
SUPPLE TOWN THUMB TROUT GOLD

List 6 (261–305)

QUILT SWITCH *swither* TWENTY TWINS TWISTER WHIN WHIP WHISKEY
WHISKERS WHISPER WHISTLE WHITLOW WHITTLE *whittret* ('*stoat*')
WILDERNESS WILL WIND WINDOW WINNOW WINTER WISH WISP WIT
WITCH WITHER WITHY WIZARD WRINKLE WRIST MANY (ANY) *burn*
('*stream*') FOUND GROUND MOUNTAIN MOURN POUND (£) POUND (*lb.*)
POUND (*for animals*) BRITTLE *chullers* CINDERS *lum* STEADY STITHY

List 7 (306–361)

attercap caup CHOP CROP ('*harvest*') CROP (*of bird*) DROP HOP LOPSIDED
PROP SHOP *slap* SOB STOP TOP OPEN BOB HOB HOBBLE JOB KNOB
LOBSTER LOFT OFF OFTEN SOFT TOM BOTTLE (*hay, etc.*) FOND MUST
PORRIDGE ALONG AMONG BELONG LONG SONG STRONG THONGS THRONG
TONGS WRONG QUIT SWELL TWELVE WEATHER WEB WEDDING WELL
(n.) WET (adj.) (WETTING) WHELM WHELP WREN WRESTLE WADE *wale*
RUSHES

List 8 (362–404)

ALL, *AT ALL, BALL CALL FALL HALL *miscall* SMALL WALL BALK BE-
HOLDEN *dwalm* SALT SCALD, *scald*, STALK TALK WALK BLOW CROW (n.)
CROW (v.) MOW ROW (*a series*) SNOW SOW (v.) *taws, thrawen, thraw hook*,
AWAY TWO WHERE WHO CLAW DRAW HAW HAWK JACKDAW JAW LAW
SAW (v.) SAW (n.) BARROW *logg moghy* TASSLE

List 9 (405–450)

BEESTINGS BLAZE BREAST BRIAR *creepie* DEVIL DIE DRIP EYE *EYES
FIELD, FLY (n.) FLY (v.) FRIEND *greet* ('*cry*') HIGH *keek* KING LIE (n.)
LIE (v.) LIVE MEADOW *reek* SICK *speel* STREET ('*farmyard*') SWIM THREAD
WET (v.) WIDOW BREAD DEAD (DIED) DEAF *DEAFEN *freet* HEAD LEAD (n.)
MARE *nieve* PEAR PHEASANT SPREAD SWEAR WEAR WELL (adv.)

List 10 (451–507)

ALONE *blate* (*'bashful'*) BONE BOTH *blae brae* BROAD CLOTH *CLOTHES
COMB FROM GABLE *graip* HOME KALE LOAD LOAN MORE MOST(LY) NO (adj.)
NONE NOTHING ONE OWN (adj.) ROPE SLOE SO SORE *spae* STONE STRAW
TOE WHOLE BEAK BEAST BEAT CHEAP CHEAT CREAM CREATURE DEATH
EASTER ELEVEN FLEA NEAT QUIET REAPER REASON SCHEME SEASON SEAT
SEVEN SHEAF SHED SPECIAL TREAT *weans hain* WEAK

List 11 (508–523)

boke bole CORD CORN DOG FROTH *glomin gopen hoke lonin* MORNING NOT
ROCK *scobe* SHORT *snoke* SORT *thole*

List 12 (570–613)

AY (*'always'*) BAY BRAY CLAY *gey* HAY MAY PAY *quey* REINS STAY STEEP
WAY WEIGH WHEY BOIL (n.) AY (*'always'*) AYE (*'yes'*) BAY BUY *gey* GUY
MINE (n.) MINE (adj.) MAY (*the month*) MY NEIGHBOUR PAY PIE STAY STY
(*for pigs*) DIE DYE EYE I LIE (*'fib'*) LIE (*'recline'*) FIFE FIVE PRICE PRIZE

List 13 (570–613)

BOLD COLD FOLD HOLD OLD SCOLD SOLD TOLD BOLSTER BOLT BOWL
COLT JOLT KNOLL MOULD (BOARD) POLE ROLL SHOULDER SOUL BESTOW
CHEW *coup* EWE FOUR *gowl goup* GROW LOOSE LOOSEN *lown loup* OVER
PONY THAW TOW *moily stoigh*

List 14 (614–665)

DO DON'T, I DON'T KNOW, DOES DOESN'T DIDN'T, (HE MADE ME) DO IT
HAVE HAVEN'T HAVE TO, HAS HASN'T, HAS TO, HADN'T, HAD HAD, BE-
HOVE TO, DAREN'T MUSTN'T CAN'T COULDN'T MIGHTN'T SHOULDN'T
WON'T WOULDN'T AMN'T ISN'T AREN'T WASN'T WEREN'T BREAK BROKE
BROKEN GIVE GAVE GIVEN TAKE TOOK TAKEN BEGAN BEGUN HIT (p.t.)
LET (p.t.) SAT SET, IS/ARE THERE? WAS/WERE THERE? *I'll have to go,
Where are you going to? I'll not be able to get, It doesn't matter about it,
Is there any more bread? He made me cry.*

7 Anglo-Welsh Dialects in South-East Wales

David R. Parry

Introduction

The present essay makes an attempt to examine the Welsh and English influences that have provided the basis of the English dialects spoken today in the counties of Radnor, Brecon, Monmouth, and Glamorgan. The twenty localities where dialect speech has been recorded[1] are shown on the accompanying map.

Three of the counties surveyed—Radnor, Brecon, and Monmouth—border English counties. Part of Glamorgan is relatively close to the Somerset-Devon coastline; trade contacts between the Gower Peninsula and the south-west coast of England during the nineteenth century led to a considerable degree of immigration into Gower

Table 1. Population Figures and Currency of Welsh in SEW

County	(a)	(b)	(c)
Radnorshire	18,471	0·1	4·5
Breconshire	55,185	0·6	28·1
Monmouthshire	444,679	0·2	3·4
Glamorganshire	1,229,728	0·4	17·2

Column (a) contains population figures.
Column (b) contains percentage of population aged three years and above speaking only Welsh.
Column (c) contains percentage of population aged three years and above able to speak both Welsh and English.

[1] Part of the material contained in the present discussion originally appeared in a dissertation submitted for the degree of M.A. of the University of Leeds in 1964 (D. R. Parry, 'Studies in the Linguistic Geography of Radnorshire, Breconshire, Monmouthshire and Glamorganshire'). In preparing the dissertation I was indebted to field recording books made by Mr D. R. Sykes for information about the dialects of the Monmouthshire localities of Skenfrith, Llanelen, Raglan, and Shirenewton. The whole of the dialect material contained in the present discussion was obtained by asking the questions contained in the Dieth-Orton *Questionnaire*.

140

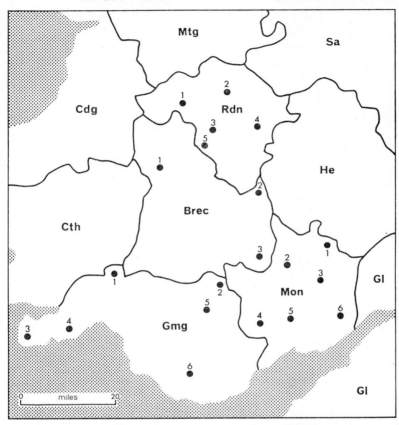

Localities investigated in South-east Wales

KEY TO ABBREVIATIONS

Brec	Breconshire	He	Herefordshire
Cdg	Cardiganshire	Mon	Monmouthshire
Cth	Carmarthenshire	Mtg	Montgomeryshire
Gl	Gloucestershire	Rdn	Radnorshire
Gmg	Glamorganshire	Sa	Shropshire

Also used in the text are D, Devonshire, and So, Somerset

KEY TO LOCALITIES

Rdn 1, Rhayader; 2, Llanbister; 3, Howey; 4, New Radnor; 5, Cwmbach Llechryd.

Brec 1, Llanwrtyd; 2, Hay-on-Wye; 3, Llangattock.

Mon 1, Skenfrith; 2, Llanelen; 3, Raglan; 4, Crosskeys; 5, Llanfrechfa; 6, Shirenewton.

Gmg 1, Cwmllynfell; 2, Pontlottyn; 3, Middleton; 4, Bishopston; 5, Miskin; 6, Cowbridge.

141

that has had its effect upon the dialects of the area, as we shall see later on. Communications within Wales itself have never been particularly good, and even today Shrewsbury is considered the most convenient central meeting-place for the Principality as a whole. Apart from Cardiff, Swansea, Newport, and perhaps Merthyr Tydfil, large towns have always been unknown in Wales, and so for business and social amenities not provided near home the natives of our four counties have been orientated towards such English centres as Shrewsbury, Hereford, Gloucester, and Bristol. This, of course, has contributed to the decline in the use of Welsh and the acquisition by the natives of south-east Wales of English speech that often resembles that of Shropshire, Herefordshire, Gloucestershire, Somerset and Devon. Table 1 shows that comparatively few bilingual, and hardly any monoglot, Welsh-speakers remain in south-east Wales at the present day.[2]

Nevertheless, the speech of these four counties clearly owes much of its character to the influence of Welsh. As one would expect in places where English has occupied the position of a deliberately acquired 'second language', there has evidently been a tendency for speakers to substitute familar Welsh sounds, words, and grammatical constructions for their unfamiliar modern English counterparts. Hence we can isolate a clearly discernible 'Welsh element' in the dialects with which we are dealing, just as there are also recognizable 'west-Midland' and 'south-western' elements. There remain, however, many features of the dialects of our four counties that are difficult or impossible to categorize with any certainty, owing to the close similarities between (i) certain English and Welsh phonemes and (ii) various features of the dialects of the west-Midland and south-western counties of England.

The method of investigation to be adopted is as follows. First, we shall examine some details of all aspects of the dialects of south-east Wales with a view to isolating and classifying those features that can safely be assumed to result from specific linguistic influences, such as spoken Welsh, or the English of the west Midlands (i.e. Shropshire, Herefordshire, north Gloucestershire), or that of the neighbouring south-western counties (south Gloucestershire, Somerset, Devon). Often, however, we shall have to be content, at least temporarily, to group these two English areas together under the heading 'general western English', owing to their frequently shared characteristics.

[2] The figures are based upon *Census 1961: Welsh County Reports* (London, 1963) and *Census 1961: Wales (Including Monmouthshire): Report on Welsh Speaking Population* (London, 1962).

Secondly, we shall then gather together in connected fashion those features of the dialects of south-east Wales that we have found to be attributable to one or other of the specific linguistic influences mentioned above, and in the process of doing this we shall try also to sub-categorize the 'general western English' influences wherever the possibility of a reasonable hypothesis exists. In this way we shall hope to establish the distribution-patterns of these various influences throughout the four counties under investigation.

In what follows, the designation SEW is used as an abbreviation for south-east Wales and as a code-name for the dialects of the area as a whole. County-names will be abbreviated in the way shown on the map, and so likewise the code-names for the various localities. When dialect-features are cited for areas outside SEW, our authority will be Joseph Wright's *English Dialect Dictionary* or his *English Dialect Grammar*. Otherwise, the abbreviations used are conventional.

I

The Consonants

1. Table 2 lists the members of the SEW consonant system, each being placed opposite to the ME phoneme it represents.

Table 2. The SEW Representatives of the ME Consonants

ME Sounds	SEW Sounds and Representative Words
w	[w] *wear, west, wool*; also zero (sec. 5i)
initial *wr*	[ɹ], [r] *write*
1ME/eNE *w* between cons.–back vowel	zero *two, who*
j	[j] *years, yesterday*
sj-	[ʃ] *sugar, sure*
m and final *mb*	[m] *mother, among, arm*; *climb*
n	[n] *north, evening, ten*
[ŋ]	[ŋ] *finger, uncle*; but [n] finally in unaccented syllables as in *morning*

ME Sounds	SEW Sounds and Representative Words
p	[p] *pears, apples, sheep*; see also secs. 2ii and 2v
t	[t̪] *take, kettle, foot*; see also secs. 2i, ii, v
k	[k] *calf, pockets, make*; see also secs. 2ii, v
kn-	[n] *knead, knife*
b	[b] *bread, rabbits, rub*; see also sec. 2iv
d, dd	[d̪] *dozen, saddle, had, ladder*; see sec. 2i
g, medial *gg*	[g] *gate, wagon, dog; sugar*
[ç], [x]	zero *fight, light, brought, daughter* (sec. 5i)
f	[f] *farm, barefoot, deaf*; also [fj] (sec. 3), [v] (sec. 5ii)
v	[v] *vest, harvest, give*
þ, ð	[θ] *third, tooth*
	[ð] *brother, father*
s	[s] *seven, first, house*; also [z] (sec. 4)
z	[z] *busy, cheese*
[ʃ]	[ʃ] *sheep, ashes, fresh*
h	zero *hair, hoof*
r (initial)	[ɹ], [r] *run*
r (medial, and final after vowels)	zero, [r] *arm, floor* — For [r] see sec. 2iii
[tʃ]	[tʃ] *church, butcher, catch*
[dʒ]	[dʒ] *jump, ridges, bridge*
l (initial)	[l] *lamb, loaf*
l (medial/final)	[l], [ɫ] *colt, meal, wool*

2. Certain features of this consonant system have arisen through the influence of spoken Welsh:

(i) Dental [t̪] and [d̪] exemplify the substitution of Welsh consonants for the NE developments of ME ones, since Welsh *t*, *d* are regularly dental rather than alveolar.

(ii) The voiceless plosives [p], [t̪], [k] have aspirated variants [pʰ], [t̪ʰ], [kʰ] that are the normal articulations of Welsh *p*, *t*, *c*.

[pʰ] represents ME *p* in *pea, pears, porridge, pound, put* (Brec 1, Gmg 1.2.5.6), and sporadically elsewhere, as in *porridge, pound* (Brec 2), *put* (Mon 4).

[t̪ʰ] represents ME *t* in *take, tongue, daughter* (Brec 1, Gmg 1.2.5), also in *tongue* (Brec 2).

[kʰ] represents ME *k* in *calf, carrots, coal, cold, colt, comb, corn, cow, curds, pockets, second, uncle* (Brec 1, Mon 4, Gmg 1.2.5), also sporadically in *calf, carrots* (Mon 4), *coal* (Mon 4, Gmg 6), *corn* (Brec 2.3), *cow* (Brec 2.3, Mon 4), *curds* and *second* (Mon 4).

(iii) Welsh rolled [r] varies with [ɹ] as representative of ME *r* in *rabbits, arm, furrow, floor* (Rdn 1, Brec 1, Gmg 1.2.6).

(iv) Soft mutation of Welsh initial consonants causes, int. al., the change [b] > [v] in certain syntactical and articulatory positions. The related [β] occurs as representative of ME *b* in *birds, boy* (Brec 1, Mon 4).

(v) Geminate voiceless plosives, paralleling Welsh lengthened *pp, tt, cc* that occur medially between vowels after accented syllables, occur as variants of SEW [p], [t̪], [k], although only sporadically:

[pp] represents ME *p* in *apples* (Brec 1, Gmg 5);

[t̪t̪] represents ME *t* in *butter* (Gmg 5);

[kk] represents ME *k* in *second* (Gmg 6).

3. Of the SEW consonantal sounds paralleling those of the neighbouring English dialects, only one, the representation of ME initial *f* by [fj] in Rdn *fern, fine*, is traceable to an unequivocally west-Midland source. It occurs in mid-Sa, Denbighshire, and south Ch, but is unrecorded by Wright for any other English county.

4. Only one phonemic variant appears to arise from a specifically south-western source, and it is possible to isolate this one only because its currency in SEW is limited to the Gower Peninsula (cf. page 140 above). SEW [z] varies with [s] as representative of ME initial *s*, and although Wright records this for both west-Midland and south-western counties, the obvious assumption is that it is the latter influence that explains initial [z] in *seven, sight, silver, six, south, sow* n. at Gmg 3.4.

5. Other notable features of the SEW consonant-system are recorded for wide areas of adjacent English territory in both the west Midlands and south-west. For the present, we shall designate such features 'general western English'.

(i) Throughout much of SEW zero represents:

(a) ME initial *w* before back vowels, as in *woman* (Rdn 2.4, Brec 2, Mon 1–3.6, Gmg 2.3) and *wool* (Rdn 4, Brec 2, Mon 1, Gmg 2–4); cf. Wright's findings for Sa, Gl, So.

(b) ME final *d* in *second* (Rdn 3.4, Mon 1.4.5, Gmg 1.2–4); cf. Wright's findings for Gl and south-western counties.

(c) ME [x] in *trough* [tɹou], [tɹɔː], [trɔː] (Rdn 1.3.4, Brec, Mon, Gmg 2.4–6); cf. Wright's findings for Sa, He, So, D.

(ii) SEW [v] varies with [f] as representative of ME initial *f* in *fellies* (Brec, Mon 1.3.6, Gmg 3.4), *fields, fifth, five* (Gmg 3.4), *furrow*

145

Mon 1.3.6, Gmg 3.4). Wright found this to be general in east He and parts of Gl, So, D.

The Vowels and Diphthongs

6. Table 3 lists the SEW vowels and diphthongs, each being placed opposite to the ME phoneme it represents.

Table 3. The SEW Representatives of the ME Vowels and Diphthongs

ME Sounds	SEW Sounds and Representative Words
a	[a], [a̧], [æ], [e̜ː] *apples, catch, saddle; began, hammer, hand*; see secs. 8i, 13
a before *f*	[a] *chaff*; [aː] *laughing*
a before *s*	[aː] *grass*
a after (*k*)*w*	[ɔ], [a] *quarry, wasps* (sec. 8i)
al+consonant	[ɔː] *bald*; [ɔ] *halter*; [aː] *calf*; [eɪ] *ha'penny*
ar+consonant	[aː] *arm, darning*
a in *war*+cons.	[ɔː] *quart, warts*; see also sec. 11
e	[ɛ] *any, herrings, yellow*; also [ɪ] in *kettle* (sec. 14)
er+consonant	[aː] *barn, harvest, stars*; see also sec. 11
eNE *er*	[œː], [ɛr] *earth, herd, hearse* (secs. 8ii, 11)
i	[ɪ] *window, busy, string, Christmas, thimble*
ir+consonant	[œː] *birch, birds, Church*; see also sec. 11
o	[ɔ] *dog, tongs, hot, porridge*
o before *f*	[ɔː] *off*
o before *s, þ*	[ɔ] *cross* n., *broth*
ol+consonant	[ou], [o̧ː] *gold, yolk* (sec. 7ii)
or+consonant	[ɔː], [ɔr] *corn, morning, north* (sec. 8ii, 11)
u	[ʌ̈] *sun, butter, such, uncle, dust*
ul+consonant	[ou], [o̧ː] *coulter, shoulder* (sec. 7ii)
u before final *l*	[ɷ] *wool*
ur+consonant	[œː] *curse, worms, work* n.
ā	[eɪ], [e̜ː] *gate, make, take* (sec. 7i)
ār+consonant	[ɛː] *dare, hare, mare*

ME Sounds	SEW Sounds and Representative Words
ẹ̄	[iː], [ɪ] *he, feet, creep, cheese, needle, sheep, week, niece* (sec. 12)
ẹ̄r	[jœː] *hear, year* (sec. 11); [ɛː] *where*
ē̩	[iː] *reach, east, weak, eat, grease*; [eɪ], [ẹ̄ː] *break, great* (sec. 7i)
ē̩ shortened	[ɛ] *deaf, head, sweat*; [ɛː] *bread*
ē̩r	[ɛː] *pears, swearing*
ē̩r > NE [ɪə]	[ijʌ̈] *shears*
ī	[ʌ̈i] *ice, lice, nine, thigh, find, light*
īr	[ʌ̈ijʌ̈] *fire, iron*
ō	[uː] *goose, moon, root*; but [ɷ] in *tooth*
ō shortened	[ʌ̈] *brother, Monday*; but [ɷ] in *foot, soot*
ōr	[ɔː] *door, floor*
ǭ	[ou], [ǭː] *both, oak, road, broke, nose* (sec. 7ii); but [ʌ̈] in *none, once, one*
ǭr	[ɔː], [ǭː] *boar*
ǭ + ld	[ou], [ǭː], [äu] *cold, old* (secs. 7ii, 9)
ū	[ʌ̈u] *cow, drought, plough, ground, round*
ūr	[ʌ̈uʌ̈] *hour, flour, flower*
ūr + consonant	[ɔː] *mourners*
AN ṻ	[juː] *tune*; [ɷ] *sugar*
ai (ei)	[eɪ], [ẹ̄ː] *snails, weight, clay, eight, they, chain*, (sec. 7i)
air (eir)	[ɛː], [ɛr] *chair* (sec. 8ii)
au	[ɔː] *straw, saw* n., *autumn*; [aː] *laugh*
e̩u, iu, ṻ	[uː], [ɪu] *blue, Tuesday*; also [əu] in *chewing*; see sec. 10
e̩u	[juː] *ewe, dew*
ǫu	[ou], [ǭː] *mow, dough, grow, trough* (sec. 7ii)
ǫur	[ɔː] *forty, four*
ui	[əi] *boiling, oil*

7. Varying with diphthongal [eɪ], [ou] we find vocalic [ẹ:], [ọ:] distributed over a wide area of SEW. These latter sounds are not unrecorded in some of the neighbouring English dialects, but there appears to be good reason for assuming that their use in SEW arises from Welsh sound-substitution. Modern Welsh uses the long vowels but not the diphthongs. The latter occur consistently in SEW only in the most easterly and anglicized localities, whereas the former are found in not only the localities where, as we shall see, Welsh influence generally is at its strongest, but also in a considerable number of places where other kinds of Welsh influence are less remarkable. Hence so far as these two groups of sounds are concerned, it appears that Welsh influence has given rise to [ẹ:], [ọ:], English to [eɪ], [ou].

(i) [ẹ:] varies with [eɪ] as representative of:

(a) ME *ā* in *gate, grave, make* (all localities except Brec 2);

(b) ME *ę̄* in *break, great* (all localities except Brec 2);

(c) ME *ai (ei)* in *tail* (Brec 1.3, Mon, Gmg 2.3.5.6), *weigh, chain* (Rdn 1, Brec 1.3, Mon, Gmg), *clay, eight, they* (sporadically in west Mon, Gmg 2.3.5.6).

(ii) [ọ:] varies with [ou] as representative of:

(a) ME *ol*+consonant in *gold, yolk* (Rdn 1, Brec 1.3, Mon, Gmg);

(b) ME *ọ̄* in *both, home, loaf, oak, road* (Rdn 1.2, Brec 1, Mon 2–6, Gmg);

(c) ME *ọ̄r* in *boar* (Rdn 1, Brec 1.3, Mon, Gmg);

(d) ME *ọ̄*+*ld* in *cold, old* (Rdn 1, Brec 1, Mon 2–6, Gmg 2.5.6);

(e) ME *ul*+consonant in *coulter, shoulder* (Rdn 1, Brec 1, Gmg);

(f) ME *ou* in *mow, dough, grow, trough* (Rdn 1, Brec 1, Mon, Gmg).

(iii) Welsh *iw* [ɪu] varies with [u:], [ju:] as representative of:

(a) ME *ęu, iu, ū* in *blue* (Gmg 1.4.6), *Tuesday* (Mon 4, Gmg 1.3.5);

(b) ME *ęu* in *ewe* (Mon 4.5, Gmg 1.2.6), *dew* (Rdn 1, Brec 3, Gmg 1.2.4.6).

8. One or two other vowel variants arise from spelling-pronunciation of English words where Welsh values are given to orthographic vowels and no account taken of their English phonetic context:

(i) Unrounded [a] occurs as representative of ME *a* preceded by (*k*)*w*, just as Welsh *a* remains unrounded in similar contexts. Hence [a] in *quarry* (Brec 1), *wasps* (Rdn 1.2.4, Brec 1.3, Mon 1.2.4, Gmg 1.2.5).

(ii) The substitution of Welsh [r] in some localities for the NE development of ME *r* means that:

(a) eNE *er* is represented by [ɛr] in *earth, hearse* (Rdn 1);

(b) ME *or*+consonant is represented by [ər] in *corn, fork, horses, morning, north* (Gmg 1);

(c) ME *air (eir)* is represented by [ɛr] in *chair* (Gmg 1).

9. Only one sound in the SEW vowel-diphthong series seems to arise from a specifically west-Midland source, and it is confined to Rdn, where [äu] varies with other SEW representatives of ME $\bar{\varrho}+ld$ in *old*; cf. the form *auld* recorded for north He by Wright.

10. At Gmg 3.4 the diphthong [əu] varies with other SEW representatives of ME *ęu* in *chewing*; cf. perhaps Wright's *ɒi* form recorded for west So. The phonetic resemblance is not of course close, but *EDG* appears to record no more similar form for adjacent English counties, and substitution of the Welsh [au] or [əu] seems scarcely likely.

11. Other noteworthy vowel and diphthong sounds arise from more general western English influences. But let us first deal with the retroflexion that affects three of the vowels in quite a large part of the area.

[œː] is retroflected as representative of:

(a) eNE *er* in *earth, heard, hearse* (Rdn 4, Brec 2, Mon 1.6);

(b) ME *ir* in *birch* (Rdn 2–4, Brec 2, Mon 1.2.6, Gmg 3); *birds* (Rdn, Brec 2, Mon 1.2.6, Gmg 3);

(c) ME *ẹr* in *hear, year* (Rdn 3.4, Brec 2, Mon 1.2.6).

[aː] is retroflected as representative of ME *er*+consonant in *stars, darning, barn* (Rdn 3.4, Brec 2, Mon 1.2.6), *partridge* (Mon 1.6), *harvest* (Rdn 1–4, Brec 2, Mon, Gmg 2–4).

[ɔː] is retroflected as representative of:

(a) ME *a* in the combination *war*+consonant in *quart, quarter, warts* (Mon 1.6);

(b) ME *or*+consonant in *corn, fork* (Rdn 1.2.4, Mon 1.6), *horses* (Rdn 2–4).

Similar retroflex vowels in similar positions occur in the dialects of Gl, parts of He, all southern and south-western counties of England, and in south Pembrokeshire.

12. ME *ẹ̄*=OE *i*-mutation of *ō*, and ME *ę̄*=WS *ēa*, non-WS *ē* are both represented by [ɩ] in *feet, teeth* (Rdn 3–5, Gmg 3.4); *sheep* (Rdn 1.4, Gmg 3.4), as is true also in He, Gl, So, D.

13. ME *a* is represented by [a̭], [æ] throughout Rdn in *apples, carrots, catch, saddle*. So also in Sa, Gl, and the south-western counties.

14. ME *e* is represented by [ɩ] in *kettle* (Mon 6, Gmg 3.4), similar forms being recorded for He, Gl, D, south Pembrokeshire.

Lexicon

15. About the only Welsh words used in the English speech of the whole area are *flummery* (Welsh *llymry*) that is in general use, with

meanings 'porridge' and (figuratively) 'flattery' in Scotland, Ireland, and England likewise; *tollent* (Welsh *taflawd*) 'hay-loft', also in common dialectal use in the western counties of England from Co to Ch; and *tump* (Welsh *twmp, twmpath*) 'hillock' that is in general use in western English dialects.

16. Other Welsh words occur only, or predominantly, at Brec 1, where Welsh itself retains considerable currency. Such are: *beudy* 'cow-house' (used also at Gmg 2); *cae* in *cae hospital* 'field where sick animals are kept'; *ffwlbart* 'polecat' (but cf. English dialectal *foul-mart*); *pwll* 'pool'; and *gwaddottyn* 'smallest and weakest pig in a litter'–this same notion is denoted by *cardydwyn* at Rdn 1.

Dôl 'meadow' is the usual generic term throughout Rdn, perhaps because of the large number of specific field-names that contain it. Another Rdn word, *gweddill*, is known also across the border in He.

Two Welsh words found not only at Brec 1 but also, rather surprisingly, in the very anglicized Gower Peninsula (Gmg 3.4) are *bwbach* 'scarecrow' and *pantun* (Welsh *pen tân*) 'hob'; these have perhaps been borrowed from the more northerly areas of Gower, which are Welsh-speaking.

17. A significant part of the vocabulary consists in borrowings, particularly by Rdn, from the west Midlands.

(i) Common throughout most of Rdn, Brec, Mon are *askel* (OE *āðexe*) 'newt'; *cratch* (ME *crecche*) 'hay-loft'. Rdn and Brec share *bing* 'gangway in a cow-house'; *hopper* (ME *hoper*) 'seed-basket used when sowing by hand'; *larper* and *lumper*, both of which denote a young boy up to the age of about sixteen.

(ii) Peculiar, within SEW, to Rdn are *bodge* 'to pleach'; *brevit about* 'to rummage'; *cank* 'tantrum'; *hespel* 'to harass'; *sclem* 'to steal food'; *simple* 'in poor (physical) health'; *skelt* 'to wander'; *sniving* 'abundant'; and *soller* (OE *solor*) 'upper floor'.

(iii) *Putchen* 'salmon-basket' is apparently peculiar, within SEW, to Mon, although recorded by Wright for four west-Midland counties.

18. Rather fewer lexical borrowings come from specifically southwestern sources, but common to the whole of SEW are *dap* 'to bounce' and *pine-end* 'gable-end'. Most other words in this group are peculiar to Gmg 3.4. They include *jugglemire* 'bog'; *lancher* (*land shard*) 'boundary path in a field'; *nestletrip* 'smallest and weakest pig in a litter'; *pilm* (cf. Cornish *pilm*) 'dust'; *plud* 'puddle' (recorded otherwise only for So and Y); and *voriers* (cf. Med. Lat. *forarium*) 'headlands in a field'.

19. Words recorded for both west-Midland and south-western counties that also have considerable currency in SEW include *oont*

(OE *wand*) 'mole'; *prill* 'pool'; *quist* 'woodpigeon'; *sally* (OE *sealh*, Lat. *salix*) 'willow'. These are known throughout SEW except Brec 1, Gmg 1. Rdn has, in addition, *briff* 'to beg'; *clem* 'to starve' (trans. and intrans.); *ean* (OE *ēanian*) 'to lamb'; and *keck* 'throat'. Gmg 3.4 have *evil* (OE **gifel*) 'dungfork'.

20. SEW also shares a few words that are in *general* use in the English dialects. Such are *tup* 'ram' (all localities except Gmg); *close* 'paddock', *dubbit* 'blunt', *quaily* 'sick', *stean* (OE *stǣne*) 'breadbin', all current throughout Rdn; and *raisty* 'rancid' (throughout Mon, Gmg).

21. A few words remain that occur sporadically in SEW and are either in very general dialectal use or else difficult to trace elsewhere. These include *coopy down* 'to squat' (Mon 4.5); *spag* 'to claw' (Mon 4); *steep* and *wet* 'to infuse tea' (Mon, Gmg); and *tundish* that alternates with *funnel*, the latter occurring only at Rdn 1.2.5, Mon 1, Gmg 3.

Morphology

22. Welsh influence upon the morphology appears only slight.
(i) Such reflexive pronouns as *his self*, *their selves* that occur everywhere except Rdn 1.2.5 could conceivably be translations of Welsh *ei hun*, *eu hunain*, but such forms are so widespread in English dialects too that it seems easier to assume borrowing from English sources.
(ii) Often, especially in Rdn, Gmg, the habitual forms of the present tense of a verb follow the pattern (pronoun + auxiliary *be* + present participle), a parallel to Welsh (auxiliary *bod* + pronoun + *yn* + verbnoun). Hence *I'm going to town every Friday; she's wearing the trousers in that family; they are going to Chapel twice every Sunday*, and the like, Rdn 1–3, Gmg 1.2.

23. About the only forms derived, apparently, from specifically west-Midland sources are the negatives *she inna, we doona, he anna, I munna, you shanna*, 'she isn't', 'we don't', 'he hasn't', 'I mustn't', 'you shan't', all used with or without stress, and the confirmatory negatives *binna, canna* of *be* and *can* (all persons singular and plural). Such forms are confined to Rdn, especially Rdn 2–5, where they are almost universal amongst dialect speakers when the occasion is informal. These forms are of course attested by some of the novels of George Eliot, especially *Adam Bede*.[3]

24. Other verb-forms parallel those characteristic of the southwest.

[3] Cf. also Georgina Jackson, *Shropshire Word-Book* (London, 1879).

(i) Some localities use a present-tense habitual form constructed on the pattern (pronoun + auxiliary unstressed *do* + infinitive), as *she do wear the trousers* (Mon 4, Gmg 5); *they do keep hens* (Brec 3, Mon 4.5, Gmg 2.3); *they do go to Chapel on a Sunday* (Mon). *EDG* § 345 states that similar forms are in general use in south-western dialects.

(ii) When inflected forms of the present tense are used, we find third person singular forms ending in [θ], [ð] in use amongst elderly speakers at Gmg 3, as *look(e)th, runn(e)th, com(e)th* and the like. Wright recorded these 'among the older generation of dialect speakers' in So, D.

(iii) The verb *be* has the forms *we am, you am* (especially unstressed as *we'm, you'm* before following adjective or participle) in general use at Mon 4. This is recorded also for western and southern So, D, Co and some south-eastern counties.

25. Next, we find a number of morphological features that seem to arise from general western English sources.

(i) Amongst the pronouns we find the disjunctive possessives *yourn, ourn, theirn* (Rdn 4, Mon 1.3.4.6); *thine* (Mon 1, Gmg 3.4); *hisn, hern* (Mon 1.3.6), similar forms being recorded also for Midland, eastern, southern, and south-western counties of England.

(ii) Verbs with weak past tense in SEW include *bring* (Gmg 3); *catch* (Rdn 4, Mon 1.3.6, Gmg 3–5); *draw* (Rdn 4); *see* (Rdn 1.4, Gmg 3); and *grow* (Rdn 3.4, Brec 2, Mon 1.4.5.6, Gmg 3.4). Wright records weak past tense for *bring* in east D, and for all other verbs here mentioned in both west-Midland and south-western counties.

(iii) *Break, eat, steal, speak* have past participles *broke* (Rdn 4, Brec, Mon, Gmg 3–5); *ate* (Mon, Gmg 4); *stole, spoke* (Rdn 4, Brec, Mon, Gmg 3–5). Cf. Wright's findings: *broke* for Gl, south-western counties et al.; *ate* for Sa, Gl, west So, east D; *stole* for Sa and south-western counties; *spoke* for Sa, D.

26. Certain features remain that are either in very general dialectal use or else difficult to attribute to particular external influences.

(i) *House* makes plural *housen* at Rdn 3, a form that Wright designates 'general in England except north country'.

(ii) *Enough* has plural form *enowe* at Gmg 3.4, and is recorded for the Midlands and south-west, although of course the latter is the more likely source in this particular case. So far as comparative forms of the adjectives are concerned, *bad* makes *worser* (Gmg 4) that is in general use in English dialects, also comparative *worst* (Rdn 1.4, Mon 5, Gmg 1.2.5). *Usefuller* occurs at Rdn 4.

(iii) The pronouns *thee, thy* survive over a considerable area of SEW, especially Rdn, east Mon, Gmg 3.4, their use being restricted to familiar conversation between intimates.

152

(iv) The third person singular feminine pronoun has nominative (*h*)*er* in Rdn, Brec, parts of Mon. In northern Rdn the nominative and objective forms of the first person plural agree in *we*.

(v) Forms of *be* derived from OE *bēon* are current over a large part of our area. *Be* occurs for all persons in the present tense everywhere except Brec 1, Gmg 1, as do interrogative forms such as *be I? bist thee? be her? be they?* in stressed and unstressed positions. Also current are confirmatory negatives such as *bistn't thee?, binna we?* (these latter especially in Rdn).

(vi) *Do, have* have third person singular *do, have* (Rdn 3.5, Brec 2, Mon, Gmg 1.2.4–6), and the present participle *a-doing* (recorded by Wright for west Midlands, south-east, and many other English areas) occurs at Rdn 4, Mon 1–3, Gmg 3.

Syntax

27. Not specifically Welsh, but characteristic of English spoken in Celtic areas of Britain, is the use in SEW of *will* as stressed form of the first person singular and plural of the future tense of *be* in stressed positions (*I'm old-fashioned; I've always done it like this and I think I always will*). It also occurs as a stressed auxiliary (*we will come; will I finish it for you or won't I?*) These usages are most common in Brec and Gmg. Cf. *EDG* § 440: 'the future tense of verbs is formed in the dialects the same as in literary English except that in Scotland, Wales, Ireland *will* is used for first person singular and first person plural'.

28. Certain idioms occur that are literal translations of Welsh constructions, e.g. the extremely common *there's nice it is, it's happy I am*; and at Rdn 1 *to rise up in one's sitting* ('sit up in bed') is sometimes heard.

29. Welsh word-order is exemplified over almost the whole of SEW in such sentences as *saw him yesterday, I did; coming round soon he'll be*. A word requiring sense-stress may receive it by being placed at the head of the sentence, as *now* (i.e. only now) *you're finishing, is it?*

30. The only other noteworthy syntactical features of SEW are in general use in many English areas too.

(i) The definite article precedes the names of diseases, as *the head-ache, the rheumatics, the toothache, the whooping-cough* (Brec 2, Mon), also the pronoun *both* throughout SEW. The same is true in Ireland and most parts of England. But the definite article is omitted before *same* (*he lives in same place as she do*) throughout SEW, as also in the Midlands and south-west.

(ii) *An* is a rare form of the indefinite article, *a* being preferred even when the following noun begins with a vowel.

153

(iii) *Enough*, or its plural *enowe*, where found, is followed by *of* before following noun in Rdn, as also in Gmg 3.4 (*enough of flour, enowe o' chickens*).

(iv) The relative pronoun *as* occurs at Rdn 1–4, Brec 2.3, Mon, Gmg 2.5.6. Often, too, the relative pronoun is omitted altogether, even when a verb immediately follows, as *he's a man can't see very well*.

II

We now attempt to assess the extent of the respective linguistic influences upon SEW that have been discussed in the foregoing pages.

The Welsh Influence

Considerable significance attaches, of course, to the fact that the consonants [d̪], [t̪] are articulated, throughout SEW, in a way that is characteristically Welsh but that is not, so far as can be ascertained, characteristic of cognate phonemes in any of the neighbouring dialects of England. Only slightly less widespread is the distribution of [eː] that is completely absent only from Brec 2 on the border of He, and of [ọː] that is current everywhere except eastern Rdn, Brec 2, and Mon 1 in the north-eastern corner of the county, bordering upon He. The existence of these dental plosives and Welsh long vowels serves as a constant reminder that English in south-east Wales is still, as it were, an imperfectly acquired foreign language, even in counties like Rdn and Mon that have a considerable English-speaking tradition behind them.

The survival of Welsh words in English speech is something that is much less extensive, the only three words found to be current throughout the *whole* of SEW being forms that have obviously been widely absorbed into English regional dialects as well. Even the number of Welsh words resorted to by SEW speakers in moments of intense feeling (such as colloquial *ach-y-fi!* expressing disgust) or when a precise English equivalent is hard to find or seems to lack the precise nuance of the Welsh (as with *hiraeth*, *hwyl* 'nostalgia', 'feeling') is comparatively small. Welsh words that have an inevitable place in ordinary conversation—the place-names—are frequently anglicized in pronunciation, except in the few areas where Welsh itself remains current. Hence *Llanddewi* (Rdn), *Maesmynis* (Brec), *Ynysddu* (Mon), and *Cwmrhydyceirw* (Gmg) are current in the forms [lǎnˈdjuwi], [mɛsˈmɪnɪs], [ǎnɪsˈdiː], and [kɒmɹɪdiˈkǎiɹuː]. In other

154

words, there seems to be an increasing tendency for Welsh to be regarded as an alien tongue, at least where the more universally recognizable forms of Welsh—words and pronunciations that are consciously felt to be non-English—are concerned.

More significant than the survival of actual Welsh words is the use of syntactical and idiomatic forms that are immediately recognizable as following Welsh patterns. These are current throughout the whole area, and perhaps imply Welsh thought-forms in the minds even of English speakers who would deny any knowledge of Welsh itself. So well-known a phenomenon in Celtic areas requires little further comment.

If such forms as *his self, their selves* were demonstrably due to translation of their Welsh equivalents, their existence as pronominal forms over the whole of SEW would of course furnish very significant evidence for the continuing influence of Welsh upon Anglo-Welsh. But since the same forms are common in England too (cf. *EDG* § 415) the most we can safely claim for Welsh is that its influence may have strengthened the position of these words when they were borrowed, along with so much else, from neighbouring English dialects. There seems less strength in the reverse argument—that the existence of these forms in neighbouring English dialects strengthened the position of literal translations from Welsh into English—since other 'translated forms' thrive lustily enough without reinforcement from English dialects, as is the case with the syntactical and idiomatic forms referred to in the preceding paragraph.

One Welsh feature that is extremely pervasive and that has not hitherto been mentioned in the present discussion is the intonation. Precise notation of speech-tunes is of course difficult to devise, and in any case the use of the apparatus placed at our disposal by such scholars as Daniel Jones and A. C. Gimson[4] would be somewhat beyond the scope of the present paper. Hence we make no attempt to provide specific illustrative details of the similarity between Welsh intonation patterns and those of SEW, but can only offer the subjective observation that this similarity is so remarkable over so wide an area (except perhaps the extreme easterly parts of Rdn, Brec, Mon, and the southernmost tip of the Gower Peninsula) that it constitutes one of the most obvious characteristics of all that strike the average English ear as a mark of the Welsh colouring of the SEW dialects. Perhaps the most noticeable of these Welsh intonation tunes are those used in asking questions beginning with interrogative

---

[4] Daniel Jones, *The Pronunciation of English* (4th edn., Cambridge, 1963), Chap. XIV; A. C. Gimson, *An Introduction to the Pronunciation of English* (London, 1962).

particles, when many dialects end the question on a note remarkably higher-pitched than any in the preceding part of the sentence.

Apart from these, the almost *universal* Welsh features, a few others emerged that although not general were found to be characteristic of what may for the sake of convenience be called an 'inner Welsh core' of SEW where the native language is either (i) generally current or (ii) spoken at least by the elderly or (iii) current in one of these ways in immediately adjacent territory.

At Brec 1 Welsh and English are about equally current at least amongst elderly speakers; at Gmg 1 Welsh probably has marginal ascendancy over English amongst most native speakers; at Gmg 2 and Gmg 5 Welsh retains a more limited currency, being confined almost exclusively to the older generations. It is in localities such as these that we find the most consistent use of aspirated voiceless plosives, although these do occur sporadically even in anglicized localities like Brec 2 and Mon 4. It is noticeable that they occur nowhere in Rdn. Rolled [r] occurs in these same Welsh-speaking localities and also at Rdn 1, where Welsh seems to have been regularly heard, at least, up till the beginning of the present century or perhaps a little earlier. The [r] occurring at Gmg 6 is more surprising, since this locality is in the much more anglicized Vale of Glamorgan.

Spelling pronunciations are not so widespread as one might perhaps have expected, although [wasps] does have currency in all the Welsh-speaking localities mentioned above, as also in some of the more anglicized ones (Rdn 2.4, Brec 2.3, Mon 1.2.4). It is surprising that [kwari] is confined to Brec 1, but it will be recalled that rolled [r] causes further spelling pronunciations at Rdn 1 and Gmg 1.

In addition to the above obviously Welsh consonantal features, we may recall at this juncture some points that were made above, in section 5, about SEW zero that represents ME initial *w* before a back vowel, zero that represents ME final *d* in *second*, and [v] that represents ME initial *f*. All three phenomena were grouped under the heading 'general western English' because they have been recorded by Wright for both west-Midland and south-western counties of England. Attempts will be made in the next two sections to subclassify the SEW occurrences of some of these phenomena under one or other of the two specific English headings. Yet amongst the SEW localities where zero represents ME initial *w* before back vowel is Gmg 2, a place so far from an English border as to have little apparent connection with either the west Midlands or the south-west. Is the real explanation of the zero to be found, therefore, not in terms of English influences at all, but in the unfamiliarity in Welsh of radical forms of nouns with initial consonantal *w*? Secondly, one of the occurrences of SEW zero representing ME final *d* in *second* is at Gmg 1, where an explanation in terms of Welsh is even more attractive than at Gmg 2. Every British final *nd* became Welsh *nn*, hence Welsh has no native words ending in *nd* except where a vowel has been lost between the two sounds in the Modern Welsh period.[5] Thirdly, SEW [v] representing ME initial *f* in *fellies*, *furrow* at Brec 1 is perhaps after all a Welsh spelling pronunciation, since Welsh orthographical *f* = [v]. These explanations are no more than hypotheses, however, and must at present remain so, owing to the similarity, in these three cases, between sounds in Welsh and in English.

It is these same Welsh-speaking areas that are most consistent in their use not only of [ẹː] and [ǫː] but also of the [ɪu] diphthong, although it is true that this is also found in a few of the more anglicized localities, such as Mon 4, Brec 3, Gmg 4.

The dialect where most Welsh words are current seems to be that of Brec 1, where the majority of these lexical forms denote objects common in the everyday life of a farm. Outside this locality, the number of current Welsh words diminishes dramatically; apart from *dôl* and *gweddill* that are widespread in Rdn, we find one word each at Rdn 1 and Gmg 2, and two further words that Gmg 3.4 share with Brec 1. Along with the three forms *flummery, tollent, tump* that are found in all localities, this gives a total of only just over a dozen Welsh words in twenty localities.

Rdn 1 uses present-tense habitual forms with *be* + present participle, and this spreads across to Rdn 2.3 and is found also at Gmg 1.2. Equally sparse is the distribution of consonant gemination (found consistently only at Brec 1, Gmg 5, and sporadically at Gmg 6) and of the pseudo-mutation of initial consonants (sporadic at Brec 1 and at Mon 4 that is part of Monmouthshire's Western Valley).

Hence it seems true to say that Welsh influence, very marked in respect of a small number of sound-substitutions, lexical forms, and of a larger number of idiomatic sentence-structures and intonation patterns, is nevertheless something that is really strong only in the most expected places: those localities where, or near which, Welsh is still spoken to a greater or lesser degree, side by side with English.

The West-Midland Influence

Specifically west-Midland features are rather sparse, except of course in Rdn, but a good many of the features ascribed earlier (sections 5,

[5] Cf. Sir John Morris Jones, *A Welsh Grammar—Historical and Comparative* (Oxford, 1913), p. 169.

11–14, 19, 25, 26, 30) to 'general western English' influences will find a fairly credible place in this section.

Only one consonantal feature of SEW is recorded by Wright exclusively for the west Midlands, and this is confined to Rdn, where the combination [fj] representing ME initial *f* is widely current, especially amongst the more elderly speakers. We may add, here, however, the zero representing ME initial *w* before back vowel found at Rdn 2.4 and Mon 1.3.6, which Wright records for Sa and Gl, int. al. Zero representing ME final *d* in *second* has probably reached Mon 1.4.5 from Gl. Similarly, zero representing ME [x] in *trough* in Rdn, Brec, Mon is most probably due to the parallel forms recorded for Sa and He. Although ME initial *f* is represented by [v] most consistently in the Gower Peninsula, its occurrence at Brec 2.3, Mon 1.3.6 in *fellies*, *furrow* is no doubt due to the influence of parallel forms recorded in He and parts of Gl.

Returning to Rdn, we find that [äu] is fairly general amongst all speakers in words containing the development of ME $\bar{\varrho}+ld$. Furthermore, the vowels of many localities in Rdn, Brec, Mon show several of the 'general western English' qualities mentioned above in sections 11–14. Retroflexion of vowels is carried out most consistently at Rdn 2–4, Brec 2, Mon, where it affects [œː], [aː] and [ɔː]. Of these places, all except Rdn 2.3, it will be noticed, are the most easterly localities surveyed in their respective counties and hence are the nearest to the west Midlands. Even Rdn 2.3 are the next most easterly after Rdn 4. It is Rdn 1.5 that show least retroflexion in their county, although even here it is not entirely absent. In Mon, too, we find some degree of retroflexion in all localities. Brec 2 fulfils one's expectations by showing a considerable degree of retroflexion, Brec 1 likewise by showing none at all. It is somewhat surprising, however, that Brec 3 also shows none, despite its proximity to Mon 1.2 and Brec 2. Only a little retroflexion is found in Gmg, where it is confined almost entirely to Gmg 3 and hence is probably due to the influence of the south-west. Thus it seems true to say that the retroflex vowels we find in SEW are due almost entirely to the influence of the west Midlands.

Also noteworthy here are SEW [ɪ] representing ME $\bar{e}$=OE *i*-mutation of $\bar{o}$ and WS *ēa*, non-WS *ē* that occurs in Rdn and is recorded by Wright for, int. al., He, Gl; also SEW [ạ], [æ] that are found exclusively in Rdn representing ME *a* and recorded by Wright for Sa.

By far the strongest of the west-Midland influences are upon the vocabulary. *Cank* is recorded by Wright for Sa only, and *lump* (cf. SEW *lumper* 'young boy') only for Sa and the Isle of Man. Three further words, *bodge*, *sclem*, and *skelt*, Wright records only for He.

Another small group of words, *bing, hespel, putchen*, is recorded only for the west-Midland counties, and yet another, *askel, brevit about, simple* 'in poor physical health', *sniving, soller* for west-Midland counties and for some other areas with no obvious connection with SEW, although not for the south-west. The distribution-pattern of these words within SEW shows, not surprisingly, that they are most current in the more easterly areas of our territory. They all occur in Rdn, rather fewer are found in Brec, only one (*putchen*, a technical word known only in connection with a local salmon-fishing industry) occurs in Mon, and none at all in Gmg. We may also add here *briff, clem, ean, keck* that are confined, within SEW, to Rdn, also *close, dubbit, quaily, stean* in the same county that have *general* currency in the English dialects. *Oont, prill, quist, sally, tup* occur only in localities in Rdn, Brec. Mon, and never in Gmg, hence west-Midland borrowing seems a safe assumption in respect of these, too. *Raisty*, one assumes, reached Mon from the west Midlands and spread thence to Gmg, perhaps being reinforced there by the south-western influences felt in the Gower Peninsula.

The specifically west-Midland morphological features (the negative and confirmatory negative forms of verbs mentioned in section 23) are confined, within SEW, to Rdn, and even here there is a consciousness, on the part of some speakers, that such forms are dialectal and their use therefore to be discouraged amongst their children and grandchildren—although this of course has not noticeably diminished their currency. From the 'general western English' sources we may add here some of the SEW occurrences of those weak past tenses that are recorded also for the west Midlands and south-west: *catched* (Rdn 4, Mon 1.3.6); *drawed* (Rdn 4); *seed* (Rdn 1.4); *growed* (Rdn 3.4, Brec 2, Mon 1.4–6). Likewise the past participles *broke* (Rdn 4, Brec, Mon); *ate* (Mon), both of which Wright records for Gl; *stole* (Rdn 4, Brec, Mon) recorded for Sa but no other adjacent English counties. We may also add most of the syntactical features mentioned in section 30 as having general currency in the Midlands and in other English localities.

West-Midland influences, then, are felt over most parts of Rdn, Brec, Mon, although many of these are in fact common also to the south-west and are attributed to the west Midlands because of the greater proximity of this area to the three counties in which the relevant characteristics most commonly occur.

The South-Western Influence

The influence of south-western English upon SEW is clearly strongest in the Gower Peninsula, Gmg 3.4.

Only one consonant ([z] representing ME initial *s*) and one diphthong ([əu] representing ME *ēu* in *chewing*) constitute the phonological material that is peculiarly south-western, and the currency of these is confined to Gmg 3.4. An examination of some of the 'general western English' features, however, that are mentioned in sections 5, 11–14, reveals a number of further phonological features for which south-western origins are at least highly probable. So far as consonants are concerned, it seems possible to add to the above the zero that represents ME initial *w* before back vowels at Gmg 3.4; the zero that represents ME final *d* in *second* at the same localities; and the zero representing ME [x] in *trough* at Gmg 4–6, since So and D are amongst the counties for which Wright also records them. Similarly, the [v] representing ME initial *f* at Gmg 3.4 is in this case clearly attributable to south-western influences; indeed, the south-west has given this phenomenon greater currency in SEW than have the west Midlands, since Gmg 3.4 show it in *all* the words cited in section 5 (ii), and it is not confined to the more 'technical' words like *fellies* and *furrow* there as it is in the other SEW localities where it is current.

Retroflexion of vowels that is due to south-western influences does not appear to be very widespread. The only Gmg locality where it occurs to any appreciable extent is Gmg 3; at Gmg 4 it is only very slight. Three localities—Gmg 1.5.6—show no retroflexion at all. The fact that Gmg has no English border is of obvious significance. Two other vowel sounds can be added to those occurring at Gmg 3.4: the [ι] representing ME *ē̜* = OE *i*-mutation of *ō* and = WS *ēa*, non-WS *ē*, recorded for, int. al., So, D; and the [ι] representing ME *e* in *kettle*.

Two words that Wright records for the south-west, including in this case Gl and W, but not for the west Midlands, are in general use throughout SEW: *dap* and *pine-end*. The other lexical forms that come indisputably from this source—*evil* 'dungfork', *jugglemire*, *lancher*, *nestletrip*, *pilm*, *plud*, *voriers*—are widely used amongst all generations of dialect speakers at Gmg 3.4 but are unknown elsewhere in SEW.

So far as morphology is concerned, the present-tense habitual forms with unstressed *do* + infinitive have limited currency at Brec 3 and somewhat more general currency in Mon (especially Mon 4 which saw considerable immigration from the south-west of England during the nineteenth century). The surprising fact here is that Gmg 3.4 are *not* notable for their use of such forms, even though another morphological feature, the use by elderly speakers of third-person present-tense forms in [θ], [ð] that Wright recorded—as long ago as 1905, one recalls—as being confined to elderly speakers in So and D, is something occurring at Gmg 3 but apparently nowhere else in SEW. To the foregoing we may add, from the 'general western English' influences, the disjunctive possessive *thine* (Gmg 3.4), and weak past tenses *growed, bringed* (Gmg 3), *seed* (Gmg 3.4), and also participles *broke, ate, stole, spoke* (Gmg 3–5), all recorded by Wright in south-western counties.

We may also of course add many of the syntactical features listed above in section 30.

Hence although south-western influence is very obviously at its strongest in Gmg 3.4, the existence of the present-tense habitual forms with unstressed *do*+infinitive shows that this influence is by no means insignificant in some of the other parts of SEW as well.

III

Some Tentative Conclusions

What, then, are the final patterns that emerge amongst the dialects that have been engaging our attention?

Clearly, we have had to deal with a linguistically complex area containing a considerable variety of dialectal phenomena. But if our theories about the various origins of these phenomena are sound, and particularly if our sub-classification of what in Part 1 were called 'general western English' influences was correctly carried out in Part 2, certain distribution-patterns can be discerned, even though they will not always be very clearly defined.

Rdn 1 is a locality where Welsh influence is noticeably stronger than in the rest of Rdn. Although little Welsh is heard in Rhayader today, the area to the west, across the Cardiganshire border, is one in which Welsh retains considerable currency. At Ysbyty Ystwyth, for instance, out of a population aged three-years-and-over numbering 279, 252 can speak Welsh.[6] Rdn 1 also shares many of the west-Midland features that characterize the other Rdn localities, and is thus part of a border area that sees the merging of the two sets of influences.

Rdn 2–5, on the other hand, have little more of the Welsh colouring than is common to *all* the SEW dialects, but these four localities form a neatly defined unit of territory wherein west-Midland influence is clearly dominant, increasing in strength from Rdn 5 in the south-western part of the county till it reaches its peak in the east at Rdn 4; it is here that retroflexion of vowels is carried out most

---

[6] Cf. *Census 1961: Wales (Including Monmouthshire): Report on Welsh Speaking Population* (London, 1962).

consistently and here that we find most examples of west-Midland weak past tenses and past participles.

Moving southwards, we find that these latter features are only slightly less prominent at Brec 2 which, like Rdn 4, borders upon western He. In several respects Brec 2 agrees with the Rdn 2–5 group of dialects, but it cannot finally be grouped with them because it diverges from them in respect of a number of its phonological features. Nor does it have a great deal in common with Brec 3 or the localities in eastern Mon.

Brec 1 has very few west-Midland characteristics apart from a few lexical forms, three past participles, and [v] representing ME initial *f* in the single form *fellies*. In other respects its English is heavily influenced by the Welsh that is current locally and in much of the surrounding district to the west and south-west. Gmg 1 lies at what is perhaps the other end of the same dialect area, since it too adjoins the Welsh-speaking eastern borders of Carmarthenshire, although the Welsh characteristics of the English spoken at Gmg 1 are slightly less numerous than those of Brec 1. The former locality is of course far less isolated than the latter; even though so many people at Gmg 1 habitually speak Welsh, their fluency in English is probably greater than that of the Welsh-speakers at Brec 1.

Brec 3 and Mon 1.2.3.5.6 are alike in showing only slight Welsh colouring additional to that which characterizes the whole of SEW anyway, and they also agree in their use of south-western present-tense habitual forms with *do* + present participle. Of these localities, Mon 1.2.6 show considerably more vowel-retroflexion than do the other three. Brec 3 shows rather fewer west-Midland characteristics than do the Mon localities.

Mon 4, Gmg 2, and Gmg 5 are typical Welsh-valley industrial communities and all show a degree of Welsh influence in excess of that affecting SEW generally. Mon 4 has, in addition, a more prominent south-western element than the other two localities, being notable particularly for its use of *am* forms of the verb *be* in first and second persons singular and plural. Gmg 6 in the Vale of Glamorgan is a very different kind of place from these three industrial localities, but can perhaps be included in the same group on the grounds that it shows only slightly less Welsh colouring than they do, and because it has certain south-western and west-Midland characteristics that give it a degree of affinity with Mon 4.

Of Gmg 3.4 little more need be said, except that the extent of the Welsh influence upon both of these dialects seems to be exactly the same, despite the differing percentages of Welsh-speakers in the two localities. The south-western characteristics of which we have seen so much are marginally more prominent at Gmg 4 than at Gmg 3, although it is the latter that has retained the [θ], [ð] endings in the third persons, being even today considerably more isolated than Gmg 4.

Such are the necessarily rough and ready groupings with which we conclude our survey of the dialects of south-east Wales. In parts, the picture is neat and clearly defined: a degree of Welsh colouring throughout; Rdn 2–5 clearly very west-Midland; Gmg 3.4 equally clearly south-western. For the rest, the outlines are more blurred; one can perhaps do little more than distinguish strongly Welsh-coloured dialects like Brec 3, Gmg 1, and perhaps Rdn 1 on the one hand, and then propose the sub-groupings suggested above for all the remaining localities, where it is a complex picture of part-Welsh, part-west-Midland, and part-south-western that goes to make up the character of these borderland dialects.

8 The Morphemic Distribution of the Definite Article in Contemporary Regional English

Michael V. Barry

Brief Summary of the History of the Definite Article

In Standard English the definite article is [ðiː] in stressed positions. There are two main allomorphs, [ðɪ], before an initial vowel (V.), and [ðə] before an initial consonant (C.). The main outline of the development of these forms is generally agreed among philologists.[1] The regional forms have received rather less attention and most scholars have based their views largely on the findings of A. J. Ellis's *On Early English Pronunciation*, Part v (*EEP*).[2]

The Standard forms are believed to have developed from early ME *þē*, which was firmly entrenched by 1296, as is evidenced by such texts as *The Owl and the Nightingale* and *Poema Morale*. *Þē* is thought to have arisen from the first person nominative singular of the OE demonstrative *sě*. The oblique cases of the demonstrative had initial *þ* or *ð*, which are thought to have been [θ] everywhere. The initial [s] of the nominative must at some stage have been completely levelled with the [θ] of the other cases.[3] The demonstrative evidently came to be used grammatically as an article during the OE period.[4] In ME a

---

[1] E. J. Dobson, *English Pronunciation, 1500–1700* (2nd edn., Oxford, 1968), i, 5–6, 55, 77, 129, 252, 274, 279, 316, 345, 387, 391, 399, and ii, 457, 616–18, 634–5, 836–8, 874, 936, 948. S. Moore and A. M. Markwardt, *Historical Outlines of English Sounds and Inflections* (Ann Arbor, Michigan, 1951), pp. 95–6, 154. J. and E. M. Wright, *Old English Grammar* (3rd rev. edn., Oxford, 1925), pp. 465–466; *An Elementary Middle English Grammar* (2nd rev. edn., Oxford, 1928), pp. 8, 10–11, 107–8, 166–7; *An Elementary Historical New English Grammar* (Oxford, 1924), pp. 3, 47, 113, 155. H. C. Wyld, *A Short History of English* (3rd rev. edn., London, 1927), pp. 61, 222–6.

[2] See map in flyleaf, 'English Dialect Districts', and pp. 15–22. Also see his *dialect tests* and *comparative specimens* for each dialect region in pp. 23–820; *EDG*, pp. 65, 71.

[3] A. Campbell, *Old English Grammar* (Oxford, 1959), p. 290; R. Quirk and C. L. Wrenn, *An Old English Grammar* (2nd rev. edn., London 1958), p. 20. *Þe* occurs beside *se* in the nominative singular masculine in OE; see Cambell, op. cit., p. 291.

[4] K. Brunner, *Die englische Sprache* (Max Niemeyer, Verlag, 1951), pp. 120–8; Quirk and Wrenn, op. cit., p. 69.

164

gradual loss took place of the number and gender distinctions of the demonstratives in all dialects. This process may have been more rapid in the north and Midlands than in the south. By the late fourteenth century *þē* was almost exclusively used for the definite article. Chaucer, Gower, and Wycliffe all have *þe* or *the* spellings, in the singular and plural, with no inflected forms.

The initial [θ] was probably voiced to [ð] early in the southern dialects in *the* and certain other words, mainly pronouns and adverbs. Initial [θ] was voiced to [ð] in all words in the dialects south of the Thames and Severn, but this voicing eventually began to die out in Standard English. In RP this voicing is retained only in *the* and the pronouns and adverbs referred to above. More widespread voicing of initial fricatives is confined in present-day English to the south-western dialects.[5] The existence of initial [d] in Kent, Sussex, and Surrey suggests that the voicing of the [θ] in these words took place earlier than voicing in other words containing initial [θ] in OE, otherwise presumably they too would have developed a [d]. The voicing of [θ] in *the* and the pronouns and adverbs is usually attributed to loss of stress. One occurrence of *the* with initial [θ] has been recorded as late as the fifteenth century[6] before an initial V. Dobson considers that in late ME, apparently in all cases by the fourteenth century, initial [θ] became [ð] in unstressed words.[7] It is assumed that [ð] then spread from the unstressed forms to the stressed ones. Dobson notes that Bullokar gives the first record of [d] in Sussex in the mid-sixteenth century, but he apparently did not record [d] in *the*.[8]

The development of the vowels of the unstressed article must derive from the development of the stressed form. *Sě*, later *þě*, is thought to have had [e(ː)] in OE. These vowels continued in ME.[9] In the late fifteenth century, ME *ę̄* became [i(ː)], presumably after ME *ī* had become diphthongized to *ei* (*c.* 1500).

In early NE, all ME vowels and diphthongs were reduced to [ə] or [ɩ] in initial unstressed syllables. Thus, unaccented *the* became [ðə] before a C. or [ðɩ] before a V. Very few instances of the strong form [ðiː] are recorded. An earlier weak form appears to have been [ð]

---

[5] M. F. Wakelin and M. V. Barry, 'The Voicing of Initial Fricative Consonants in Present-Day Dialectal English', *Leeds Studies in English*, N.S. ii (1968), 47–64. See also Campbell, op. cit., pp. 20, 29.

[6] Dobson, op. cit., i, 5–6.   [7] Ibid., ii, 948.

[8] Ibid., ii, 948. See also M. V. Barry, 'Studies in the Linguistic Geography of Kent, Sussex and Surrey' (unpublished M.A. thesis, University of Leeds, 1960), i, 199–200, and ii, 140; Ellis, op. cit., p. 108.

[9] R. Jordan, *Handbuch der mittel-englischen Grammatik* (Heidelberg, 1934), p. 140.

when *the* preceded an initial V., and occasionally before an initial C. This form is widely attested when occurring before a V. Dobson concluded that in late ME and early NE unstressed Vs. were in hiatus before main or secondarily stressed initial Vs.[10] He considers that the [ɪ] developed in Standard English as a compensatory lengthening in order to avoid this elision.[11]

The history of the [t] for *the* in the North of England seems not to have been investigated thoroughly. The York and Towneley plays and the thirteenth-century *Cursor Mundi* all have *þe/the* spellings. It would be difficult to attribute this [t] to the same source as the [t] in *tother* (i.e. from *þæt ōþer*) since this would imply *þæt* becoming acceptable in all cases and genders, and besides, the distribution of *tother* does not parallel that of [t] for *the*, as Map 5 below reveals. However, it may be assumed, broadly, that when the voicing of OE [θ] took place, at least the areas delimited by Ellis's line 4 and line 7[12] failed to take part,[13] and that [θ] continued to be used in the north-west Midlands and [t] developed apparently at some later date, in certain areas only before a V., and other areas, before a V. or a C. The date of the emergence of this [t] is obscure.

Map 1

A. J. Ellis's findings concerning the forms of *the* are summed up by his lines 4, 5, and 7 which are to be found on his map 'English Dialect Districts', first printed in 1887. To these are added subdivisions indicating the presence of *zero* allomorphs in south-east Y and [d] allomorphs in south-east England. The position of these areas may be determined by an examination of the data in Ellis's *dialect tests* and *comparative specimens* for each region, as well as in his general comments.[14]

Unfortunately, in drawing his transverse lines, Ellis did not distinguish between data on *the*+V. and that for *the*+C., nor did he examine the important variations occurring in the north when *the* precedes initial [t]. Thus, at best, his map is a broad generalization. His *dialect tests* and *comparative specimens* also reveal a regional distribution of [ðə]+V. and [ð]+V. and [ðɪ]+V., which he failed to comment upon.

---

[10] Dobson, op. cit., i, 220. See also Jordan, op. cit. § 154, K. Luick, *Historische Grammatik der englischen sprache* (Leipzig, 1921–), p. 503, and H. Kökeritz, *Shakespeare's Pronunciation* (Yale, 1953), p. 274.

[11] Dobson, op. cit., ii, 837.

[12] Ellis, op. cit., see map in flyleaf. Occasional spellings with *te/ta/t* did occur in early ME but apparently not in northern texts: see *OED*, s.v.

[13] See *SED*, I, 515, 990.   [14] Ellis, loc. cit.

166

The present data is based upon the findings of the *Survey of English Dialects*. It reveals that apart perhaps from drawing line 4 too far south in Derbyshire and Nottinghamshire, and line 5 too far north and east in Yorkshire, Ellis's general conclusions are valid.[15] Joseph Wright clearly agreed with the findings of Ellis.[16]

The before an Initial Vowel (Map 2)

SED question V.6.6, Where do you bake the bread?
In the oven.

The map is based upon the responses to the question only.

The question was intended to elicit information concerning the form of the article used before an initial V. The responses reveal that in south Nb, Du, Cu (except the region around Carlisle), north We, north and east Y (except Holderness), an initial [j] appears in the word *oven*. However, this does not seem to have affected the results significantly, perhaps because of its semi-vocalic nature. The preceding phonetic context (at least in Standard English) is the consonant [n] in *in*, but this [n] was lost in Y (except in the extreme north-east corner), La, north Db, and in scattered instances in south Du, east Nb, Nt, and St. This loss does not appear to have affected the distribution pattern of the various allomorphs recorded.

Map 2 reveals a clearly-defined region in which the voiceless allomorph [t] precedes an initial V. The northern boundary of the [t] is almost exactly that drawn by Ellis, passing from the Solway Firth, south of Carlisle, cutting east to the point where the Nb, Cu, and We boundaries meet, then curving south to exclude Wearhead in Du, and passing east to the North Sea. The southern boundary of the region, however, differs from that suggested by Ellis in various respects. He has two isoglosses, one (line 5) showing the southern boundary of an area in which [t] is the only morph no matter what the succeeding context, and a more southerly one (line 4) including central and south La, most of Ch, north St, Db, Nt, and the West Riding of Y, as far north as the river Wharfe. This extension of the occurrence of [t] must have arisen because his map included data for *the* + C., which

---

[15] Ellis, loc. cit. The distribution pattern will probably have altered since 1887, but Ellis's material was often obtained second-hand, and his data for La seems to have been influenced by Standard English more than that for Y. It seems unlikely that the division of the [t] and the [ð] areas would have been less clear in the late nineteenth century than now. Yet this is suggested by Ellis's map.

[16] *EDG*, p. 65.

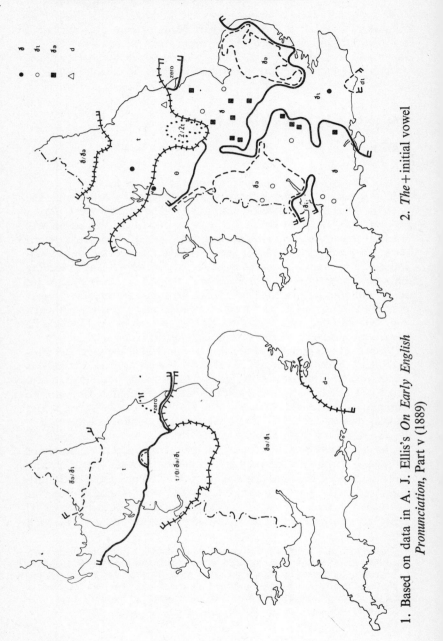

1. Based on data in A. J. Ellis's *On Early English Pronunciation*, Part v (1889)

2. *The* + initial vowel

produced [t] in La in *SED* also.[17] For a consideration of *the* + V., therefore, only Ellis's line 5 should be taken into account. The present data reveals agreement with Ellis in excluding Man, and dividing La a few miles north of Fleetwood, and in cutting east to the Y border. At this point, however, the boundary suggested by *SED* bears south-south-east to exclude only Y 21/29/30.[18] It then continues south to include two localities in the north-east of Db and Nt 2. From the most northerly point of Nt, it agrees with Ellis in following the Humber estuary but passing sharply to the north-east to exclude Holderness.

Isolated examples of [t] outside these boundaries are few and occur only in the incidental material for Du 4, Ch 2, Db 4, Y 29 and St 1/2. These may perhaps suggest a tendency for the region to be extended to the south-west.

Other phonetically related allomorphs within the [t] area are *zero*, [d], [t°], [ʔ], and [ʔt]. The [d] occurs only in the incidental material at Y 11/20 and in the response at Y 25. This may suggest a small subdivision of the [t] area in which the voiced plosive occurs. This is situated in the Wolds of the East Riding. This [d] must have a different history from that of south-east England.[19] [t°] occurs only once, as the response at Y 34, and has no particular significance, distributionally. A clear sub-region emerges in the extreme southwest of Y and north Nt in which [ʔ] or [ʔt] commonly occur. The incidental material reveals [t] also in this region and [ð] at Y 27. Isolated instances of glottalized allomorphs also occur in this material at Y 2/9.[20]

A *zero* allomorph occurs in Holderness at Y 28 only, though also at Y 11/20/25 in the incidental material. This seems to indicate the dip-slope of the Wolds as the boundary for *zero* forms.[21] This is slightly more westerly in position than that suggested by Ellis. Isolated cases of *zero* also occur at Y 7/22/31 and Cu 2/5, in the incidental material.

The influence of the RP allomorph [ðɪ] in the [t] region is slight and examples are only recorded in the incidental material at Y 2/7/16/22 and La 2. Isolated instances of the non-standard form [ðə]

[17] See Map 3, below.
[18] See also W. E. Jones, 'The Definite Article in Living Yorkshire Dialect', *Leeds Studies in English* (1951), 81–91, and B. R. Dyson, 'A Synchronic Study of the Dialect of the Upper Holme Valley' (unpublished Ph.D. dissertation, University of Leeds, 1960), ii, 271–97.
[19] Barry, loc. cit.
[20] For a discussion of the phonetic character of the glottalized forms of *the* in Y, see Jones, op. cit., 87, and Dyson, loc. cit.
[21] Jones, op. cit., 86.

+V. were recorded at Y 16/27, and of [ð] at Y 7/29, La 3 and We 2, in the incidental material.

The north-west Midlands present a complicated and less clearly defined picture. The principal allomorph is again voiceless, but in this case the fricative [θ] emerges. [ʔθ] is the most common variant. The region in which these allomorphs predominate is defined in the north by the boundary of the [t] area as far as the centre of Db, where a new boundary must be drawn towards the west so as to include only central and south La, north Ch, north-west Db, and a very small section of the Pennine region of the West Riding of Y. It will be noted that this is rather smaller than the area allowed for [θ] by Ellis. In this case, *the*+C. gives no support for the wider region shown by Ellis and one must conclude that the [θ] area is shrinking, if his information was correct. No evidence emerges to suggest an extension of [θ] into the Washburn area north of Wharfedale.[22]

The responses reveal that [θ] has a rather scattered provenance in the region, with an isolated example at St 6, but in the incidental material [θ] appears more frequently and is recorded at La 3–4/7–8/ 10–13, Y 21/29/30, Ch 2 and Db 1.[23] In the responses [ʔθ] is more common than [θ]. [tθ] occurs in the west of the West Riding and occasionally in south La, in the responses. An incidental material example is recorded at Ch 2. [tð] occurs at La 7 and [ʔtð] at Ch 2. These allomorphs suggest that there is some blurring of the boundary of the stop [t] and fricative [θ] areas leading to a compromise morph with both. The widespread use of [ʔθ] rather than [θ] may possibly be accounted for in the same way.

Ellis allows [ð] and [t] allomorphs in the [θ] area. The *SED* data reveals [ðə] only in the incidental material at Ch 2. [ð] was recorded at La 6 in the response, and at La 7/9 and Ch 2 in the incidental material. [dð] occurs in the incidental material for La 6. This evidence shows a slight tendency for [ð] to appear in a sub-region centred around La 6/7 and 9. This is of interest in that Ellis[24] groups Man with the Fylde. The responses for Man in *SED* reveal [ðə], which at first sight appears to suggest a link with the west Midlands, but the incidental material shows that [ð] is much more common before an initial V. The allomorph [ðəʔ] also occurs in Man. Alternatively, the frequency of [ð] in Man could suggest a link with south La and Ch where [ð]+V. is normal. Man has links with both the Fylde

[22] Ibid., 84–5.
[23] A confusion has sometimes emerged between the [θ] form of the article and the initial consonant of words beginning with [θ] in the north-west of England. See *SED*, II, 70, 73, 136–7.
[24] Ellis, op. cit., pp. 351–63.

and Merseyside through shipping and the tourist trade. *SED* does not offer much evidence for [t]+V. in the [θ] area and this allomorph is only recorded in the incidental material for Ch 2, Db 4, and St 1/2, all of which are close to the [t] boundary. Ellis allowed [ðɪ]+V. in the [θ] area but this is not confirmed by *SED*.

Everywhere south of the [t] and [θ] regions, *the* is represented by voiced initial consonants with or without a vowel. It is possible to subdivide these in more detail than was done by Ellis on the basis mainly of the nature of the vocalic element. These subdivisions are into [ðə], [ð], [ðɪ], [ðiː], and [d] areas.

The [ðə] area includes south Ch, almost all of Sa, Wo, He, north and central Mon, north and west Gl, and central Wa. No data is available in *SED* on the forms found across the Welsh border. Ellis's data for his Districts 13/14 confirms [ðə] in Sa, He, Mon, west Wo, and east Radnor with scattered examples in central La, Man, Ch, north Gl, Do, north D, So, and O. He also recorded [ðə] in Bd and Hrt. If his information was correct, the [ðə] in some of these areas must have been replaced by [ð] or the RP allomorph [ðɪ] and this is almost certainly the case in the south-east Midland counties of Bd and Hrt.

Another [ðə] nucleus is found in East Anglia. This includes central Nf, central and west Sf, north and west Ess. Ellis's data also confirms this distribution in general terms. He recorded [ðə] occasionally in north-west, north-east, and south Nf, east Sf and Ess and, more frequently, in west Sf.

[ðə] also occurs north of the [t] region, in Nb, north-east Cu and north-east Du. This distribution is identical to that suggested by Ellis and delimited by his line 7. The [ð] allomorph is also found at Nb 3/4 and Cu 1. The incidental material reveals that [ð] is in widespread use in Nb and north Du. Ellis also recorded [ðɪ] in this area but this is not confirmed by *SED*. [θ] occurs, unaccountably, at Nb 7 in the incidental material. The situation of this area of voiceless fricative forms of the article may be related to the proximity of Lowland Scots dialects which, according to Ellis, have [ðə ∼ ð ∼ ðɪ].[25]

The incidental material confirms these three main [ðə] areas but isolated examples of [ðɪ] occur at Sa 7, Wo 2/3 in the incidental material. He 1/7 have [ðɪ] in the response. These cases may be the result of RP influence, especially at Wo 2/3, which are close to Birmingham.

Isolated incidental material examples of [ð] occur in the [ðə] area at Ch 4, Sa 5/11, He 2, Wo 3, Wa 5, and Mon 5. All of these, except

25 Ibid., pp. 681 ff.

Mon 5, occur on the boundary of the [ð ~ ðə] morphs and may indicate a blurring of it. In the East Anglian [ðə] area, [ð] is common in the incidental material, perhaps because the region is surrounded by localities in which [ð] is normal.

It is noteworthy that no field worker recorded [ʔ] between the [ðə] and the initial V., except in Man. This presumably means that a vowel glide occurs between the [ə] of the article and the following V. As a result, the [ðə] must be phonetically closely related to the [ð] morphs in which this V. has been elided.

The most widely distributed allomorph of all is [ð]. It occurs as the response in the north-west Midlands, L, north-west Nt, Hu, R, and Lei, as well as north Ess and the south-western counties. Scattered examples occur in the [θ] and [ðə] areas. The incidental material shows [ð] to be common in the south-east of England, especially in west Sx and south Sr, with scattered examples in K. This may suggest that the RP [ðɪ] forms have only recently ousted a traditional [ð] in these parts.

The RP form [ðɪ], as might be expected, is recorded in London,[26] the south-east of England, and much of the south-east Midlands, and appears to be fingering outwards along the East Anglian coast and north-west through the Birmingham and Midland industrial areas into central Wa and south St. It has also penetrated into Wight and south Brk. This indicates a considerable spread since Ellis's investigation. *EEP* records [ðɪ] chiefly in central Nth, and C, with scattered examples in Nt, central L, north Wa, east He, W, O, and north-east Nf.

The *SED* incidental material shows [ðɪ] to be common outside the main area indicated on Map 2, in west L, central Wo, east Do, Lei, Wa, and south St. Scattered isolated examples occur at So 3/10, in the response, and at Ha 4, He 2/4, O 4, and L 12 in the incidental material. In the [t] area of the north, [ðɪ] occurs at Y 2/7/16/22 and Db 6, in the incidental material.

A notable subdivision of the [ðɪ] area is found in east Sx where [dɪ] is recorded. According to Ellis, this feature once occurred throughout east Sx and K, except north of the North Downs, and he used the [d] forms as a basis for his division of the south-east into his regions D 9, as opposed to D 5 and D 8. Clearly the use of [d] allomorphs has declined considerably through the strong influence of London speech and RP. Only Sx 6 has [dɪ] in the response, and K 7 and Sx 4 in the incidental material. [d] also occurs at Sx 6 in the incidental material. The fact that the form is more common in the incidental material

---

[26] E. Sivertsen, *Cockney Phonology* (Oslo, 1960), p. 51, records [i/ij] as the vowel in *the* in Cockney English.

may suggest that it is preferred in informal and uninhibited speech and might not emerge too readily when a questionnaire is in use. [də] does not emerge before an initial V. The opposition of [də~dɪ] seems to follow the pattern of the RP [ðə~ðɪ] which are so influential in the same area.

The allomorph [ðiː] occurs in a small area in Mon and So 1, and in the incidental material at So 3, W 5/6/8/9, and Ha 1/5/6. Isolated examples occur in the response at Nf 6 and in the incidental material at K 1/6. This form may represent the survival of an older form of the RP [ðɪ], which derived from [ði(ː)] in early ME. The nucleus in Mon might, however, arise through the influence of Welsh in which the close, short [i] tends to be used in preference to [ɪ].

The before an Initial Consonant (Map 3)

SED question IX.2.3, In summer you don't water your garden in the middle of the day; you wait [g. the sun going down]...*till the sun* goes down.

The map is based on the responses to the question only.

The [t] allomorph is again found in a clearly defined area of the north of England and, in this map, extends to Du 4 and into La, except for loc. 14, the north-eastern arm of Ch, central and north Db. In the incidental material, where a complicated pattern is revealed, [t] is also found in north-west L, Nt 2, Db 6, and Ch 3, as well as Cu 1.

A phonetically related allomorph [ʔ] occurs in central La and La 2, with an isolated example at Y 30. [tʔ] occurs at Y 4, La 9, and Ch 2. The area in which glottalized forms are found is much extended by the incidental material data but the heaviest concentration is still in La, the West Riding of Y, north Db, central Db, north-west Nt, and north-east Ch, with a scatter of [tʔ] types in north-east and north-west Y. This indicates the Pennines as the main nucleus of these forms. In contrast with *the*+V., Map 2, glottalized forms do not occur in south-west Y and north Nt except in the incidental material.[27]

The [d] allomorph in the [t] area occurs only at Nt 1 ([d°]), and in the incidental material at Y 6 and Nt 1. [d°] also occurs at Du 3 in

---

[27] Vol. I of *SED* unfortunately does not give the phonetic context of the incidental material examples of *the*+C. cited at IX.2.3. It is possible therefore that a few of the glottalized and zero allomorphs and perhaps other forms did in fact precede an initial [t] and should properly be considered in relation to Map 4, below. Time did not permit the elimination of this data by checking with the original field-workers' recording books.

the incidental material. This distribution in no way parallels the northern [d] in Map 2.

Zero is again recorded as the response at Y 28 (Holderness) and at L 2. Isolated cases occur in the responses at Y 6/26, St 1/2, and Brk 2, and D 10 in the south. The incidental material reveals that *zero* is common in Lei, south-east England, D, and Co, with a scatter in W, Ha, Wight, Brk, and west So, central and south L, Nf, R, La, and Man. At L 1/3/8/12 the response was *while night*, and at Nf 3, St 7, Ess 8, K 3, *till sundown*. Absence of the article in these cases is attributable to the syntactical context.

A small region in which [ð] (and occasionally [θ]) occurs is located in central and south Ch, north St, and south-west Db. The form [θ] occurs within this region at St 3 and La 14. In the incidental material, however, [θ] is found more widely in Fylde, Central and north Ch, north and west Db, north and central St, and Y 30. This would suggest that there may have been too arbitrary a dismissal of the possibility of [θ] before C. in the past.[28] The provenance of [ð] will be seen to be much diminished from that shown on Map 2. Man has no examples and, in this map, adheres to the west-Midland [ðə]. Isolated examples of [ð] occur in the responses for L 4/14.

The RP form [ðə] occurs everywhere south of the [t] and [ð~θ] areas, with a few minor exceptions in the south-east. The northern [ðə] nucleus emerges clearly throughout Nb and also in Cu 1 and Du 1. [ðə] occurs in the [t] area only in the incidental material but is more widespread there than in that for *SED* question V.6.6 (*the* + V.). This occurrence of [ðə] is most concentrated in north Y, the West Riding, north L, north Ch, and west Db. Since these examples are mostly in localities adjacent to the main [ðə] areas to the north and south, this suggests that a gradual invasion of the [t] area by the RP forms is taking place, especially in the industrial West Riding of Y.

The [ðɪ] allomorph occurs only in a very limited area comprising Sr 3, east Sx, south-west K, with one example in south Ess. No isolated cases occur in the responses. The incidental material extends the area to cover all K, Sx, Sr, Brk, south-west O, and Ess 12, with isolated instances at Wa 2, He 7, and Man 2. The use of [ðɪ] in the south-east is not in line with RP practice but might be accounted for by analogy or levelling with the [ðɪ] + V. or by hypercorrection, once the notion that [ðɪ] is 'right' in some contexts has become established. This is more credible if indeed the [ðɪ] + V. has replaced an older [ð] quite recently in the south-east. Ellis recorded [ðɪ] + C. in central L, south Du, Nb, Lothian, and also in west Do, east He, O, south-west

---

[28] G. L. Brook, *English Dialects* (London, 1965), p. 103.

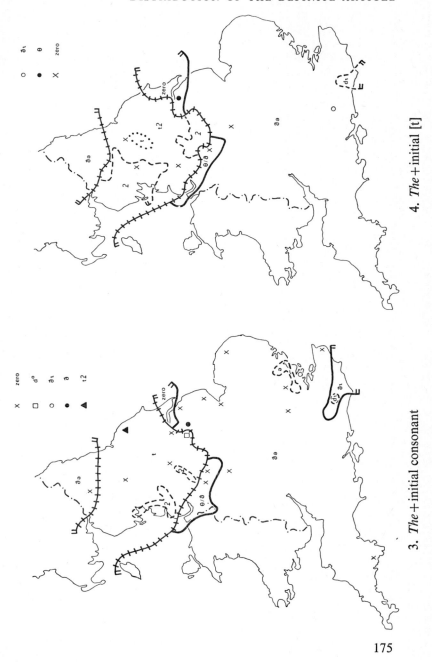

3. *The* + initial consonant

4. *The* + initial [t]

D, Nth, north Wa, Gl, and So. Only the north Wa occurrence is confirmed by *SED*. The disparity between *SED* and *EEP* on the distribution of [ðɪ] could be accounted for either by inaccuracy of information in Ellis, perhaps arising from his use of educated agents such as schoolmasters and clergymen to collect his material at second-hand, or by a survival of [ðɪ] from the earlier and universal stressed form [ðiː] of early NE, which has been gradually overwhelmed since the nineteenth century by the RP [ðə] in unstressed positions before initial C.

The [d]-area is again evident as a subdivision of the [ðɪ] area, in the south-east. In the responses, [dɪ] only occurs at Sx 4 but the incidental material adds Sx 2/5/6, K 4/7, Sr 5, and Brk 5. [də] is recorded in the incidental material at Sr 1/2, Sx 4/5/6, and K 7. This allomorph is presumably based on the RP contrast of [ðə~ðɪ].

In Ess a morph [ə] is recorded in the responses at localities 6/10/14. A second response at 8 also produced [ə]. This form is difficult to explain and was not recorded in Ess by Ellis.[29] Perhaps this may be

---

[29] Ellis did record loss of the initial fricative in Scotland, op. cit., pp. 747, 786. Cf. *The Scottish National Dictionary*, vol. i, ed. W. Grant (Edinburgh, 1931–4), §§ 96–156.

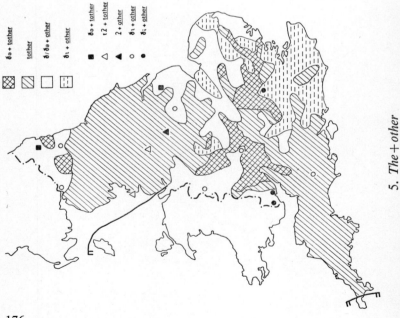

5. *The + other*

accounted for by the loss of the initial fricative in unstressed positions. The form cannot, in the context, represent the indefinite article. An isolated example of [ə] in the incidental material at St 10 occurs in the phrase [woz ə maɹə] *what's the matter*. Here the loss of [ð] may be explained by absorption into the preceding voiced fricative [z].

The before an Initial [t] (Map 4)

SED question V.8.12, When you put things on the table ready for a meal, what do you say you do?
To lay the table.

No incidental material was collected for *the* + [t] under this question.

The northern region in which [t] is usually found only has this allomorph at Y 3 (second response)/8/15. Elsewhere, glottalized morphs are usual. Cu, except 1/5, We, north La and La 9, Y 12/13, and Du 6 have [ʔ]. Another nucleus of [ʔ] is found in south-west Y, north Db, except loc. 3, and north Nt. An isolated case of [ʔ] occurs at La 13. The rest of the localities in the region have [tʔ]. The glottalized morphs are presumably brought about by the juxtaposition of the [t] of the northern article and the [t] in *table*. Ellis did not distinguish between [t] + V., [t] + C., and this [ʔ ~ tʔ] + [t]. He appears to subsume them all under his 'suspended t'. The boundaries within which the glottalized forms occur almost exactly parallel those within which the [t] forms occur in Map 3.

The *zero* allomorph is recorded in a slightly wider area before initial [t]. This includes Y 20/28 and L 1/3. Isolated examples occur at L 10 [sɛtː tɛɪbl],[30] Y 1/5, La 12 and St 1, Lei 2.

In north Ch (except 2), north St, and west Db, [θ ~ ð] occur. These allomorphs occupy only the southernmost section of the region delineated by Ellis for [θ]. The [ð] may indicate a transition of the northern forms towards the border of the [ðə] region. The distribution of [θ] and [ð] closely parallels that in Map 3. An unaccountable example of [θ] occurs at L 2.

The [ðə] areas are almost exactly the same as in Map 3 and clearly are not affected by the [t] of *table*. This agrees with the findings of Ellis.

[ðɪ] occurs only at Sr 5. The allomorph [dɪ] was recorded in Sx 4/6. It is perhaps a little surprising that [də] was not recorded in the south-east.

---

[30] The form in the preliminary manuscript of *SED*, III, pts. 2–3, March, 1970.

The before Other (Map 5)

SED question IX.8.8, (a) You cut an apple in half, and to your
little girl you give [g.]...*one* half
(b) And to your boy you give [g.]...*the other*

The map is based upon the responses to part (b) of the question
only.

The pattern is complicated by the occurrence of the reflexes of OE
þæt ōþer.[31] The semantic significance of the [t] representing *þæt* has
often been lost. Presumably *tother* originally arose by wrong syllabic
division of *þæt ōþer*. The informants in certain regions now seem to
regard *tother* as a single word and the *þæ*- has been completely lost.
In the south, where [ðə] occurs before *tother*, the [t] has become part
of the word *other*, and it has been assumed that *þæ*- represents *the*.
The occurrence of these various forms, therefore, presents a pattern
which at several points diverges from that normal for *the*+V.

(a) Examples of *tother* with loss of preceding *the* < OE *þæ*-

A northern region in which *tother* normally occurs emerges very
clearly and reaches to the south-east into north L, and south-west
through St, east Sa, north Wo, and also into the Midlands through
Db, north Wa, north and east Lei, with scattered examples in central
L and north Nf. Within this area, the only instances of *the*+*tother*
are at La 5 and Y 29, which have [tʔ]+*tother*. A [ʔ] occurs at Y 34,
which is the sub-region having glottalized morphs in Map 2.

Tother is also found throughout the south-west of England, from
Ha and W to Co (except the extreme western tip), with an extension
north-east into O, north-west Bk, and south-east Nth. Isolated
cases occur in Hu 1/2, Nf 12, Ess 9/11/14, and a small nucleus in
Sr 4 and Sx 4/5. Another small extension reaches up the east of Mon
and into west He. These examples may suggest a once more widely-
spread distribution. The incidental material tends to confirm this
view and reveals more examples in the south-eastern counties except
K, where *tother* only occurs in 4/7, while a broad 'corridor' of *tother*
forms also links the northern and southern regions through central
and east Wo and Wa. The incidental material reveals initial [d°] at
Ess 10, and [t]+*tother* at Ess 7 ([tˑtʌðə]).

The region of Holderness in which *zero* allomorphs occur has
tother, but an (unpublished) phrase [ɪntɪ ɷðə] is noted in the field-
worker's recording book at Y 25, under question IV.8.9.

[31] See Brook, loc. cit.

(b) Examples of *the + other*, with no residual [t] from OE *þæt*

The article takes the form [ð] in some instances just south of the northern *tother* area. These occur in places where [ð] is normal before a V. Presumably this has developed in the usual way, by absorption of the final vowel of *the* before an initial V. Groups of [ð] occur in Man, south Ch, St, south Nt, central L, north Wa, south Lei, central Nth, Nf, C, and east Sf. Isolated cases were recorded in O 4, W 3, Brk 4, and Wight. The form is also found in the western extremity of Co. In the case of west Co, the [ð] may have arisen by the late introduction of English leading to the adoption of the standard form of *other*, thus enabling the article to develop as it would in the southwest before any other word with an initial V.[32] Incidental material examples of [ð] are frequent in Lei, St, west O, west Brk, west Ha, and north Ess. The St examples form a 'corridor' linking the nucleus of [ð] in Ch with the Midlands as a whole.

In the extreme north-east of England, [ð] is normal, rather than [ðə], but the latter occurs at Nb 2. This region however also has a small area in which *the + tother* occurs.

[θ] does not emerge at all in the responses but the incidental material reveals it in Y 21/30, Ch 2, Db 1/3 before *other*.

[ðə] + *other* occurs in the same area as [ðə] in Map 2, but with a slightly more restricted provenance. In the response, [ðə] is confined to Ch 5, Sa, except for locs. 4 and 5/8 (in the east of the county), He 1/3/5, Mon 2/5/7, and Wo 4/6. There is a small nucleus of [ðə] in central and west L with isolated examples in central Wa, south Nth, west Bk, and east Sx. These scattered forms in no way parallel the occurrence of [ðə] in Map 2. The incidental material adds nothing of significance to this pattern.

[ðɪ] + *other* parallels the distribution of the same allomorph on Map 2, but without the extension north-west into the Midlands. Here [ðɪ] is confined to K, most of Sx, east and central Sr, London, Mx, east and north Brk, with a fingering out into east Ess, south Sf, north Sf, and north-east Nf. A small nucleus occurs in south L, north-east Nth and another (perhaps through the RP influence in the industrial Midlands) in south St and north Wa. Isolated examples occur at Nt 3, Sa 4, Wo 7, So 11, and at Cu 1 and Nb 8 in the north. Presumably these are the result of the spreading influence of RP. The incidental material adds further examples at He 7, Wo 3, Bk 6, Nf 10, L 8 and We 4.

The related allomorph [ðiː] is found in Mon 4/5, as in Map 2, and a few isolated cases in Hrt 3, and in the incidental material at K 1/6.

---

[32] Wakelin and Barry, op. cit., 47–63.

The [d] allomorphs do not emerge in the south-east except in incidental material examples of [dɪ] at Sx 3/5/6.

(c) Examples of *the* followed by *tother*

The complicating factor in the distribution of *the* + *other* lies in the mixture of forms derived simply from *other* with those derived from *þæt ōþer*. The key to the interpretation of Map 5 therefore lies in a collation of the data of Map 2 with that on Map 3. *The* + *other* presents the phonetic context of *the* + V. and *the tother* of *the* + C. Thus it is to be expected that [ðə] would emerge in the Midlands since [ðə] is the usual form preceding initial C. This occurs in the responses in two large areas, firstly south-east Sa, north-east Wo, south Wa, south-west Nth, south-east He, north and central Gl, and So 1; secondly Bd, east Bk, south-east O, north and central Hrt, north and central Ess with isolated cases in central Sf and central C. Another small nucleus occurs in south and east Nb. This latter case may arise because of the influence of the *tother* forms in Y. An isolated example of [ðə] + *tother* is found in L 5 as a second response. The incidental material adds two further cases in L at 8/9. It also extends the northern nucleus to Cu 5 and Nb 6. The west-Midland area is protruded by the incidental material into south-east Ch, east St, and west Lei. A 'corridor' is created linking the west Midlands with the south Midlands through north O and east Bk. Further isolated examples occur in Du 5, La 7, Ha 4, Sr 1, and D 4. These seem to have no distributional significance.

[ðɪ] + *tother* only occurs in the incidental material at Mx 1. This is presumably a merging of the RP [ðɪ] + *other* and the traditional [ðə] + *tother*.

In the northern *tother* area, the article occurs only before *tother* in the form [tʔ] at La 5 and Y 29. This may represent a small sub-region for the incidental material adds Y 21/30, adjacent localities, and Y 16. [tʔ] before initial [t] is common in much of Y, as Map 4 above reveals.

[θ] + *tother* occurs only in the incidental material at Ch 2 and St 2. This is in the region where [θ] appeared in Map 4.

There seems to be no geographical link between the areas of [tʔ] or [θ] + *tother* and those of [ðə] + *tother*.

Further detailed research which would provide considerably more data on the morphemic distribution of the definite article is clearly required. *SED* has indicated some of the main bones of the skeleton, but finer details will emerge only from close, localized studies such as those undertaken by Jones[33] and Dyson[34] on the complicated

[33] Op. cit.   [34] Op. cit.

patterns in Yorkshire. Similar field-work covering the Pennine areas of Cheshire and Derbyshire as well as the whole of Lancashire would complete the picture they have begun to draw. A diachronic study of the spread of the [ðɪ] + V. morph pushing its way from the south-east-Midland region towards the north-west, north-east, and west of the country would throw light on the strength of the influence of RP emanating from the London area. An examination of its progress should be made each five or ten years. Ellis's failure to note the geographical patterning of [ðə] + V. has been partially remedied by *SED*. Information about the allomorphs of *the* before an initial V. west of the Welsh border would be valuable in this connection, and such information might also confirm whether the [ðiː] + V. in Monmouthshire is to be explained by Welsh influence. Further research on these and other aspects of the morphology of *the* are awaited with interest, and information about present-day *the* in Scotland and Ireland would also be welcome.

9 Forms of the Feminine Pronoun in Modern English Dialects

Pauline Duncan

The feminine pronoun has long been recognized as an interesting phenomenon in English, both because of the rather puzzling history of its standard form and because of the variety of forms in which it still appears in the various regional dialects. In this essay I propose to trace the forms and their present distribution and perhaps make some suggestions for more detailed study.

The evidence for my statements about the distribution of *she* is material contained in the *Survey of English Dialects*. In nine questions (VI.14.14; VIII.9.5(a)/(b); IX.7.2/3/6/7/9/10) the nominative form is expected as part of the response, whilst in question IX.7.8, and several questions in Book III, which were 'completing questions' intended to elicit a verbal form, the pronominal subject was often recorded as well. These, together with examples recorded in the 'incidental material', are the examples dealt with.

Whilst the questions demanding *she* for the most part elicited it, there were a few localities where for some reason the question was not asked or not answered. The questions where the pronoun was not specifically required yielded numbers of examples varying widely from locality to locality, and a similar disparity is found in the number of examples collected in the incidental material. From this it will be realized that the total 'sampling' is somewhat uneven, and for this reason a table has been included indicating the number of examples dealt with in each locality, sub-divided into forms. (A key to the names of the localities may be found on p. 31 of the *Introduction* to *SED*.)

There are a large number of phonetic variants, as one might expect, particularly since the notation of the field workers is, on the whole, fairly narrow. However, the variant forms may be classified as *she*, *shoo*, *hoo*, and *her*. Before we consider these any more closely, let us take a look at the history of *she*. Much has been written on the subject of the origin of the standard form, and no new theory is to be expounded here, but a brief resumé of the various explanations which have been advanced for its development may be deemed helpful.

182

Early suggestions that [ʃ-] forms represented, on the one hand, a new formation developed from the OE feminine singular demonstrative *sēo*, or, on the other, a hybrid of the OE demonstrative and personal pronouns, *sēo* and *hēo*, seem now to have been invalidated. As Flom[1] and, more particularly, Lindkvist[2] so forcefully pointed out, *sēo* had become obsolete by the end of the OE period (replaced by *þēo*), at which time *hēo* was still flourishing. It was hardly likely, therefore, that the feminine pronoun would have been replaced by, or hybridized with, this obsolete form. The usual view taken by scholars since these two articles is that [ʃ-] forms represent new formations developed direct from earlier *hēo*.

Because no straightforward English sound-change seems to explain it, and because the [ʃ-] form first appeared in the area of Scandinavian settlement, the usual assumption is that the [h] > [ʃ] change originated in the influence of the Scandinavian pronunciation of English. Late Norwegian had rising diphthongs where the OE ones were falling. A stress shift *hēo > heó, hió > hjó* is therefore assumed. With evidence from place-names like *Shetland, Shapinsay*, and *Shap* (Norse *Hjaltland, Hjalpandis-ey*, and OE *Hepp(e) > Yhep*) it has been argued, originally by Smith,[3] and later by scholars such as Dieth,[4] that [hj-] became [ç-], which was then interpreted as [ʃ-]. Dieth gives examples of [hj-] in Scandinavian dialects becoming [ç-], [ʃ-] and even [tʃ-], and assumes that the settlers must have dealt with English words, like *hēope* and *hēo*, similarly. The implication, then, is that the Scandinavians heard and pronounced English *hēo* as *hjó*, and the Angles heard this as [ço] or [ʃo], which they in turn adopted, usually in the latter form.

Dieth points out that stress-shift of diphthongs does occur under certain conditions in the native English phonology before the end of the OE period, one being after a palatal consonant. This is probably responsible for NE *choose* < *ceósan* < OE *cēosan*. However, he also points out that *hēo-, hēa-* > *sho-, sha-* has not been evidenced outside the Scandinavianized area.

The timing for this is not altogether reliable, however. Dieth admits that for his argument he is 'assuming a somewhat advanced

[1] G. T. Flom, 'The Origin of the Pronoun *she*', *JEGP*, vii (1908), 115–25.
[2] H. Lindkvist, 'On the Origin of the English Pronoun *she*', *Anglia*, xlv (1921), 1–50.
[3] A. H. Smith, 'Some Place Names and the Etymology of *she*', *RES*, i (1925), 437–40.
[4] E. Dieth, '*Hips*: A Geographical Contribution to the *she* Puzzle', *English Studies*, xxxvi (1955), 208–17.

stage of Norwegian', whilst Gordon[5] states that the stress shift in diphthongs had not taken place, except initially, in Norse at the time of settlement. Stevick[6] criticises the theory on these grounds and also points out that the 'unusually complex socio-linguistic sequence' implied 'though not inconceivable is not readily credible'. A one-stage development (Scandinavian [hj-] becoming [ʃ-]) in a few place-names and nouns is credible and well documented, but this is a very different thing from the many steps postulated for the change in the English feminine pronoun, which is a form of very high frequency.

A further suggested explanation of the development of forms is that put forward by Lindkvist[7] in 1921. He presumes that old Mercian and old Northumbrian *hīo*, *hīu* became stress-shifted *hjó*, which in turn became *jó*, and then posits sandhi occurrences of a preceding -*s*, the inflection of the third person singular, present tense, of the verb. We then have $s+j->$ [ʃ-], a well recognized English sound change (cf. *sugar* [ʃʊgə] and the [tʃu] pronunciation of *issue*).

This explanation too, then, is dependent upon an assumed stress shift due to Scandinavian influence—an assumption which we have seen is unreliable. In addition, it depends on reversed word order, not a very common occurrence even in old Northumbrian, for the opportunity for metanalysis to be there.

Stevick[8] himself postulates an explanation based on phonemic and morphemic considerations. [heo] > [ʃo], he points out, presumes an intermediate [ç] stage. This [ç], he suggests, would quite naturally arise as a phonetic realization of /h-/ before a high front sound, and since the Northumbrian and Mercian allomorphs of *hēo* were *hīo*, *hīw*, *hīe*, and some variants with a short *i*, [ç-] forms would be expected to occur. No difficulties would be caused with similar allophones of /x/, because its distributional pattern was mutually exclusive with that of /h/.

There then followed the reassignment, in the area of Norse settlement, of [ç] to the /ʃ/ rather than to the /h/ phoneme. This, he suggests, was made less obtrusive by the fact that new borrowings of Scandinavian words with /sk-/ had caused /ʃ-/ forms, the developments of earlier /sk-/, to be redistributed in line with initial spirants /f, θ, s/, whose distribution was vitually identical with that of /h/.

He links this with the argument that after monophthongization of the OE diphthong *ēo* (*ēo* > *ē* in the east, and a rounded *ȫ* elsewhere)

---

[5] E. V. Gordon, *An Introduction to Old Norse* (Oxford, 1927), quoted in R. D. Stevick, 'The Morphemic Evolution of *she*', *English Studies*, xlv (1964), 381–8.
[6] Stevick, op. cit., 382. [7] Lindkvist, ibid. [8] Stevick, op. cit., 384–5.

the nominative masculine/nominative feminine pronominal distinction, V/Vv, was obscured and was carried by merely an /ē/, /ō/ contrast, or, in some districts, was left temporarily undistinguished. 'Clearly contrasting allophones of /h-/ and /ʃ-/ or /ē/ and /ō/, and in some cases both, were therefore selected to keep communication efficient'. Each of the two possible methods was utilized by one dialect or another, and in some cases, where *sho* appeared, both seem to have been used. 'Once [ʃ-] forms were established', he continues, 'the analogical circumstances of nominative *he* and *þei/þeʒ* etc., and the increasing dominance of east Midland speech are sufficient to account for the displacement of *sho* by *she* wherever the two existed as allomorphs.'

Samuels[9] too sees the spread of *sh-* forms as the filling of the systemic gap caused by *he* and *she* becoming not at all, or insufficiently, differentiated, although he sees it as a selection of 'the originally rare stress-shifted forms /hjo/ and /hje/' which 'probably originated in the heavily Norse influenced Cumberland/Yorkshire belt'.

The weakest point in this argument is perhaps the presumption that the new rounded monophthong still maintained the conditioning for /h/ to be realized as [ç]. Allowing that this is possible, however, and the appearance in ME of both *sho* and *she* would seem to support the inference, the argument is quite strong and has much to recommend it in its non-reliance on Norse-influenced stress shift.

[ç-] and [ʃ-] forms spread southwards during the ME period, [ç-] forms, it would appear, being used first, to be superseded shortly by [ʃ-] (cf. Samuels p. 23). The *-e* forms originating in the east predominated, *-o* variants being basically northern. In the west Midlands and south-west, where unrounding took place very late, the vowel sound seems to have been sufficiently distinct to prevent confusion with forms of *he*. /hö/, usually regarded as [hø] phonetically, remained the basic form. It was represented by many spellings: *ho(e)*, *heo*, *hu(e)*, *hy*, etc., the last three perhaps representing a raising of the vowel to [y]. In the north-west Midlands *ho* was the most common form (cf. *Pearl, Cleanness, Gawain*, etc.), and from the appearance of [hu] in the modern dialects of the area it would appear that this was realized by a phonetic variant nearer [-o] than [-ø]. A fair sprinkling of forms with an initial [ç] or [ʃ] are recorded here as well, however, as they are in the rest of the west Midlands and the south-

9 M. L. Samuels, 'The Role of Functional Selection in the History of English', *Transactions of the Philological Society*, 1965, 21–3.

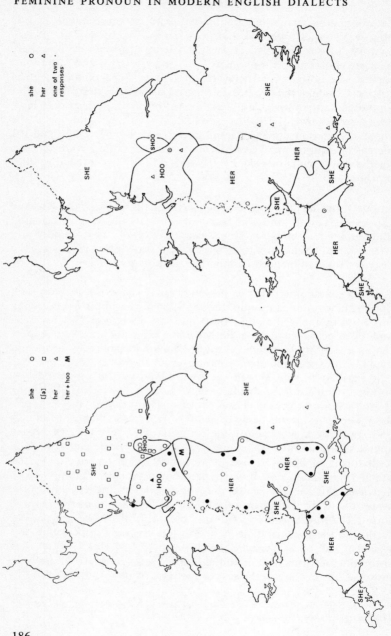

2. Stressed forms of *she*

1. Distribution of *her, hoo, she, shoo*

west (cf. the map showing the distribution of ME forms of *she* in Bloomfield and Newmark[10]).

What has happened since the end of the ME period? The material from *SED*, since it recorded in the 1950s informants who were at that time usually in their sixties, allows us to piece together the picture as it was when they were acquiring their language at about the turn of the century.

Map 1 shows a generalized isogloss drawn from all the evidence available. It plots the extent of *her*, *hoo*, and *shoo* forms against the more prevalent *she*, which is, of course, also the standard form. More than two examples of any of these three forms is taken as justification for including the locality concerned within the appropriate isogloss. If more than two instances of *she* or another form is also found in the locality, however, this is indicated by an open symbol, which is filled in if the form accounts for fifty per cent or more of the examples. This is of necessity a rather arbitrary set of criteria, but it will be recognized that the border area between forms will usually contain examples of both. With present evidence, however, the pattern is not sufficiently clear to enable one to draw the boundary of each of two forms and a straightforward area of overlap.

The influence of Standard English *she* seems to be sufficient to produce a sprinkling of examples in almost all the basically non-*she* areas. Map 2, therefore, represents the picture arising from a single question (IX.7.7 Which of you is English here? For her you could say...SHE IS) which elicits a stressed form, and Map 3 from one which generally elicits a form without strong stress (IX.7.2 To find out whether she had a husband, you'd ask me: IS SHE MARRIED?). The simple isoglosses may then be compared with the more complex picture of Map 1.

As the maps show, *she* (phonetically [ʃɪ] and [ʃi] and forms with a lengthened vowel or with an -*i* diphthong) is the most extensive form, covering almost all but the west Midlands and the south-western peninsula, as from the ME picture we might expect. In the vast majority of cases a lengthened or diphthongized form was recorded for the stress question (Map 2). In several cases this was the only occasion on which a long variant occurred. Elsewhere this appears as the general form, even where no strong stress seems to be intended. A more detailed study would need to sort out minor distribution patterns here in terms of the phonemic systems of the particular dialects. (Is the contrast, for instance, one of length or one of vowel quality; is it meaningful to equate places with identical

---

[10] M. W. Bloomfield and L. Newmark, *A Linguistic Introduction to the History of English* (New York, 1963), p. 221.

phonetic forms, when a closer study of phonemic systems might reveal them to be realizations of very different phonemes? Cf. Weinreich's suggestions.[11])

Shoo, the descendant of ME *s(c)ho*, is confined fairly closely to south-west Yorkshire. As the table shows, only four localities have three or more examples (Y 23/26/31/32) and in no case is this the exclusive form. The neighbouring *she* forms are found in all these localities, though never the *hoo* ones of the western border of the region. Synchronically, then, *shoo* seems to be a blend of the forms on either side of it.

The use of *shoo* and *she* does not on present evidence seem to fit into any very distinct pattern. *Shoo*, phonetically [ʃᵒuː] or [ʃu], was recorded in all four localities for the stressed question, but on other occasions [ʃω], [ʃə], and [ʃɩ] were all phonetic possibilities.

The phonetic form [ʃə] is, in fact, quite prevalent over the whole northern area. It is likely that historically this should be regarded as a reduced or unstressed *shoo* (cf. Dieth, p. 217), and certainly it does occur in all the localities where a definitely assignable *shoo* also

11 U. Weinreich, 'Is a Structural Dialectology Possible?' *Word*, x (1954), 391 ff.

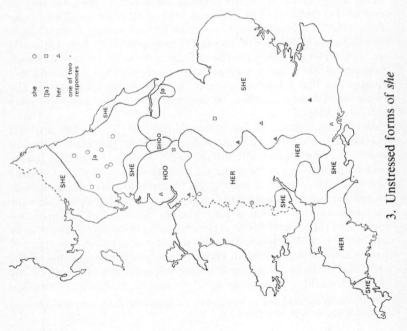

3. Unstressed forms of *she*

appears. However, synchronically it appears to be an alternative un-stressed form to [ʃɪ], where the full or stress form is [ʃiː]. (I am under the impression, as yet untested, that in this northern area [ə] is the regular unstressed vowel in most positions, even when the full vowel is a high front one. In cases where more southerly dialects, and RP, would have [ɪ]: [ɪnʌf] *enough*; [ɪksɛpt] *except*; [nidɪd] *needed*; [mɪnɪt] *minute*, etc., I suspect that [ə] will be found with a frequency equal to or greater than that of [ɪ]. Perhaps this might help to explain the [ʃə ~ ʃɪ] alternation as the unstressed form of *she*.)

Hoo in the north-west Midlands covers Lancashire from a little south of the Lune, a strip of south-west Yorkshire, all but the ex-treme southern strip of Cheshire, northern and central Derbyshire, and the extreme north-eastern tip of Staffordshire—almost exactly the area delimited by Ellis for this form towards the end of the last century. For four of the localities to the west of Lancashire *hoo* is the only form, though in Fleetwood, on the coast, virtually every ex-ample came as part of a parallel *she* OR *hoo* response. Elsewhere, in localities on the border of the region, we get a sprinkling of the ad-jacent forms: *she* on the Lancashire/Yorkshire border, except where the boundary is with *shoo* forms, where one of these is recorded in an otherwise *hoo* locality; and *her* along the south Cheshire boundary of *hoo*. Most of central Derbyshire seems to be a genuine region of overlap, in which both *hoo* and *her* are to be found in more or less equal proportions. The occasional *she* forms in the centre of the *hoo* area are probably to be explained as due to some influence from Standard English, whilst the *her* of La 12, where no *hoo* forms were recorded, appears an inexplicable exception. All the examples come from the same informant, so perhaps this is merely his idiolect and not properly representative. Alternatively, it might be that this is an isolated pocket of *her* forms which in fact includes a wider area than just this one village, but the fairly wide mesh of the network of localities at this point has not shown this up.

Hoo represents phonetically a number of forms ([uː], [üː], [ʏː], [ɔuː], [ɛɵ], etc.), although it is never recorded, even in the stress question, with an initial [h-]. The form presumably indicates a straightforward development from ME *ho*, as did the *shoo* forms from ME *sho*: ME $\bar{ọ}$ > NE $\bar{u}$. The vowel is long or has a diphthongal on-glide in all the examples recorded, for the stress question and elsewhere, with the exception only of two responses to VIII.9.5(a), which have [ʃɵ]. These are at Y 29 and Y 30, both of which are on the *shoo* border where variants with an [ɔ] vowel occur, and both of which have [uː] as their usual form.

In terms of modern developments, the widespread appearance

189

of *her* as the nominative form in the central and southern west Midlands and the south-western peninsula would seem to pose most questions. Has this somehow developed from a regular ME form of the nominative, as Ellis tentatively suggests? 'It is very common...to use *uu*, usually accepted as *uur*...and written *her*, and considered as the accusative case used for the nominative. It is possible that this is not the case, and hoo, shoo, her...may all be phonetic descendants of the WS *heo* having the same meaning.'[12] On the other hand, is it merely the accusative form which has over-run the nominative as well?

Wright's only comment on the subject is that 'the objective forms are often used for the nominative when the pronouns are unemphatic, especially in the south midland, eastern, south, and south western counties'.[13] This is a general comment on pronominal usage, however, which only partly applies to the material obtained by *SED*. *Them* occurs instead of *they* as subject sporadically in the southern area west of Sussex, in most of the west-Midland region, and in two east-Midland localities to the west of Buckinghamshire—always in unstressed conditions (questions IX.7.2/3/5/6). This is not the invariable form in any of the localities concerned, however, and it does not occur in response to the stressed question, IX.7.7, or to question IX.7.10 (If I said to you: They're drunk, you would answer: Oh no...THEY AREN'T), where the pronoun precedes the verb, and would probably carry a certain degree of stress. Likewise, there are a few examples of *us* recorded as an unstressed subject, though again these are never the invariable form, and the area covered is very small—one locality each in Gloucestershire, Oxfordshire, and Berkshire, and the whole of Devon. The area covered by these examples, then, does not completely coincide with our *her* area, and in any case, *her* is used consistently as subject, whether in stressed or unstressed position.

It does not seem to be a matter, either, of a straight reversal of the usual cases, i.e. *her* as subject, *she* as object. This does occur sporadically in some localities in Hampshire, Wiltshire, and west Berkshire (though *her* occurs more often as object), but it is never recorded in the west-Midland region. In addition, in one or two localities in north-east Somerset, and one in west Sussex, *she* is occasionally recorded as object, though it is also the regular subject form.

We seem to have synchronically, then, one form for both subject and object of the feminine pronoun. Historically it seems possible, perhaps, that the ME form for the nominative, [hø], was eventually

12 A. J. Ellis, *English Dialects, Their Sounds and Homes* (London, 1890), p. 71.
13 *EDG*, p. 271.

realized by the central vowel [ə:], and that this came to be very similar to the phonetic realization of *her* once [ə:] came to be used in this word, towards the end of the eighteenth century. The two might then have come to be thought of as the same form. This, however, is only a tentative suggestion, and does not take into account the following *r* sound, which was present originally in the accusative form (*her* < weak form of *hir* < OE *hiere*) but not in the nominative.

The actual phonetic forms recorded in the *her* area for the subject usually have a long schwa + the *r*-colouring or *r* appropriate to the region concerned (almost invariably retracted, or, to the south, retroflex). Occasionally this is reduced to schwa alone, sometimes without length. An initial [h-] occurs hardly at all, even in stress position, virtually the only examples being found in two localities, one in Somerset and the other in Wiltshire, and perhaps, therefore, being merely part of the idiolect of the informants concerned.

These forms cover the same range phonetically as those found in the oblique cases, though there are more reductions to a mere [ə] in non-subject positions. *Her* is likewise the form for the oblique cases over the rest of the country: again an almost invariable schwa (the alternative being [ə], which is found sometimes in Northumberland), long or short, + *r* or *r*-colouring (velar [ʁ] in Northumberland and Durham, the occasional [r] in north Cumberland, [ɹ] or [ɻ] in the west and south-west, and [ɹ] elsewhere). As with the west-Midland and south-western forms described above, the occasional form with initial [h] is recorded when stress is intended.

Although *her* is the basic south-western nominative form, in the extreme west of Cornwall this is rarely recorded, the main form being *she*. As Ellis points out,[14] until towards the end of the seventeenth century Cornish, a Celtic dialect, was spoken west of Truro. Since the acquisition of English in that area was therefore so late, the influence would seem to have been that of the now well-established standard, rather than of the neighbouring dialect—in this feature at least. (In fact the isogloss on the present maps is not quite as far west as that indicated by Ellis. One locality east of Truro is included in the *she* area. This might suggest that the old dialect form is losing ground to *she*, which is stronger through being also the standard form.)

The same reason will probably account for the *she* area in Monmouthshire. A late changeover to English from Welsh meant the acquisition of the standard form. Several localities on the English side of the Welsh border, as can be seen from Map 1, also show a

---

[14] Ellis, op. cit., p. 37.

majority of *she* forms—presumably the form in the adjacent Welsh territory. The Welsh Survey as yet extends only over Monmouth (also covered in the *SED* material), Glamorgan, Carmarthen, Pembroke, Breconshire, and Radnor. The forms here, as we might expect, are all *she* (with *her* as object), except for two localities with [œ˙ː] on the Herefordshire border, one in Brecon and the other in Radnor.[15]

This, then, was the distribution of forms of *she* when *SED*'s informants were acquiring their speech habits. Many questions still remain to be answered, however. What part have these forms in the total pronominal usage of the dialects, and, more particularly, how do the contrasts in stressed and unstressed forms fit into the phonemic and morphemic aspects of the stress systems of the individual dialects? (It would be difficult to study these accurately from *SED*'s written material, since stress and intonation patterns are not regularly recorded.) The division we have here is into four basic areas—including the boundary of possible [ʃə] forms, which divides the North from the east Midlands—as well as the pockets of near standard usage where Celtic was relatively recently abandoned for English. Further study of *SED*'s material will show us how basic these divisions are—how many other features follow similar distribution patterns. The isogloss enclosing [-ɪŋg] for more usual [-ɪŋ] in words like *sing*, for instance, would trace a boundary very similar to that delimiting the *hoo* area.

This is a picture, and intentionally so, of rural dialects, since *SED*'s policy was to avoid urban localities. The question arises, therefore, would the urban dialects fit into the pattern we have here, or would they form contrasting pockets of usage? Again, this is a picture somewhat 'old fashioned'. How many of the younger generation still consistently use the dialect? How far has their speech been modified by greater mobility and the effect of mass media in the direction of the standard? Are forms of *she* gaining at the expense of *shoo, hoo*, and *her*? This article has, if nothing else, I hope, shown that these questions need to be answered.

---

[15] I should like to thank Mr David Parry of the University College of Swansea, who kindly provided me with the relevant material recorded from South Wales.

Table of Forms

County/ Locality	*she* short V usu. [ɪ]	*she* long V or diph.	[ʃə]	*shoo*	*hoo*	*her*
Northern						
Nb 1	10	2	—	—	—	—
2	9	1	1	—	—	—
3	16	1	—	—	—	—
4	12	1	1	—	—	—
5	11	1	—	—	—	—
6	5	1	3	—	—	—
7	8	2	1	—	—	—
8	6	2	5	—	—	—
9	7	1	3	—	—	—
Cu 1	13	1	—	—	—	—
2	12	2	—	—	—	—
3	14	1	—	—	—	—
4	13	2	—	—	—	—
5	10	1	3	—	—	—
6	8	1	1	—	—	—
Du 1	4	2	3	—	—	—
2	9	2	1	—	—	—
3	7	1	3	—	—	—
4	7	2	4	—	—	—
5	8	1	2	—	—	—
6	11	2	2	—	—	—
We 1	9	2	2	—	—	—
2	13	1	1	—	—	—
3	12	1	1	—	—	—
4	8	1	3	—	—	—
La 1	9	1	3	—	—	—
2	11	1	1	—	—	—
3	10	1	—	—	—	—
4	10	3	—	1	1	—
5	9	1	—	—	9	—
6	—	—	—	—	18	—
7	—	—	—	—	16	—
8	5	—	—	—	8	—
9	2	—	—	—	9	—
10	—	—	—	—	13	—
11	—	—	—	—	12	—
12	1	—	1	—	—	7
13	—	—	—	—	11	2
14	4	—	—	—	11	—

Table of Forms—*cont.*

County/ Locality		*she* short V usu. [ɪ]	long V or diph.	[ʃə]	*shoo*	*hoo*	*her*
Y	1	14	—	—	—	—	—
	2	7	6	2	—	—	—
	3	8	6	—	—	—	—
	4	5	3	—	—	—	—
	5	9	1	5	—	—	—
	6	8	7	1	—	—	—
	7	6	3	8	—	—	—
	8	8	2	4	—	—	—
	9	7	6	3	—	—	—
	10	6	—	2	—	—	—
	11	5	1	2	—	—	—
	12	11	2	2	—	—	—
	13	7	3	6	—	—	—
	14	7	2	—	—	—	—
	15	6	3	7	—	—	—
	16	9	—	2	—	—	—
	17	8	6	—	—	—	—
	18	6	—	2	1	—	—
	19	8	2	2	—	—	—
	20	8	1	1	—	—	—
	21	1	—	—	—	16	—
	22	3	5	7	1	—	—
	23	3	—	4	3	—	—
	24	5	7	4	—	—	—
	25	5	2	3	—	—	—
	26	1	—	4	8	—	—
	27	11	1	—	1	—	—
	28	7	2	—	—	—	—
	29	—	—	—	1	16	—
	30	1	—	—	—	15	—
	31	5	—	1	9	—	—
	32	5	—	1	6	—	—
	33	9	5	—	—	—	—
	34	7	1 (+ [ʃe]2x)	—	—	—	—
Man	1	9	4	—	—	—	—
	2	13	1	—	—	—	—
East Midlands							
Nt	1	11	1	—	—	—	—
	2	13	1	—	—	—	—

194

County/ Locality	she short V usu. [ɪ]	she long V or diph.	[ʃə]	shoo	hoo	her
3	15	1	—	—	—	—
4	14	1	—	—	—	—
L 1	11	1	2	—	—	—
2	10	1	1	—	—	—
3	11	1	2	—	—	—
4	10	2	—	—	—	—
5	7	3	1	—	—	—
6	13	1	—	—	—	—
7	8	—	—	—	—	—
8	11	—	—	—	—	—
9	10	1	—	—	—	—
10	11	2	1	—	—	—
11	7	2	1	—	—	—
12	8	1	—	—	—	—
13	14	1	—	—	—	—
14	10	3	1	—	—	—
15	15	3	—	—	—	—
Lei 1	14	1	—	—	—	—
2	12	1	—	—	—	—
3	10	3	—	—	—	—
4	10	1	—	—	—	—
5	12	—	—	—	—	—
6	6	3	2	—	—	—
7	9	1	—	—	—	—
8	11	3	—	—	—	—
9	13	—	—	—	—	—
10	11	—	—	—	—	—
R 1	11	1	—	—	—	—
2	11	1	—	—	—	—
Nth 1	14	1	—	—	—	—
2	13	3	—	—	—	—
3	8	1	—	—	—	—
4	9	3	—	—	—	—
5	8	3	—	—	—	2
Hu 1	4	6	—	—	—	—
2	10	2	1	—	—	—
C 1	9	1	1	—	—	—
2	12	1	—	—	—	—
Nf 1	2	12	—	—	—	—
2	11	1	—	—	—	—
3	3	8	—	—	—	—

195

Table of Forms—*cont.*

County/ Locality		*she*		[ʃə]	*shoo*	*hoo*	*her*
		short V usu. [ɩ]	long V or diph.				
	4	10	2	–	–	–	–
	5	1	14	–	–	–	–
	6	7	4	–	–	–	–
	7	8	4	–	–	–	–
	8	1	2	–	–	–	–
	9	9	1	–	–	–	–
	10	10	–	–	–	–	–
	11	3	10	–	–	–	–
	12	9	1	–	–	–	–
	13	9	1	–	–	–	–
Sf	1	11	3	–	–	–	–
	2	13	3	–	–	–	–
	3	10	3	–	–	–	–
	4	8	4	–	–	–	–
	5	11	1	–	–	–	–
Bk	1	3	–	–	–	–	9
	2	10	2	–	–	–	–
	3	8	–	–	–	–	3
	4	12	5	–	–	–	–
	5	9	2	–	–	–	–
	6	1	–	–	–	–	–
Bd	1	11	1	–	–	–	–
	2	11	2	–	–	–	–
	3	11	2	–	–	–	–
Hrt	1	12	1	–	–	–	–
	2	8	2	–	–	–	–
	3	–	9	–	–	–	–
Ess	1	10	2	–	–	–	–
	2	12	1	–	–	–	–
	3	8	1	–	–	–	–
	4	8	2	–	–	–	–
	5	8	1	–	–	–	–
	6	5	5	–	–	–	–
	7	6	8	–	–	–	–
	8	7	4	–	–	–	–
	9	7	6	–	–	–	–
	10	9	2	–	–	–	–
	11	6	6	–	–	–	–
	12	1	10	–	–	–	–
	13	9	3	–	–	–	–

County/ Locality	she		[ʃə]	shoo	hoo	her
	short V usu. [ɪ]	long V or diph.				
14	9	3	—	—	—	—
15	2	9	—	—	—	—
MxL 1	9	8	—	—	—	—
2	2	8	—	—	—	—
West Midlands						
Ch 1	5	—	—	—	13	—
2	12	—	—	—	12	1
3	—	—	—	—	12	2
4	—	—	—	—	12	2
5	1	—	—	—	—	13
6	3	—	—	—	—	12
Db 1	3	—	—	—	10	—
2	10	1	1	—	4	—
3	—	—	—	—	10	2
4	—	—	—	—	9	7
5	2	—	—	—	5	4
6	—	—	—	—	5	5
7	—	—	—	—	—	14
Sa 1	1	1	—	—	—	9
2	—	—	—	—	—	20
3	3	—	—	—	—	9
4	3	2	—	—	—	5
5	—	—	—	—	—	13
6	7	—	—	—	—	9
7	2	—	—	—	—	13
8	—	—	—	—	—	11
9	—	—	—	—	—	14
10	—	—	—	—	—	17
11	—	—	—	—	—	14
St 1	—	—	—	—	5	5
2	2	1	—	—	—	11
3	—	—	—	—	—	14
4	—	—	—	—	—	9
5	—	—	—	—	—	18
6	—	—	—	—	—	18
7	1	—	—	—	—	12
8	1	—	—	—	—	10
9	—	—	—	—	—	17
10	—	1	—	—	—	10
11	3	2	—	—	—	9
He 1	—	—	—	—	—	13

Table of Forms—*cont.*

County/ Locality	*she* short V usu. [ɪ]	*she* long V or diph.	[ʃə]	*shoo*	*hoo*	*her*
2	—	—	—	—	—	16
3	—	—	—	—	—	12
4	—	—	—	—	—	13
5	—	—	—	—	—	14
6	—	—	—	—	—	13
7	17	7	—	—	—	10
Wo 1	—	—	—	—	—	14
2	1	—	—	—	—	12
3	—	—	—	—	—	22
4	—	—	—	—	—	18
5	—	—	—	—	—	17
6	—	—	—	—	—	25
7	9	3	—	—	—	8
Wa 1	2	6	—	—	—	4
2	21	2	—	—	—	6
3	5	3	—	—	—	1*

* ('rare')

County/ Locality	*she* short V usu. [ɪ]	*she* long V or diph.	[ʃə]	*shoo*	*hoo*	*her*
4	4	1	—	—	—	11
5	—	—	—	—	—	17
6	—	—	—	—	—	11
7	—	—	—	—	—	14
Mon 1	—	—	—	—	—	11
2	4	1	—	—	—	9
3	10	2	—	—	—	—
4	1	12	—	—	—	—
5	1	22	—	—	—	—
6	9	3	—	—	—	—
7	—	—	—	—	—	—
Gl 1	—	—	—	—	—	13
2	1	1	—	—	—	13
3	—	—	—	—	—	10
4	1	—	—	—	—	10
5	—	—	—	—	—	12
6	—	—	—	—	—	9
7	4	1	—	—	—	7
O 1	4	5	—	—	—	4
2	3	8	—	—	—	—
3	5	6	—	—	—	—

County/ Locality		*she* short V usu. [ɪ]	*she* long V or diph.	[ʃə]	*shoo*	*hoo*	*her*
	4	12	9	—	—	—	—
	5	5	6	1	—	—	—
	6	9	2	—	—	—	—
Southern							
So	1	2	15	—	—	—	—
	2	2	8	—	—	—	—
	3	1	8	—	—	—	—
	4	9	1	—	—	—	—
	5	—	3	—	—	—	11
	6	3	5	—	—	—	7
	7	—	2	—	—	—	9
	8	1	—	—	—	—	11
	9	—	3	—	—	—	13
	10	—	6	—	—	—	3
	11	6	8	—	—	—	1
	12	—	6	—	—	—	5
	13	1	2	—	—	—	13
W	1	—	6	—	—	—	8
	2	—	2	—	—	—	10
	3	—	4	—	—	—	8
	4	—	2	—	—	—	10
	5	—	15	—	—	—	1
	6	—	2	—	—	—	9
	7	2	7	—	—	—	8
	8	—	15	—	—	—	—
	9	—	4	—	—	—	9
Brk	1	2	4	—	—	—	9
	2	1	—	—	—	—	10
	3	3	6	—	—	—	—
	4	—	4	—	—	—	9
	5	9	2	—	—	—	—
Sr	1	10	11	—	—	—	—
	2	2	7	—	—	—	3
	3	7	9	—	—	—	—
	4	—	10	—	—	—	—
	5	6	8	—	—	—	—
K	1	10	1	—	—	—	—
	2	7	10	—	—	—	—
	3	8	2	—	—	—	—
	4	10	1	—	—	—	—
	5	9	1	—	—	—	—

199

Table of Forms—*cont.*

County/ Locality		*she* short V usu. [ɪ]	long V or diph.	[ʃə]	*shoo*	*hoo*	*her*
	6	9	3	—	—	—	—
	7	8	1	—	—	—	—
Co	1	—	—	—	—	—	21
	2	—	—	—	—	—	19
	3	—	2	—	—	—	20
	4	—	16	—	—	—	1
	5	—	12	—	—	—	5
	6	1	20	—	—	—	2
	7	—	17	—	—	—	—
D	1	—	—	—	—	—	20
	2	—	—	—	—	—	19
	3	—	—	—	—	—	26
	4	—	—	—	—	—	18
	5	—	—	—	—	—	21
	6	—	—	—	—	—	19
	7	—	—	—	—	—	16
	8	—	—	—	—	—	22
	9	—	—	—	—	—	19
	10	—	4	—	—	—	13
	11	—	—	—	—	—	21
Do	1	3	17	—	—	—	1
	2	—	13	—	—	—	—
	3	—	1	—	—	—	10
	4	—	10	—	—	—	5
	5	1	10	—	—	—	1
Ha	1	—	9	—	—	—	7
	2	3	11	—	—	—	—
	3	—	9	—	—	—	3
	4	5	10	—	—	—	—
	5	—	5	—	—	—	9
	6	—	12	—	—	—	5
	7	—	9	—	—	—	1
Sx	1	9	6	—	—	—	—
	2	4	6	—	—	—	—
	3	—	10	—	—	—	1
	4	6	8	—	—	—	—
	5	4	7	—	—	—	1
	6	6	8	—	—	—	—

Index

201